# THE LIFE AND WORKS OF
## DAVID LINDSAY

# THE LIFE AND WORKS OF
# DAVID LINDSAY

BERNARD SELLIN
*University of Brest, France*

*Translated by*
KENNETH GUNNELL

CAMBRIDGE UNIVERSITY PRESS
*Cambridge*
*London   New York   New Rochelle*
*Melbourne   Sydney*

Published by the Press Syndicate of the University of Cambridge
The Pitt Building, Trumpington Street, Cambridge CB2 1RP
32 East 57th Street, New York, NY 10022, USA
296 Beaconsfield Parade, Middle Park, Melbourne 3206, Australia

First published 1981

Photoset and printed in Malta
by Interprint Limited

*British Library Cataloguing in Publication Data*
Sellin, Bernard
The life and works of David Lindsay.
1. Lindsay, David, b. 1876 – Criticism and
interpretation
I. Title
823′.912   PR6023.I58115Z/   80-41330
ISBN 0 521 22768 2

*For Faouzia, Karim and Yann*

# CONTENTS

# ACKNOWLEDGEMENTS

The author, translator and publisher are grateful to the following for giving their permission to quote copyright material: Mrs Diana Moon, for David Lindsay's books, and especially for the extracts from the *Philosophical Notes*; Victor Gollancz, Ltd, for the extracts from *A Voyage to Arcturus* and *The Haunted Woman*; Putnam & Co., Ltd, for the extracts from *Devil's Tor*; John Long, Ltd, for the extracts from *Sphinx*; Sidgwick & Jackson, Ltd, for the extracts from *The Violet Apple*.

# FOREWORD

*Colin Wilson*

When David Lindsay died in July 1945, I doubt whether even his closest friends would have prophesied a 'Lindsay revival'. The reason will be clear to anyone who has ever glanced into a Lindsay novel: the style is hopelessly amateurish. And there is, unfortunately, a great gulf fixed between amateur and professional writers. It is not, of course, unbridgeable – every young writer has to learn to bridge it (unless he is one of those lucky ones who is 'born with style'). But if a writer has still not crossed it by the time he approaches middle age, then the case is hopeless. He probably lacks some quality of judgement that blinds him to his own naivety – like the extraordinary Amanda McKittrick Ros, who never realised that her novels were regarded as a joke.

But Lindsay's work somehow continued to live. Gollancz decided to reprint *A Voyage to Arcturus*, as part of a series of 'rare imaginative fiction', which included two other 'amateur' writers, E. H. Visiak and M. P. Shiel. I doubt whether Gollancz regarded *Arcturus* as an unrecognised masterpiece; if he had, he would have agreed to reprint it a quarter of a century earlier, when it would have done Lindsay's reputation some good. I think it more probable that he had noted the increasing popularity of fantasy – works like *The Lord of the Rings* and Peake's Gormenghast books – and decided that he could hardly lose. New readers discovered Lindsay's astonishing imagination, and became curious about his other books. I played my own small part when I became acquainted with Lindsay's friend E. H. Visiak, and proposed writing a joint book about Lindsay – to take Visiak's mind off his aches and pains. Our *Strange Genius of David Lindsay* was read by Alexander Besher, of the Chicago Review Press, who decided to try to print the two unpublished books *The Violet Apple* and *The Witch*. Another American publisher – Arno Press – decided to reissue *Devil's Tor* and *Sphinx*. And so, one by one, all the works of David Lindsay have crept back into print.

Yet to reprint him is one thing; to take him seriously another. For, as I pointed out in *The Strange Genius*, Lindsay is a curious border-line case. There can be no possible doubt about his genius, and the uniqueness of his vision. But when five out of the six novels are failures (I except *The Adventures of Monsieur de Mailly* because it is a potboiler), it is difficult to see how admirers can build up the requisite enthusiasm; the leaden prose and unmemorable characters of *Devil's Tor* or *The Witch* are enough to discourage anybody. I have periodically returned to Lindsay's books – sometimes for the purpose of writing introductions like this one – and have continued to be impressed by this imaginative vision; but I would be most unwilling to attempt any lengthy commentary on the six novels after *Arcturus*.

And now, fortunately, I have been relieved of any such temptation – or obligation. When Kenneth Gunnell told me that a French professor had written a long book on Lindsay, I was astonished. I knew that Lindsay's grand-daughter Rosamund Moon intended to write her thesis on him; but that was a family affair, so to speak. But I found it difficult to imagine how anyone could write a lengthy book about Lindsay. It is true that the French critic Michel Foucault has said that a commentary on a text ought to be more interesting than the text itself; but I found it hard to imagine how anyone could muster the enthusiasm to be interesting about *Sphinx* and *The Violet Apple*.

In fact, I have found Professor Sellin's text a revelation. What he has done is to examine Lindsay with the care and precision that his fellow countryman Roland Barthes has brought to the text of Balzac. Not that Sellin is a structuralist or 'textualist' in the ordinary sense of the word. He is not concerned, as Barthes is, to examine every phrase and every expression, to squeeze but the last drop of meaning. What he does, rather, is to examine Lindsay's work with the kind of affectionate care that dedicated Sherlockians put into books about the chronology of Holmes's life. As to the question of Lindsay's amateurishness, he examines it briefly, then firmly waves it behind him, and proceeds, quite simply, upon the assumption that Lindsay is a great writer. And I am convinced he is right to do so. For although Lindsay's style often sounds more like that of *Chums Annual* than a modern classic, the world he has created has an extraordinary consistency, and can be treated as a self-contained entity. Sellin has not exaggerated Lindsay's importance, or tried to sidestep the issue of his 'abominable writing' (Gollancz's expression). He has simply made it his business to try to uncover the greatness. And I feel he has been entirely successful.

I would like, nevertheless, to try to express my own sense of what went wrong with Lindsay's career as a writer. On the simplest level, it can be seen in the opening paragraph of his final novel *The Witch*:

'Ragnar Pole trod noiselessly into the large, hushed drawing-room at the Waylands' Kensington house. The piano was being played in another room, with both doors open, and the atmosphere was intense ... He sank down in the cushions of a solitary chair, and covered his eyes with a hand, to listen. Surely she was playing with a strangely daring sympathy of understanding and passionateness of heart?'

What is wrong is immediately clear. There is a clumsy humour-lessness about the writing, and an insensitivity to cliché. It hardly helps the reader to tell him the atmosphere was 'intense' – it conjures up visions of one of Ronald Searle's cartoons of a would-be literary lady asking a poet 'Are you *intense*?' The 'hushed' atmos-phere, the large drawing room (it *would* be in Kensington), the man covering his eyes to listen, the phrase 'passionateness of heart', all reinforce the slight but jarring impression of phoniness. One anony-mous critic, quoted in my own essay on Lindsay, talked about his 'nickel-plated style'. 'His characters never go, they proceed, they can't just get into a train, they must journey by first-class, they don't leave, they take departure, they don't say yes, they assent.' We get the impression of someone who has led a cloistered life, trying to convince us that he is used to Kensington drawing rooms. There is a touch of *The Young Visiters* about it.

Now Lindsay was not, in any sense, a phoney. The clumsiness springs from his Scots rigidity of temperament. Bernard Shaw has a passage about the Scottish critic William Archer that reminds me of Lindsay:

'... the reserve was real; it was a habit that had become second nature to him. In modern psycho-pathological terms it was a repression that had become a complex. Accustomed as I was to this, he amazed even me once. He had just completed his translation of Ibsen's *Little Eyolf*; and he read it to two or three friends of whom I was one. His reading was clear, intelligent, cold, without a trace of emotion, and rather wooden in the more moving passages. When he came to the last pages he suddenly handed me the book, and said, formally and with a marked access of woodenness, "Shaw,: I must ask you to finish the reading for me. My feelings will not allow me to proceed." The contrast between the matter and the manner of this speech would have been irresistibly comic had any doubt of the sincerity of his distress been possible . . .'

Lindsay also had this wooden exterior – although, like Archer, he could be charming, humorous and relaxed. Visiak has described how, at their first meeting, Lindsay was unbending and formal; and he told me that, to the end, this formality persisted between them. Lindsay was the kind of man to whom the use of a Christian name, or the personal pronoun, came with immense difficulty.

But most spontaneous writing springs from the ability to say 'I'. Once a man can write – or speak – easily of himself, he has lost self-consciousness, and can concentrate all his attention on his precise meaning. Shaw's early novels display the same clumsiness; it was public speaking that changed his style, and gave it precision and balance.

This is obviously why music meant so much to Lindsay. The musician expresses 'himself' directly, yet is never forced to say 'I'. So he can pour out his feelings without embarrassment.

Lindsay was fortunate to start his literary career with a fantastic allegory. Because he was writing about alien beings on a remote star, he could allow his fantasy the kind of freedom possessed by the musician. Anything could happen.

Once Lindsay came back to earth, and began writing *The Haunted Woman*, he suddenly found himself subject to the old force of gravity. That is to say, he was suddenly tied hand and foot by inhibitions. He was, for example, a man who found the opposite sex boundlessly attractive. And it would not seem at all inconsistent if Maskull, in *Arcturus*, had become the lover of Oceaxe or Sullenbode. It is almost impossible to imagine any of his other heroes – Henry Judge, Anthony Kerr, Nicholas Cabot – having sexual intercourse with the women with whom they fall in love, except behind the locked doors of a honeymoon suite. Like Lindsay himself, his heroes are rigidly bound by social conventions and their own shy and puritanical temperaments.

Now writing is subject to its own peculiar laws. The writer spends his time trying to trap reality; but reality also tries to trap the writer. He is attempting to rebuild the world until it is 'nearer to the heart's desire.' That is to say, the world limits our freedom, but creative writing is an attempt to express the freedom that is normally repressed. At its best, great writing, like great music, awakens a sense of freedom. It also awakens in the reader a sense of expectation. Of what? Of *surprise*. A writer on jazz caught the essence of jazz improvisation in his title *The Sound of Surprise*. When a writer's imagination has taken wing, the reader abandons himself to the excitement of the journey, convinced that his conductor will continue to surprise him in the way that a child experiences continual surprise on a train journey. And this enables me to speak of the basic theme of all creative writing: the *hidden meaning* of the external world. The harshness of experience teaches us to mistrust reality, so that our attitude to new experience always involves some element of doubt, of 'shrinking'. But this mistrust in turn, this 'negative expectation', causes a sinking of the heart, a loss of vitality; and this negative expectation limits our perceptions. If you expect something to be boring, then in most cases you will be bored by it. This is because you have actually 'switched off' that element in the mind that *expects* surprise. So we live in a world which is limited by our own negative expectation and mistrust. Things, we believe, 'are what they are'. When, in fact, nothing could be more absurdly untrue. They are not. As we realise every time eager anticipation fills us with new energy, and we realise with astonishment that *everything* is more interesting than we gave it credit for. We close our minds, and force meaning to wait outside the door.

But then, it is quite easy to open them. Someone only has to raise his finger and say 'Listen!' to place you in an attitude of receptivity. Or to point at a picture and say 'Look closely'.

This, in fact, is what the writer attempts to do. The moment he says 'Once upon a time . . .' (or its equivalent), he is promising to surprise you. And Lindsay *does* surprise us, again and again, throughout *Arcturus*. And *Arcturus* possesses philosophical as well as imaginative stature because he understands that reality is always more surprising than we give it credit for. Lindsay's constant theme is the hidden meaning of actuality.

But when he tries to express this theme in terms of his contemporary world, he encounters a problem. Our perception of this reality is booby-trapped with our own expectation of boredom – that is to say, with negative expectation, which, in turn, induces what it anticipates. The writer who wishes to express new depths of intensity in terms of everyday reality must choose themes that will jar the reader out of the 'triviality of everydayness'. Dostoievsky expressed grim satisfaction when he heard that the murder scene in *Crime and Punishment* had made some readers physically sick. Some of the most powerful writing in the twentieth century has made deliberate use of violence – Lindsay might have picked up some interesting hints from Hemingway and Faulkner.

But then, Lindsay was a rather repressed Scot, who would probably have been irritated by Hemingway's style and shocked by Faulkner's sexual violence. No one could have been further away from Jane Austen as far as creative intentions were concerned; yet the social milieu he portrays is closer to Jane Austen than to the kind of writers he might have found more sympathetic – say Balzac or Dostoievsky. And in a sense, Lindsay's politeness, his good manners, prevented him from transforming Jane Austen into something more stormy and violent. He actually makes this frustration the subject of *The Haunted Woman*, where it is clearly implied that Isbel and Judge are stunted and limited by their middle-class lives, prevented from developing a dimension of strength and purpose (which Lindsay identifies with tragedy). And the heroes of the other books – Nicholas Cabot, Anthony Kerr, even Henry Saltfleet – are quite simply trapped in it.

So in spite of his consciousness of 'other realities', Lindsay confines himself, in practice, to the same kind of world as in the dramas of Pinero or Galsworthy. And as he lacks Galsworthy's interest in the details of middle-class life, he treats them rather perfunctorily, as a tedious duty. Yet he feels a conscientious need – characteristic of the amateur writer – to 'render' his social scenes in all their boring detail. The result is that the reader who has been invited to experience 'surprise' soon begins to mistrust his conductor, and ends by feeling thoroughly bogged down in the minutiae of every day. As this was precisely the reverse of the effect Lindsay was aiming at, it is difficult not to regard these later novels as failures. Like Shaw's 'novels of his nonage' (which also become weighed down with social detail), they seem to hint at fascinating developments to come. But, in Lindsay's case, the development was never to occur. Looked down upon by his wife, bored by his 'friends', Lindsay seems to have reconciled himself to being misunderstood, and turned his face grimly to the wall.

It would certainly have amazed him if he could have looked into the future and foreseen Professor Sellin's book. No doubt it would have stirred him to a fury of activity, a determined attempt to produce at least one masterpiece in which his message was stated definitively. For the irony is that his one indisputable masterpiece, *Arcturus*, is, from the philosophical point of view, his least mature work. It has all the force of unalloyed pessimism. The optimism that slowly developed thereafter is to be found in glowing fragments, like potsherds from the palace of Knossos, among the rubble of the later novels.

Professor Sellin, like a gifted archaeologist, has sifted through the rubble and brought the fragments together. In doing so, he has performed an inestimable service for Lindsay – and for those who believe that the author of *Arcturus* was one of the great spirits of our time.

# AUTHOR'S PREFACE

A few years ago, a friend of mine, returning from Scotland, gave me a copy of *A Voyage to Arcturus*. I can still remember the effect upon me of reading this book. Baffled and enraptured, I had the impression, not just of reading, but of participating in a game whose rules, instead of being given at the outset, would be revealed only to the reader who really scrutinised the theme. *A Voyage to Arcturus* was for me, at first, an enigma that had to be unravelled little by little.

David Lindsay's novels are often difficult, and confusing, for anyone not perceiving the author's intention. In bringing to light the richness of his books, and the task of symbolic elaboration to which the author dedicated himself, I hope to convince some readers, who see Lindsay as little more than a whimsical science-fiction author, that his work is more serious than it appears, and that it deserves to be known in its entirety. This view is supported by the increasingly favourable acclaim that is being accorded to him by the general reading public.

In my study, *A Voyage to Arcturus* takes pride of place, but only a comprehensive analysis of Lindsay's work was capable of illuminating his masterpiece, and of revealing the web of metaphors that underlie the novels. The complexity of ideas will be the more easily apparent the more one considers this work in its context.

If there are fantasy stories, it is certainly because there exists, Lindsay tells us, 'another world' more real than the one we know. Most of his books have the theme of putting man in touch with this transcendent universe. To-day, it has had to be recognised that science and rationalism have not succeeded in solving all problems. If readers to-day turn towards fantastic literature, is this not because there they find comfort? It is accordingly necessary to remember the place occupied by Lindsay in this trend of modern literature. It seems no exaggeration to rank him amongst the best, even if, as we shall point out, his books are not without their limitations. The indisputable gifts of the visionary, fertile imagination and original thinking are a few of the qualities that one readily recognises in him. His view of mankind, to be pessimistic, is in many respects a valid one.

The gift of imagination does not aim to astonish the reader but to make use of a poetic image; nothing that bears much relation to a philosophy of life. His own life, the structure of his novels, built around the pattern of his quest, the difficulty of expressing himself as regards women, the cruel deceit of a usurping God, Crystalman, the fascination of a universe beyond understanding, in which there mingle music and death, dreams and imagination; each of these ingredients bears witness to a sad malaise experienced in his life, which he strove to exorcise with literature and philosophy.

The preparation of this book extended from 1972 to 1977. I was not then able to gain access to the unpublished texts of Lindsay's books, *The Violet Apple* and *The Witch*, the manuscripts of which were in the United States, awaiting publication there. A supplementary chapter has accordingly been added to what was, originally, a doctorate thesis submitted to the *Université de la Sorbonne Nouvelle–Paris III*. I must express my gratitude to Professor Jacques Cabau, whose comments have been as valuable as they have been stimulating. Among the many other people who have shared in the production of this work, I should particularly like to thank Mrs Diana Moon, David Lindsay's daughter, Robert Barnes and F. D. Bacon for the information that they have so willingly given me, Georges Prudhomme who suggested this study, and similarly my friend and translator, Kenneth Gunnell, for the support that he has brought to me, and also his wife, Jean, for undertaking the considerable task of compiling the voluminous Index. Colin Wilson, quite apart from writing the Foreword, has always been most helpful towards the project.

BERNARD SELLIN

Université de Bretagne Occidentale,
Brest, France
1 October 1979

It must have been in the summer of 1938 that I first met David Lindsay, and by no stretch of the imagination could our initial encounter have been attributed to literature in any way.

Aged sixty-two at the time, Lindsay could only contemplate a writing career that was sadly in the doldrums, as it was to remain, indeed, until his death, seven years later, whilst I was just twenty years of age, with my own literary status completely non-existent.

The truth, as it usually is, was much more prosaic. In fact, at this period, I had not read a single line of any of the five books by Lindsay then published, and I came to know the author of *A Voyage to Arcturus* solely through moving in the same circle of friends as his two daughters: Diana, then aged nineteen, and Helen, who was two years younger. Indeed, even this bland admission needs some peripheral qualification, because, if my memory, forty years on, is to be relied upon, I am inclined to think that I was first invited to the Lindsay household by a girl called Jacqueline, not to be confused with Lindsay's wife, more than twenty years his junior, who bore the same name.

This younger Jacqueline was a French student, spending that summer at the house in Pembroke Crescent, Hove, which was by now being used by Jacqueline Lindsay for receiving foreign guests, in her effort to restore some degree of solvency to the family budget, after repeated literary setbacks suffered by her husband. This enterprise of hers is so well documented by Bernard Sellin, later in this book, that it would scarcely serve any useful purpose for me to enlarge upon it here from my personal recollection. Suffice it to say that, following this first visit of mine, I soon came to know both Lindsay's daughters, as well as their mother, very well indeed.

Getting to know Lindsay himself took rather longer, for, as Professor Sellin rightly stresses, his was a most withdrawn and complex character; indeed, it was this very complexity, even more pronounced than in most writers, that was arguably impossible of real penetration by a twenty-year-old. Nevertheless, by degrees, I did eventually get to know him a little better, and even came to admire his dry, abstract wit.

Lindsay was very fond of chess, and so it was scarcely surprising that the day soon came when Mrs Lindsay, knowing my own interest in the game, urged that I should accompany her husband to his study for a game or two. The exercise was emphatically not a success, however, and was made even worse by my own maladroitness.

By that time, I had been a County player for several years, and it soon became embarrassingly obvious that Lindsay's standard of play was, at best, no more than that of a very average club player. Accordingly, after winning a couple of games quite easily, I was ill-advised enough to decide that, with a little manipulation by me, my older host should win the third game. In the event, of course, Lindsay was shrewd enough to see through my clumsy attempt at diplomacy, and soon pushed all the pieces wearily to one side, admonishing 'Look, Ken, this is a sheer waste of your time and mine. Why don't you just go and join the girls?' We never played again.

On a rather more light-hearted note, I well recall the occasion when a number of guests, of all age-groups, were gathered in the lounge at Pembroke Crescent, which was so inadequate for seating so many people that Lindsay proceeded to share an upright chair with a lady well into her seventies, with whom he embarked upon an intensive discussion of metaphysics, a subject always obsessing him, as shown in so much of his writing. Not long afterwards, Jacqueline Lindsay summoned everyone present to an adjoining room, where she had prepared a buffet snack, and where nobody noticed the absence of Lindsay and his aging companion. It must have been nearly half an hour later that we returned to the lounge, there to find the two of them, still perched incongruously, and assuredly most uncomfortably, on the same small chair in the empty room, so engrossed in their discussion as to be unaware of the comic spectacle they presented.

If it can perhaps be said that this last anecdote illustrates the single-mindedness of Lindsay, there were occasionally grimmer reminders of his commercial failure as a writer, as evidenced by the occasion when a number of those of us of the younger generation were invited to express our personal ambitions in life. When it came to my own turn, I was brash enough to assert that I wanted to be a writer, whereupon Lindsay's face seemed to become contorted with pain, as he observed, gently enough, 'Young man, no power on earth can help you!'

Other writers did appear in the Lindsay household from time to time, however. Harold Visiak, in fact, lived just a few minutes' walk away, and was to survive long enough to write me a charming letter only a few years ago, just before his death, when he was well into his nineties. The careful reader will not fail to notice the many relevant references in Bernard Sellin's text to this literary figure, who came nearer, perhaps, than anyone to being Lindsay's intimate friend, even though their correspondence always began 'My dear Visiak' and 'My dear Lindsay'.

Another literary guest was Leo Huberman, who had just scored such a success with his *Man's Worldly Goods*, chosen by Victor Gollancz for production by his then lately-formed Left Book Club. Jacqueline Lindsay, ever the aspiring literary hostess, had invited a small group of her daughters' friends to meet the great man on the evening of his arrival, but, here again, her plans somewhat miscarried. Huberman certainly arrived, shortly after nine o'clock, but, upon being told that we were all gathered there to meet him, his reaction was not quite what had been expected. Uncoiling from his neck an enormous scarf, which he handed ceremoniously to his nonplussed hostess, he addressed himself to everyone present in the following terms: 'So, you have met me. I am Huberman. I have been writing a history of the world. It has made me very tired. Now, please, I go to my room.'

I last saw David Lindsay in 1944, and he died in the following year.

KENNETH GUNNELL

*Cornwall, England*
*15 October 1979*

# INTRODUCTION

David Lindsay is a little-known writer. When he died in 1945, in his house on the outskirts of Brighton,[1] it was difficult not to accept the evidence: his writing career had been a failure in many respects. His books, apart from the first two, had encountered great difficulty in finding a publisher. Public reaction had been luke-warm. None of Lindsay's novels had been republished during his lifetime.

The fact that his writings were not well-received by either publishers or the general public, however, did not mean that his name remained unknown within a literary circle of critics and other writers, amongst whom could be mentioned Robert Lynd, E. J. King Bull and Roger Lancelyn Green. At the time Lindsay's books appeared, literary critics did not fail to emphasise his shortcomings; nevertheless, there clearly emerges from these reviews the conviction that Lindsay was a writer worthy of interest. L. P. Hartley, Rebecca West, Hugh L'Ansson Fausset and J. B. Priestley are a few of the celebrities of that time who declared themselves impressed by the force of certain passages, the power of the imagination, and the originality of thought.

These qualities must, moreover, have been confirmed by the unconcealed interest shown in Lindsay's work by two eminent writers, C. S. Lewis and L. H. Myers. The former was well-known in the literary and university life of the inter-War years. Best remembered of his works are *The Allegory of Love*, a critical work on medieval literature, and his 'fantasies', a trilogy of novels which established Lewis as a master of this literary genre that is so successful to-day. C. S. Lewis drew attention to Lindsay's book, *A Voyage to Arcturus*, which he declared had influenced him in the production of his own works. Hence, Lewis placed Lindsay in the field of modern 'fantasy', as distinct from science-fiction, which had its origin in the writings of, amongst others, George MacDonald, and diversified itself through the inspiration of Charles Williams, Mervyn Peake and J. R. R. Tolkien, to mention only the most famous of such authors.

1

As regards L. H. Myers, although he was little known to the public at large, he attained a solid reputation as both writer and philosopher. With more insight than Lewis, Myers was to remember less of Lindsay's gift of imagination than his capacity for thought. Behind these qualities emphasised by Lewis and Myers respectively, there are noticeable the two aspects of Lindsay which to-day attract the attention of readers and critics; his imaginative and philosophical writings.

This brief historical survey shows that, in spite of a set-back as regards readers and publishers, Lindsay's work had nevertheless found a few adherents. From 1945, the year that Lindsay died, a kind of reverse process developed. Readers and publishers who, until then, had shown coolness towards his writing, began to display interest. His books did not have to wait long to be republished, with a success that was moderate at first, but which soon grew enormously, and the paperback market got hold of *A Voyage to Arcturus*, thanks to a boom in works of science-fiction and the fantastic. Publishers, hitherto cautious, wanted Lindsay. A French version of *A Voyage to Arcturus* appeared in translation.[2] In the United States, and also in England, two novels, long-unpublished, suddenly appeared. Already, there was talk of a new edition of *The Adventures of Monsieur de Mailly*. Lindsay's *Philosophical Notes*, edited from his notebooks, were deposited at the Scottish National Library, at the request of the Curator, anxious to stimulate the interest being shown in Scotland in Lindsay's writing. It is probable that, before very long, *Philosophical Notes* will in turn be published, as they provide a wealth of information on Lindsay's thinking. One important study of Lindsay's life and work has already seen the light of day, *The Strange Genius of David Lindsay*,[3] followed by other critical appraisals. Finally, and significantly, the magazine, *Adam International Review*, known for its integrity, international enlightenment and good taste, devoted some thirty pages to Lindsay's correspondence.[4]

Latterly, the number of admirers of *A Voyage to Arcturus* has continued to increase. Eulogies were soon showered on the book. For *The Sunday Telegraph* reviewer, it was 'undoubtedly a work of genius'.[5] According to Lin Carter, *A Voyage to Arcturus* is 'an extraordinary novel'. Colin Wilson goes even further: the book deserves to become 'a twentieth-century classic', in the same category as the long-unrecognised works of Kafka, J. C. Powys and M. Lowry.[6]

Here, then, rather than any disagreement, is a consensus of opinion signifying a rebirth of interest in the work and ideas of David Lindsay.

Lindsay turned to literature rather late in life. He was past forty before he wrote his first novel. The early part of his life had been devoted to a business career in the City of London. Certainly, literature interested him. He read a great deal, and reflected upon what he read. Lindsay's decision to bring to an end his career as an insurance broker, apparently highly successful, was a great surprise to his family and friends. This decision also revealed a courageous spirit which was not to desert him. It is true that Lindsay had never concealed the fact that he felt ill at ease in the environment in which he then found himself. Literature seemed to constitute both a haven and a redemption. He also felt the need to express ideas to which he had been drawn as the result of some twenty years of reading and reflection. The urge towards expression and the feeling of frustration were released by a marriage in many respects surprising. These, broadly speaking, were the conditions which led to the birth of his career as a writer.

Lindsay's output stretches between the two World Wars. He started writing immediately after his demobilisation, in 191 and died in the last months of the Second World War. This historical background shows itself clearly throughout his writing, his thinking and his feeling. Criticism of society in the name of threatened spiritual values, condemnation of the falsity of human relations, the allure of a transcendent, supernatural reality, inquests into the nature of Evil, the reassessment of suffering, the recurrent themes of the Fall and defeat, are so clearly the dominant features of the inter-War English novel. The names of D. H. Lawrence, L. H. Myers, E. M. Forster, J. C. Powys, Graham Greene, Evelyn Waugh, Bernard Shaw and many others can be cited in this context.

As the result of coming late to literature, Lindsay did not write very much. The obstacles that he encountered in getting his work published and the difficulty that he experienced in editing, explain why his work appears meagre; *A Voyage to Arcturus* (1920), *The Haunted Woman* (1922), *Sphinx* (1923), *The Adventures of Monsieur de Mailly* (1926), *Devil's Tor* (1932). To these, there can be added *Philosophical Notes*, or *Sketch Notes towards a New System of Philosophy*, an unpublished work which is a selection of reflections collected by Lindsay from his notebooks as a writer. Finally, there are two more novels, *The Violet Apple* and *The Witch*, both long unpublished, which have appeared only posthumously.

The interest of a book has never been in proportion to the number of its pages. The same is true in respect of the entire output of a writer. Content, presentation and insight are infinitely more important. Lindsay's limited output is evidence of a concentration of ideas, and of a depth that is all too rare. Only a few pages need be read to reveal an abundance of thought, of a kind that one might well wish to find more often in authors who are more famous and more prolific.

*A Voyage to Arcturus* alone could constitute the basis of a study longer than the book itself! If we have chosen not to limit our analysis to the better-known Lindsay novels, at the risk of being accused of wallowing in the obscurity of unobtainable books, this is primarily because all narrative is the expression of its author, and it would seem arbitrary to isolate one text from his creative work as a whole. David Lindsay's first book, *A Voyage to Arcturus*, condenses his thinking at the precise moment that he became a writer. It covers the process of transformation that preceded the act of writing. It is no more than the departure-point of an experience that was to develop over the course of years, from one book to the next. New developments, doubts, strains, all appear elsewhere. Taken in isolation from the other books, *A Voyage to Arcturus* is often incomprehensible; right down to the present day, critics, genuinely anxious to clarify the texts, have been only too ready to present each of Lindsay's novels on its own. It is accordingly necessary to approach the works in their entirety, and to study them in depth.

The field of research is enormous. The works, by reason of their form which is so often baffling, are a constant invitation to question, contemplate, indeed to try to understand; an invitation all the more enticing as research into Lindsay's life and works is still in a state of gestation. The major critical work, *The Strange Genius of David Lindsay*, although it certainly defines the direction of his thinking, is none the less rudimentary, and, indeed, even inaccurate, in so far as concerns the first, biographical, section of this three-part book. It is fundamentally a picture of a little-known writer, an invitation to discover him, and a valuable guide for the reader. Our own analysis tries to be more detailed, in the light of recent studies of Lindsay,[7] approaching the works, not simply to present them, but in the hope of unveiling their unsuspected riches, and also their limitations. Our path has led us from the outside to the inside; from the man to his works, from the life to the personality, from the concrete to the abstract, from the tangible world to the intangible.

If we concentrate at first on Lindsay's life and personality, it is because we feel it to be essential to complete the available biographical data. We are not so much advocating a biographical approach to the works, which course would be open to criticism. The stories of Lindsay are not some kind of intimate self-revelation. Art is not the expression, pure and simple, of the personality, nor is it the realisation of individual experience. Our approach is dictated by the need to inform, to outline a biography of Lindsay, and is justifiable since the spiritual experience at the centre of his work is related to one event: the decision to change his life, to sacrifice his comfort, in order to devote the rest of his days to literature. The act of writing identifies itself in the episodes of a life; accordingly, it seems essential to shed some light upon the personal motives, and the consequences, of Lindsay's decision. I have, to this end, met Lindsay's children, friends and relations, whose testimony, as rare as it is valuable, has greatly facilitated our task. The publication of Lindsay's letters to E. H. Visiak, here analysed for the first time, has allowed me to present Lindsay in his relations with other writers, and to follow the development of his career.

Far from vindicating any kind of sincerity in a writer, a better acquaintance with his life tends to reveal the man and his pretences; disguise, compromises, travesties. We have had to play at 'secret agents', as Armand Hoog puts it,[8] to manipulate the 'false passports' that the writer offers us. The work is not a confession; it is often the very reverse, a kind of double-dealing. As with music, one must know how to appreciate the value of silence. However tempting may be the psychoanalytical approach, it can only be one among other methods of interpretation. Psychoanalysis is, first and foremost, a therapeutic technique that must be applied to the man himself at the moment when he expresses himself. In literature, according to all the evidence, one of the elements is missing; namely, the man. The mystery which surrounds certain biographical aspects of Lindsay, the personality of his mother, his relations with women, counsels prudence. It is also true that the secrets of psychoanalysis do not easily reveal themselves to the layman. Though convinced that psychoanalysis constitutes the most systematic investigation of the human spirit that exists in our time, we should content ourselves with noting the existence of this kind of approach, without running the risk of venturing too far.

Having outlined the life and literary career of Lindsay, we turn towards his writing, and begin by describing the background to his work. Initially a means of escape, Lindsay's work had to anchor itself to concrete experience. If the first book prolongs this escape in fantasy, the subsequent writing lies within a framework of reality, as if the adult, ashamed of his fantasies, were seeking to excuse them by a return to the intimacy of the home; an obscure intimacy, however, where the secret mingles with the dismal; the disturbing strangeness of Freud, 'this kind of terror which links up with things long known, and always familiar'.[9]

The background of Lindsay's novels will be thoroughly examined to bring out the main factors; Nature, on the one hand, the family and its unhappiness, on the other. Lindsay's plots oscillate between these two extremes. Their recurrence compels us to pay particular attention to them. In the realistic framework, there will be substituted, or superimposed, a symbolic, or emblematic, scenery, based on a scale of values that is at once both personal and general. We mistakenly think it is enough that we should speak of an object to feel ourselves objective. Bachelard assures us, however, that 'the object denotes us more than we denote the object'.[10] Behind the background of his books, whether hills, sunshine, houses, hotels or gardens, it is still Lindsay who expresses himself. The object has nothing but a utilitarian value; often, it is a form of expression, sometimes coarse, sometimes refined, sharing simultaneously the author's consciousness and the dream-world, common to all men.

The study of the backgrounds will make apparent a certain attachment to places, or, conversely, a sudden recoil and embarrassment. The characters, like the backgrounds, must not be taken for what they appear to be. Behind a placid appearance, there is hidden complexity which is, no doubt, related to Lindsay's character. Without being openly autobiographical, his writing reveals, to those who know how to unravel it, the author's innumerable facets. In this picture of a 'human world', the interest in the woman is predominant. She, too, is seldom presented as being constructed as a single entity. She is a kind of composite portrait that Lindsay never tires of examining with alternating irritation and fascination; an important consideration, since she goes on to colour the theories, not to mention the philosophy, of Lindsay.

The dialectic of the visible and the invisible, of reality and unreality, animates the entire work in varying degrees. Between the 'two worlds', the frontier is blurred. One passes almost imperceptibly from one to the other. The writer becomes a magician and, at the touch of a wand, can transmute background and characters. The man, hitherto normal, finds himself, on waking, endowed with new faculties, created in terms of the imaginary world he penetrates. Henceforward, the laws of Nature no longer obtain. The cosmic voyage leads the reader into a strange, baffling world, born out of the fantasies and dreams of the author, but also out of contemplation of considerable philosophical importance.

*A Voyage to Arcturus* reconciles, more than any other book by Lindsay, the two main directions of his work; imagination and philosophical speculation. Whilst the former will lead us through the fantastic and the supernatural, as far as the very frontiers of Utopia, his philosophical inspiration will reveal an affinity with the thinking of Plato, Schopenhauer, Nietzsche and Buddhism. Behind the recurring theme of the journey, there develops a spiritual quest, having as its objective the 'Sublime', the parallel world whose manifestations of occultism, the unconscious and music' have tinged the physical world with such unreality that life seems a long and painful burden.

In the context of this study, it should accordingly be possible to gauge the real contribution of Lindsay to the English novel, and to point out those aspects of his work which, fifty years after publication, continue to be of interest to readers and critics.

# 1

# THE LIFE AND PERSONALITY
# OF THE AUTHOR

Before studying the works, it is natural enough to try to get to know a little about the man himself. This concern becomes still more legitimate when the man is little-known. The belated 'success' of Lindsay's books, well after his death, partly explains the scant interest shown in what kind of man he was. Moreover, being quiet and shy, he lived on the fringe of his contemporaries, surrounded by only a few friends who, in any case, never came to know him really well. The scarcity of information immediately available, however, does not mean that such research is devoid of interest. There are many who, reading Lindsay's books, have tried to guess what lay hidden behind these unusual stories. Their sharpness or their extravagance are almost open invitations to discover the personality of the writer. The little evidence that we do have only confirms the wealth of this personality. Some of those who knew Lindsay, whilst testifying to the fact that his work held little attraction for them, could not refrain from stressing the fascination exercised by the man himself.[1]

## YOUTH

David Lindsay was born 3 March 1876, at Blackheath, a suburb of London. He was the youngest child of three; he had a brother, Alexander, and a sister, Margaret. His father, Alexander Lindsay, was of Scottish origin. He had left Scotland at quite an early age to come to work in London; he was employed by a City finance company, and it was in London that he met the woman he married, Bessy Bellamy, daughter of a farming family from Leamington, Warwickshire. This was scarcely a happy union, since Alexander Lindsay disappeared abruptly a few years after his marriage. For a long time, it was believed that an accident had cost him his life, but eventually it was discovered that Alexander Lindsay had emigrated to Canada, leaving his wife quite penniless in charge of three children of tender years.

8

David Lindsay spoke little of his father, doubtless because, being the youngest of the children, he had scarcely known him, but perhaps also because the circumstances of his disappearance had affected him more than he cared to say. Deprived of his father at an early age, and finding no subsequent substitute, he would be determined, in adult years, to destroy the image of this unworthy father.

The disappearance of her husband plunged Bessy Lindsay into difficulties that can easily be imagined. She would never have been able to overcome them, and raise her three young children, had it not been for the help of her sister, Mrs Couchman, then living at Lewisham, in the house adjoining that of the Lindsays. Not long after the flight of Alexander Lindsay, Mrs Couchman's husband died, following an illness, and this allowed her to invite her sister and her children to come to live under her roof, as she herself had no children, and found herself alone after her husband's death. It was in this house in Victoria Road, Blackheath Rise, that David Lindsay spent his youth.

His primary education completed, Lindsay was admitted to Lewisham Grammar School, where he showed himself to be brilliant at Mathematics and English. He won prizes in both these subjects, and would undoubtedly have taken up one or other of them if he had gone to University.

At the same time, he received a strict religious education, against which he was to react throughout his life. The severity of these English Sundays, at the end of the nineteenth century, has always been notorious. Each week, on Sunday, the entire family went three times to church. To relieve his boredom, young David would amuse himself by counting the congregation, and staring out the worshippers. One of his favourite pastimes consisted of tying his aunt's shawl to her chair, which would then fall over when she tried to get up, much to the amusement of the children. Later, when he had children of his own, he always refused to accompany them to church, leaving this duty to his wife, bestirring himself only in the case of marriages and funerals. If he did bring himself to speak to the local vicar, in the village of Ferring, conversation would be confined to non-controversial subjects, such as gardening and roses, in which both men had an abiding interest.

This very strict religious upbringing left its recognisable mark on his entire work. Lindsay's deep-rooted obsession with the hereafter is essentially religious. Underneath his 'mysticism' can be recognised

his very puritanical disgust for everything bordering upon sexuality.
His rejection of traditional religion, however, is not merely instinctive, for he studied dogma on a grand scale before finally
dispensing with everything that would not fit into his own philosophy. His notebooks contain several very strong references to
traditional religion; 'One must not', he writes, for example, 'take a
passive, defensive attitude with regard to the Church. What is false
must be attacked as poisonous.'[2]

During the holidays, it was customary for the entire family to go
to Scotland, to visit the relatives who had remained there. The
favourite holiday venue was Illston, a small village in the Border
district, near Jedburgh, where an uncle owned a textile factory.
These pilgrimages to the country of his ancestors lasted until
Lindsay's marriage. Only the financial difficulties that he then
suffered brought them to an end. It even seems likely that Lindsay
lived for a short time in Scotland, and attended a secondary school
in Jedburgh.

More, perhaps, than with most children, these youthful years
remained narrowly restricted to a family environment. Already,
there appeared a trait in Lindsay's character that would only
become more marked in the future. As a child, he took no part in
his friends' games, just as, later on, he would isolate himself from
others. It was in literature that he found his most faithful companions. The adventure novels that so absorbed him allowed him to rise
above his own solitude. He read Robert Louis Stevenson, Jules
Verne and Sir Walter Scott. Sensitive and imaginative child that he
was, he preferred their stories to the more lurid adventures of other
children of his age, just as he learned, early on, that the thoughtlessness of youth could bring unpleasant misfortunes. One day, when
swimming in a Scottish river, he was carried away a little by the
current. He called to his companions. They did nothing, not
realising the danger. David, however, was convinced that they had
acted in this way on purpose.

In later years, the adult continued to show the same distrust
towards youth. He says of one of his characters 'Arsinal, too, for all
his sapient airs, continued a boy – but boys, Saltfleet remembered,
were hard, brutal and cruel' (*Devil's Tor*, page 297).[3] So childhood
was not the kind of Paradise Lost described with so much affection
and nostalgia by his friend, E. H. Visiak.[4] Assuredly, Lindsay
admired this ability of children to transcend the actual in order to

turn towards the possible. 'Middle Age knows how to live in and enjoy the present, but on rare occasions it catches a glimpse of the noble and aspiring unrest which makes youth disdain its surroundings, as mere subject-matter for dreams and aspirations' (*Philosophical Notes*, Number 120). He takes up this theme again in associating children with the small minority of enlightened mystics, saints and musicians, all of whom know how to recognise the presence and manifestations of another world (*Devil's Tor*, page 411). Even more often, he associated children with the innocence of the world, but, on other occasions, the pessimistic nature of the author intervenes to create a barrier to any kind of nostalgic emotion. In his eyes, innocence is indistinguishable from ignorance. A young child, in his innocence, is also the most vulnerable creature. 'The politeness and honesty of rustics is like the innocence of children; it is soon destroyed by intercourse with the outer world' (*Philosophical Notes*, Number 68).

## ADULTHOOD

The discovery of the adult world came with a greater brutality than he might have wished. After the flight of his father, the family had to face considerable financial difficulties. It was because of this that the three children were obliged to abandon their education at a fairly early age in order to earn their living. Alexander Lindsay, the eldest of the three, tried several occupations before establishing himself in the Midlands at the head of a small business. Margaret found employment in a post office, and lived under the same roof as her brother, David, at Lewisham, until the latter's marriage. As for David, he was employed by an insurance brokers, Price Forbes, in the heart of the City of London. He was introduced there by an old friend of his father who worked in this field himself. The necessity to curtail his studies was, in his case, cruel, and it is not difficult to understand the hatred felt by the adolescent towards his father, when one remembers that it was the latter who was the root cause of the misfortunes of the entire family. In no way would David Lindsay have wished to undertake this kind of vocation. He was compelled to do so, in spite of himself, whilst he prepared himself for University entrance. A scholarship was even offered to him.

Although it is always dangerous to try to reconstruct the past, it needs no great stretch of the imagination to visualise the career that

Lindsay could have known if he had been able to complete his education. We know that, from his adolescence, he felt himself strongly drawn towards literature. His results at Lewisham Grammar School had pointed him in this direction. The English prize that he got there was a matter of great pride to him. He was already applying himself to the writing of short stories. So it is likely that, at University, Lindsay would have undertaken full literary studies, which would have provided him, in a few years, with the material necessary for the rapid development of his career as a writer. Moreover, he felt that dissatisfaction, recognisable in so many artists, that kept him apart from ordinary people. The brusque interruption to his education not only meant a temporary halt to his career but also helped to make Lindsay into a self-taught person who, in the event, was to have much need of guidance. As he soon had to admit, his knowledge of literature was limited to the kind of adventure stories that make their appeal in adolescence. University would not only have enabled him to extend the field of his knowledge, but would also have directed him towards a sounder critical basis, and to great writers, both English and foreign. Through failing to know them better, Lindsay came to depreciate systematically all these writers.

The need to work, however, merely served to delay by some twenty years his career, without obliterating it entirely, and these twenty years represented, in fact, the slow recapture of this career that had been crushed so soon. To accomplish this, Lindsay had to overcome many obstacles. He moved in a circle for whom literature and art generally offered no more than a very limited interest. His employment left him little free time to devote to culture, but, above all, for a man of such excessive shyness, the limits placed on his literary ambitions must have had a disastrous effect. Faced by this misfortune, the man was inclined to harp on the injustice of which he was the victim. There can be no doubt that the years of 'purgatory' which followed were a period of increasing pessimism. Lindsay immersed himself in his misery with a facility so disconcerting that nothing short of a complete upheaval could ever have got him out of this situation.

He worked in the insurance brokers' office from 1894 to 1916. The company, Price Forbes, has survived until the present day. Its size was then more modest than it is now, comprising no more than some thirty employees, distributed between four London offices, all located within the business area. Two offices were near to the Stock Exchange, another was close to the Bank of England, with the remaining one being situated in King William Street, at the present-day site of the Sedwick Forbes group. It was one of these offices that served as Lindsay's working-place, a large square room, shared by four or five employees, in which several tables were placed along the walls.

Everything points to the fact that young Lindsay eventually accepted this new profession with the versatility of a sixteen-year-old boy. He even showed himself, very quickly, to be a model employee. He began as an ordinary office-boy, but lost no time in getting more important duties entrusted to him. Quite soon, he was specialising in financial problems; a field that seemed to be his speciality throughout his career as a business-man. At the office, all cheques and letters relating to finance passed through his hands. He was put in charge of the account books, and was entrusted with the task of dealing with correspondence. This was work of great responsibility that had been given to him because of exemplary professional conscientiousness. The meticulous care which characterised him in all things could not have failed to be appreciated by superiors anxious for punctiliousness with figures and accounts. Hence, he climbed the ladder rapidly. His competence was such that, when the war was over, and he gave up this post, he found himself offered the position of office manager.

Having joined this firm, in spite of himself, Lindsay stayed there, notwithstanding his reluctance. He adapted himself to his work. How, otherwise, can one explain the professional conscientiousness which never abated? At the same time, he never ceased to repeat that this calling was not for him, that he wanted to give it up, and that he continued only through necessity in order to earn his living. Perhaps he was seeking a new post with too little conviction, with that kind of resignation so easily discernible in his nature. The years passed without any change; Lindsay remained a model insurance broker. Each day, he travelled from Lewisham, where he lived, to the centre of London. Admittedly, his dream profession was not easily accessible. There were no classified advertisements to help him, as his field of interest was books and literature. On his desk at the office, there was often, close at hand, some novel by Sir Walter Scott, waiting to be opened at the end of the day once work was finished.

In spite of his antipathy for this vocation, Lindsay remained agreeable in the eyes of his colleagues. The picture that emerges from their testimony is not that of a man embittered by his work, but rather of an employee of exemplary kindness, always polite, always courteous, and delighted to give his help to anyone who might need it. At the office, he invariably appeared to be even-tempered, calm and obliging, as if he did not know how to be impatient or surly. No doubt he was also, like Judge in *The Haunted Woman*, full of courtesy towards women.

In spite of this, he scarcely made any friends from amongst his work-mates. Liked by all, he remained nonetheless different from them by virtue of his preoccupation and temperament. He kept himself apart from others, separated from them by a barrier of shyness and reserve. Moreover, as he showed throughout his life, he was not of a sociable nature, experiencing some difficulty in mixing with his fellow-men. The easy-going camaraderie that welcomes people with hearty slaps on the back was lacking in him. He did not seek friendships, keeping his relations, though not cold, on a basis that was reserved, if courteous. It was only on rare occasions, perhaps when relating a joke, that he really relaxed in the company of his colleagues.

His work monopolised him so much that he could not devote all the time he wished to his favourite spare-time interests; reading, chess and classical music concerts. Away from the office, Lindsay lived very much within the family circle, in the company of his sister and aunt. These two remained very dear to him throughout his life. His sister, Margaret, survived him by some twelve years.

As for his brother, Lindsay's relations with him were never very good. Moreover, Alexander Lindsay was much older than David, and so much so that they never knew one another really well. Alexander Lindsay left London, at quite an early stage, for the Midlands, where he dabbled in business before emigrating. A disappointing marriage was one of his personal vexations. By the time he returned to England, he certainly had had affairs with other women, which earned him the disapprobation of his entire family, and especially that of his younger brother. On the eve of the First World War, he started to write adventure novels, later forgotten, but which then earned him some success with the general public. These books, *The Alias, Kapak, Monsieur Carnifex* and *Outside the Law*, were written between 1911 and 1914, under the pseudonym of Alexander Crawford, a name he borrowed from one of the more famous branches of the Lindsay family, that of the Dukes of

Crawford and Balcarres, in Scotland. Alexander's hectic life ended abruptly at the age of forty, when he died from a liver ailment.

This death was a warning for David Lindsay. He was approaching forty himself, and had already been attacked by the complaint that was hereditary in the family; a particularly acute kind of jaundice that required, amongst other things, a very strict diet.

This illness, if it steered Lindsay towards his artistic career, also modified the nature of this same career. Henceforward, the works would not be peopled by invalids or corpses; one does not find that obsession with illness so recognisable in the writing of his friend, L. H. Myers, for instance. His own ailment, which he knew to be hereditary and incurable, impelled him, on the contrary, to hide it. He never referred to it in his intimate writing, much less in his novels. From his writing, illness would appear to be the exception, and almost shameful. Nobody dies in the novels through illness. Death has lost its degrading hold on the body. It is the beyond which strikes, and which, in so doing, makes death glorious. There is no trace, in Lindsay, of that contemplation of degradation to be found in a John Donne, a Chateaubriand or an Edgar Allan Poe. Here, there is no drawn-out agony: the rock of Devil's Tor crashes down on Hugh Drapier during an earthquake (page 231); Nicholas Cabot dies, suddenly and calmly, in his bed, at the age of twenty-five (*Sphinx*, pages 317–318). In Lindsay's eyes, the doctor remains very much a charlatan, and it is doubtless no mere chance that one of the most disagreeable characters in his entire work is a doctor's son.[5]

In spite of the discretion of which he gave such proof, Lindsay was keenly conscious of his affliction, and it is no exaggeration to say that it gave his writing its sombre, pessimistic tone. With this ailment, tragedy was present in his own life; it was not something apart, but a living fact. The tragedy arose from the seemingly incurable nature of the illness. It was in this way that the pessimism of the author was born, reinforced by his reading of Schopenhauer.

One might even wonder whether the instinctive horror of the sun, which characterises so many of Lindsay's pages, did not have its origin in this malady which overtook him, and which inhibited him from remaining in the sunshine. From this was born all the author's Scandinavian mysticism, with its propensity for mist and cold, and the systematic denigration of the Latin races, worshippers of the sun.

These twenty-odd years remain rather obscure. It is easy to visualise Lindsay leaving his office each evening, to immerse himself in the books which fascinated him. Entirely unaided he learned German, thereby putting into practice a rule of Schopenhauer, which rejected any reading of books in translation. Little by little, he formulated his own philosophy, which would emerge in his first novel, *A Voyage to Arcturus*, the fruit of those twenty years of reflection. He already kept a diary, which would soon help him to write this novel. Lindsay thought, observed, noted, criticised, but continued to be part of the environment which became increasingly repugnant to him, though he could not succeed in leaving it. Like his first hero, Maskull, he awaited adventure, but always knowing 'There is no longer any spirit of adventure among the Earthmen. Everything is safe, vulgar and completed' (*A Voyage to Arcturus*, page 218).[6] Away from the office, adventure offered itself to him in the shape of a game of chess, to which he devoted himself with so much fervour that it brought on a nervous breakdown. Lindsay tried, in addition, to get himself introduced into London literary circles. He was a member of a literary club, which gave him the opportunity of comparing his own ideas with those of his contemporaries. At holiday time, the entire family, aunt, sister and brother, left London to go sometimes to Scotland, original home of the family, sometimes to Blankenberge, the small Belgian seaside resort, close to the Dutch border, which came to be a favourite place. Lindsay also travelled in Germany, whose art held such a strong fascination for him. He stayed in Heidelberg, and it is possible that he may also have visited Northern Italy, with its magnificent picture galleries.

When the First World War broke out in 1914, Lindsay was thirty-eight years of age. He was a bachelor and, for fifteen years, he had led a routine life. There was nothing to indicate that either his professional status or family situation could be changed by one means or another. Every evening, Lindsay came to seek, in the family circle, with his aunt and sister, the relief he needed from work that scarcely enriched his soul. For fifteen-odd years, he had been firmly established in this small household, which amply satisfied him. The family house afforded the most solid assurance of his comfort and security. He was pampered by the two mistresses of the house, who rivalled one another in their ability as cooks. Both were ready to run the household, while he could, completely at his leisure, amuse himself as he wished, without restrictions, and without having to account for himself. Why marry when woman seemed to constitute the first obstacle to all adventure? 'You are a fortunate man;' says Krag to the bachelor, Maskull, 'a bold, daring heart, and no encumbrances' (*A Voyage to Arcturus*, page 27). Lindsay's two idols, Nietzsche and Schopenhauer, preached the virtues of celibacy, and was not his brother, Alexander, the shame of the family, regretting his own marriage?

All this concurring evidence, however, was not enough to convince everyone. The family clan schemed to marry the London branch to its Scottish roots; David Lindsay would marry a cousin from Jedburgh, whom he saw each summer during his holidays in Scotland. Started in the early 1900's, the engagement slowly dragged on and on. Lindsay, with his characteristic indolence, could not bring himself to decide to leave the family circle that so suited him. Moreover, the young lady herself lacked resolution, and was somewhat reticent. Finally, this provincial girl was bereft of the kind of glamour that might appeal to a man so conscious of his own intellectual superiority. After some fourteen years of hesitation, which in fact concealed the boredom they felt for one another, the engagement was formally broken. It was now the eve of the First World War. David Lindsay resumed unmoved his normal habits; namely, work, family, reading.

Notwithstanding this, however, several important events occurred in a few years to disturb this way of life. Firstly, there was the outbreak of the First World War in August, 1914. Lindsay, like so many of his contemporaries, did not think that this war would upset his life. He had long decided that war was one of the rare activities in which man excelled. Why should he concern himself with a conflict that showed, once again, the inveterate taste of his contemporaries for lethal pastimes? As for a number of liberal intellectuals, Germany was not, in his eyes, a nation of warmongers, but the country of Beethoven, Wagner, Goethe and many other geniuses who had contributed to the greatness of their country.[7] Moreover, again like his contemporaries, he expected a war of brief duration. He certainly felt some irritation at seeing the war prolonged, but nothing comparable to his surprise and anguish when he found that he himself was going to have to take part in the hostilities. He was not opposed to the war in itself, even though his philosophy made him somewhat hostile. Like many people, he thought that this was a war which, first and foremost, concerned the young. Lindsay was then thirty-eight years of age, and regarded himself as being too old to be called up. Eventually, the belated mobilisation struck him as being completely futile at a time when, after two and a half years of exhausting struggle, several peace initiatives were in hand amongst the belligerents. Without actually becoming a conscientious objector, like so many others, from Bertrand Russell to Lytton Strachey, Lindsay managed to avoid being sent to the Front, the horror of which had been so quickly revealed in England. Lindsay refused to join the Scots Guards regiment, to which he had been detailed, and eventually found himself assigned to an Army administrative office in Birdcage Walk, in the very heart of London. His regiment was the Grenadier Guards, stationed at Caterham, Surrey.

The months which followed, notwithstanding this privilege he had been given, were nevertheless amongst the most miserable of his life. The military environment made him deeply ill at ease. He never succeeded in accustoming himself to the strict discipline. Later, he tried hard to forget this period of his life, and rarely referred to it. An entry in his journal, however, shows us clearly enough the views he held about the Army. 'After a course of years, every soldier acquires more or less *insanity*; the result of his moral training' (*Philosophical Notes*, Number 456).

## MARRIAGE

The second important event which, within a few years, was to transform Lindsay's life, occurred in this same period. Whenever he could, he got away from Birdcage Walk, in order to devote himself to his favourite activities. He went regularly to a London literary club. It was there that he met a young girl, Jacqueline Silver, for whom he felt a great attraction. She was young, only eighteen in fact. She was intelligent and lively. More than anything else, Lindsay admired the way in which she would stand up in the literary club to speak with great gusto, and hold her own with men. It turned out, moreover, that their respective grandparents knew one another quite well. From there to the making of plans for the marriage, there was only one hurdle for the two families to sur-mount. It could be argued that Lindsay was, at this time, a businessman whose success seemed to assure any wife a future sheltered from want. That, however, would take too little account of the individuals concerned, who were possessed of a measure of idealism that was quite rare, and who were scarcely inclined to lead a placid existence in a Hampstead flat. The marriage was not only a new chapter of life; for Lindsay, it was a new life completely, that of a married man, and also that of a writer.

We have already seen the attitude shown by Lindsay towards other marriage plans. A puritan in a puritanical world, he saw women as being shrouded in a mystery that, throughout his life, he would try to penetrate. If his reactions went from repulsion to attraction, this was because he was always somewhat fascinated by the mystery of the Eternal Female, in the manner of Goethe.

First of all, Jacqueline was young. Even in this, she was, for this distrustful puritan, a safeguard. The twenty-odd years that separated them, far from being a constraint, as sometimes is the case with other couples, was an advantage for him. He got to know women indirectly, starting from a vulnerable stage in their lives; their youth. The difference in age provided a means of asserting his authority; that is to say, his inexperience. He had always lived surrounded by women, but these were mother, sister and aunt. He was 'deprived of the necessary experience of women' in the sense that the women around him were mother-figures.

For both of them, this was the clap of thunder; the understanding was perfect. Each was passionately in love with the other. The youth and naiveté of the young girl prevented her from perceiving the strangeness of this self-taught person's philosophy. She was fascinated by the adult's knowledge and intelligence. She herself, notwithstanding her tender years, showed intellectual qualities that were exceptional. Topics of conversation were not lacking: art, literature and music. In her company, Lindsay forgot the narrow world of insurance. New hopes presented themselves to him, as he shed twenty years from his age. To counter the inherent indolence of David, Jacqueline was lively, with a frivolity that she took from her mother, who was French in origin. She was sentimental and unreserved, the opposite, indeed also the complement, of this intensely-serious, puritanical Scot.

The past also conspired to bring them together. Jacqueline had just known her first great disappointment in love, and threw herself heart and soul into this new experience. She had been on the point of marrying a young man of her own age, a friend of her brother, but he was killed in the War. Was it perhaps through pique that she hastened marriage? Did she, perhaps, by means of a curious transfer of rôles, see in this man the father whom she had never known, just as Lindsay sought in her the image of a benevolent mother? The two fiancés had something else in common. Both had experienced a difficult youth, in the charge of the mother, after the early disappearance of the father. Jacqueline's father, even if he did not leave his wife deliberately, as in the case of Alexander Lindsay, died young, worn out by financial worries, leaving behind him a widow of twenty-seven, with seven children. Three of these died young, while four survived; Jacqueline, and three boys who later emigrated to the United States, taking their mother with them.

If the love of the two was undeniable, there can still be no doubt that the marriage took place with some haste, on 21 December 1916, only a few months after their first meeting. Such speed contrasts strangely with the fourteen-odd years that Lindsay's first engagement had lasted. This time, the inherent caution of Lindsay found itself swept aside by the young girl's enthusiasm. It is impossible to understand the reasons for this marriage, unless one bears constantly in mind the romanticism of Jacqueline. For her, the future was planned; far from the madding crowd, there must be a little cottage, which would serve as both their love-nest and place of work, since this marriage dowry included a writer's pen. Breaking away from the world of business, both had decided to devote their life to literature, Lindsay's youthful dream that had too soon been broken. Convinced of her husband's talent, she was ready to give up everything to follow him to the end of this project, whose success seemed to her to be assured. She was soon to be disillusioned, but tribute must be paid to Jacqueline Lindsay for the courage and self-sacrifice that she showed. Without her, Lindsay would never have written a single line. Her youth, her enthusiasm and her unbounded faith made a writer out of a man who had been suffering from a psychological blockage. This burst of creative activity was too intimately bound up with Lindsay's marriage for us to ignore the tremendous liberation involved in the union. There are some psychological shocks which arrest the development of personality at certain stages of childhood, just as there are others which free tensions hitherto repressed. In the origin of *A Voyage to Arcturus*, there was this euphoria of marriage, just as in the origin of a novel like *Under the Volcano*, Malcolm Lowry's masterpiece, there was a woman's treachery and the author's alcoholic despair. In both these cases, the very special circumstances surrounding the discovery

of a vocation even explain the limitations of the entire work,
and the fact that its importance seems to rest upon a single
book.

## THE WRITER

The marriage took place at Godstone, Surrey, on 21 December
1916. Lindsay, despite his age, and henceforward, despite his ma-
rital status, would see another two years' military service before
being demobilised. It was only then that, in accordance with the
plans of the newly-weds, he left Price Forbes, the firm that employed him, and London itself, to start looking for somewhere to
live, suitable for the ambitions of a new writer. The quest must have
proved a difficult one, since it was destined to last nearly a year,
and to lead as far afield as Cornwall.

Two conditions were essential. The house must be both near to
the sea and far from London. Scotland was rejected, as being too
wet. Wales was an unknown quantity. There remained Cornwall,
whose tip plunged into the sea, as though to escape from London
and England. The married couple accordingly left for Lyme Regis,
Dorset, the first of the coastal resorts passed through on the way to
Cornwall, and then, following the coast, Torquay and Plymouth in
Devon, and Falmouth. Next, they travelled northwards as far as
Newquay. From there, a few miles further north, was the village of
Porth, about half-way between Newquay and St Columb Minor.
There, they found a house in the hollow between two hills, situated
just a few yards from the sea. One had only to walk down the
garden to reach a sloping, sandy beach. Further north was
Trevelgue Hill, at the edge of rocks and wild cliffs, which stretched
as far as the eye could see, to the cape of Trevose Head. It was an
ideal setting for walks, which could be taken across the top of the
hills, or at their foot, across the long beaches of Watergate Bay,
among the most beautiful in Europe. It was difficult to resist the
attraction of such a setting. To buy this house, Lindsay used his
savings, and also converted a pension that had been given to him by
his former employers. Neither Jacqueline nor David appeared to
give much thought to the future. The house was large, and the price
high. After the years spent in London, the marriage, the new life,
the new house were all like a breath of fresh air. London took on the
unreal hue of a nightmare soon forgotten. The true reality of life was

there, with picnics, long walks across the cliffs, and dinners which brought new friends.

Once they were installed at St Columb Minor, Lindsay got down to work, and drafted, within a few months, the first version of a book then called *Nightspore in Tormance*. It was a fantasy novel showing some features in common with the early writings of H. G. Wells, such as *The First Men in the Moon*. The writing presented no major difficulties. In the euphoria of this paradise regained, the book seemed to write itself. Indeed, the project was scarcely a new one. For twenty years, Lindsay had not ceased to imagine every stage of a journey that he wanted to describe. Long before 1919, Lindsay had developed the habit of recording in his notebooks the reflections inspired in him by what he read. The entire philosophy of this book was accordingly already well formulated before Lindsay started to write it. The novel was the fruit of twenty years of waiting.

In spite of all that, it might be wondered whether, while he was writing the book, Lindsay did not change the original idea of the novel. It has been pointed out, quite rightly,[8] that there is a kind of gap between, on the one hand, the beginning of the book, set in a real-world background, quite close to that of the later writings, and, on the other hand, the journey itself, the discovery of the imaginary planet, Tormance. Even if this form of escape appears to us to be the favourite form of the author, Lindsay himself seemed to confirm such a change of direction when he wrote to a writer friend, shortly after publication in 1921, 'I do not know how it is with you, but my books up to the present have turned out quite other than I have originally intended, so that it is all most fascinating to watch them developing themselves on their own lines'[9].

Started in April 1919, *Nightspore in Tormance* was completed in March of the following year. Offered to the publisher, Methuen, the book was immediately accepted, subject to two conditions. Firstly, the entire work was to be cut by 15,000 words, and, secondly, there would have to be a change in the title, which, according to the publisher, was too obscure to capture public interest. The publisher imposed upon Lindsay a new title that was more explicit, *A Voyage to Arcturus*, in spite of the serious misgivings of the author, who saw in this a grievous blow to the significance of the book. From now on, in the mind of many readers, the important character would no longer be Nightspore, but, contrary to the author's intentions, Maskull. Lindsay complied, however, and the book was published in September 1920. The author did not fully realise that fortune had smiled upon him in a way that was almost unbelievable. The first novel of this quite unknown author had been accepted by the first publisher to whom it had been submitted. It should be added, however, that, in this instance, it was the book's great merits that recommended it to the publisher.

*A Voyage to Arcturus* is essentially the story of a quest. The novel opens in the drawing-room of some rich London merchants who, to amuse themselves, have arranged a spiritual séance, this having been a fashionable pastime in English circles around the turn of the century. Maskull and his friend, Nightspore, have been invited to be present at an experiment designed to invoke the spirits. The medium, after passing into a kind of trance, makes a human form appear.

At the same moment, there bursts into the room an amazing character calling himself Krag, who, having contemptuously taunted everyone present, throws himself on the young man brought to life by the medium, and strangles him.

Leaving the guests in a state of bewilderment, Krag draws Maskull and his friend aside, and suggests that they should undertake a journey to an unknown country, which, he assures them, holds similar surprises for them. This country is situated on the star, Arcturus, and is called Tormance. Krag also calls it Crystalman's country.

The journey by airship takes place without incident, but, soon after arrival on the new star, Maskull loses consciousness. When he wakes up, his two travelling companions have disappeared. He sets off to look for them, determined to solve the mystery of this strange journey.

The first being he meets is a woman, Joiwind, the essence of kindness, love and tenderness. Joiwind explains to him the usefulness of the new limbs that Maskull found himself to have on awakening. She also reveals to him the laws and rules of this new universe. There can be no greater pleasure than to do good, she says. The God of this planet is Shaping, also called Crystalman, or Surtur. Eventually, Joiwind introduces Maskull to her husband, Panawe, an artist.

The following day, Maskull has to leave his kind hosts, but not without promising never to forget their kindness, and always to respect their high ideal, the sanctity of life and the need to love one's neighbour. Nothing, therefore, has prepared Maskull for his entry into the terrible world of Oceaxe, the next character he meets on his way. There, force and the desire to dominate reign supreme. Life is not governed by the kind relationships of the earlier background any longer, but by a continual struggle. Oceaxe herself is aggressive and provocative. The new law of Nature is that one must kill to live.

The humanitarian principle propounded by Joiwind cannot survive in such conditions. Maskull is compelled to kill the husband of Oceaxe, whose mistress, to avenge his death, forces Oceaxe to throw herself over a precipice.

The next character is one of those austere preachers who obeys only as a duty. Pleasure, according to Spadevil, is the root of all evil, but to hate pleasure is to discover a new pleasure; the pleasure of hating pleasure. In spite of his self-assurance, Spadevil strikes us as being a false prophet. On his death, his face becomes distorted by a horrible grin, already encountered several times in the novel, and known as Crystalman's grin. At this moment, there appears a new character, Catice, who asserts that this distorted death-mask is proof of fraud; this is Crystalman unveiled.

Catice directs Maskull to the Wombflash forest, warning him against the attraction of pleasure and beauty, both of which make one forget the real object of existence, Muspel. Dreamsinter gives him a similar answer. To Maskull's question 'What have I come to do on the planet Tormance?', Dreamsinter replies, 'You have come to steal the thunder from Muspel, in order to give men a richer life.'

From that time, Maskull is guided as much by men as by signs. In the depths of his solitude, a mysterious beating of drums leads him in the direction of Muspel. Gradually, several characters join him in his quest; first of all, Gleameil, impelled by some inner necessity, leaves her husband and children, to follow Maskull to the other side of the ocean, in an identical search for a more attractive world; next, Leehallfae, a hermaphrodite creature; then Haunte and Corpang, two mystics, also participate in this pilgrimage.

Having come to the end of his journey, however, Maskull still has to resist the temptations of Sullenbode, an amorous and devoted woman, and, particularly, the final traps of Gangnet, the Devil himself, the ultimate and true face of him who had been, from the first page to the last, none other than Crystalman.

It is only now that Maskull again finds his companions, Nightspore and Krag. In the gloom of the tower, another quest begins, also full of traps.

This first effort was unquestionably that of a master. Methuen had not made a mistake, any more than the literary critic, Robert Lynd, who defended the book with the kind of insight for which he was so well known. The reaction of the general public, however, was disappointing.

Lindsay, who did not expect to become an instant celebrity, immediately set to work on a second novel, *The Haunted Woman*. During the course of the summer of 1921, this book was published in serial form in *The Daily News*, the great liberal paper of the inter-War years, the chief literary editor of which was Robert Lynd. It was through reading *The Daily News* of this year, 1921, that Harold Visiak first discovered the name of David Lindsay, to whom he hastened to write, thus beginning one of the rare literary friendships of the author of *A Voyage to Arcturus*. *The Haunted Woman* was, in the event, published in its entirety by Methuen in January 1922, after having undergone a few detailed modifications. The principal amendments were to the titles of the chapters, which were considered too sensational. In spite of this, these bear the stamp of the first appearance of the novel in serial form, with such titles as 'Judge appears on the scene', 'Blanche speaks out', or 'What happened in the second room'.

*The Haunted Woman* is quite different from *A Voyage to Arcturus*, more subtle and better written. The imaginary adventure novel gave way to a book set in England, in a very conventional locale, of the kind which would henceforward provide the background for all Lindsay's novels.

Marshall Stokes returns from the United States, where he has just settled the matter of an inheritance on behalf of his fiancée, Isbel Loment. He rejoins, at Brighton, Isbel and her aunt, Mrs Moor. The two have lived together for some years, leading an idle, nomadic existence from one hotel to another. On the boat returning from the United States, Marshall has met a man called Judge, who has mentioned to him a property he owns near Brighton, which he wants to sell, a very old country-house called Runhill Court. Mrs Moor, tired of travelling, understandably wants to buy a house, and so is interested in this suggestion of Judge. Upon inspection, the house is exactly what Mrs Moor wants. Isbel, on the other hand, feels very uncomfortable about this house of such a different style, which makes a strange impression upon her. Remaining alone for a moment in the hall, Isbel suddenly notices a staircase in front of her, that did not exist before. All these facts seem to confirm the theory, already conveyed, that the house is haunted.

Isbel is determined to solve this mystery. She climbs the staircase, and finds herself facing three doors. The first of these leads into a small room that is almost bare. A mirror reveals an unusual image of herself; passionate, tragic, different from young girls of that period. Another mystery is that, after descending the stairs, she cannot recall what has happened above. The staircase itself has disappeared.

During the next visit, Isbel enters the second of the haunted rooms. She then finds herself face to face with Judge, the owner of the house. He, too, seems transformed, as if this room had the effect of erasing their conventional, social personalities, to reveal only their real selves, distorted by the pressures of their environment.

On the following visit that Judge and Isbel make together, their relationship becomes more intimate. Overwhelmed by the music and the scents of this new paradise of the haunted room, Isbel declares her love for Judge, and, at the same time, recognises that there is nothing in common between herself and her fiancé, Marshall.

They eventually decide to visit together the third room which, since their first meeting, has seemed to hide some disturbing secret. Upon their entry, they are blinded by a burst of sunlight, as if this room were part of some enchanted garden. By the window, they notice a strange musician who, with back turned, plays a flute, seeming to play for them, and to be the source of all this happiness. When he stops playing, they both regain their former personalities, the sunlight disappears, and the love which has just been born peters out.

Disconsolate, Judge decides to approach the musician, in the hope that the latter will help him to regain his love. Rising to his feet, he discerns for the first time the musician's face, and dies, as if struck by lightning. Even if Lindsay does not say so specifically, this musician is none other than Crystalman of *A Voyage to Arcturus*.

As soon as *The Haunted Woman* appeared, in April 1921, Lindsay undertook the writing of a third novel. 'The book will rejoice (subject, again, to the publishers' views!) in the title 'Sphinx', which, however, is only metaphorical, and consists, like its predecessor, of a blend of common and supernatural life; in other respects, however, striking a new line.'[10]

The plot of *Sphinx* begins with the arrival of a young man, Nicholas Cabot, at a small provincial railway station. A chauffeur awaits him, to drive him to 'Mereway', a country-house where Cabot is to spend a month on holiday, as a paying-guest. He also plans to take advantage of his free time to complete his experiments with a machine he has invented, designed to record dreams.

Nicholas Cabot soon realises that the place is scarcely suitable for work. He quickly clashes with the people at the house. The mistress shows herself to be particularly obtrusive, as she sees in this young man a good match for one of her three daughters. The daughters themselves are frivolous. As for the husband, one Sturt, he is a pretentious ex-actor, living only in the past.

Cabot seeks refuge with neighbours; Celia Hantish, a flirtatious woman who is basically subtle and calculating, and Lore Jensen, a well-known musician, whose inspiration has dried up through contact with the frivolous people surrounding her.

Lore is the composer of a tune called 'Sphinx' which symbolises the novel, to which it gives the title. The riddle of the Sphinx, we are told, may represent the riddle of existence, and of why we are living.

Cabot, for his part, suggests a different answer. We die, like the victims of the Sphinx, not because we cannot discover the meaning of our lives, but because we do not understand the significance of our dreams, the part of ourselves hidden in the depths of our souls.

The machine that he has just started to use allows him to penetrate outward appearances to reach the secret depths of everyone. He succeeds in revealing Lore's moral suffering, and even predicts her suicide, after a number of amatory setbacks.

*Sphinx* was written quite quickly between April 1921 and January 1922. From January to May, Lindsay revised his typescript, without becoming completely satisfied with it. It was true that the book lacked clarity, in spite of the method followed, henceforward characteristic of the author; the intrusion of the supernatural into ordinary reality. If this plot of recording the unconscious is not as improbable as it might seem at first sight, in the age of the encephalograph and other modern techniques, the fact remains that it does little to explain how the unconscious, even collectively, can have the value of an oracle. The end of the book, itself very dream-like, seems too implausible to be accepted as a mere supernatural fact. Nicholas Cabot dies abruptly, killed by an overdose of sleeping-pills, and, in Sturt's dream, rejoins Lore in the hereafter, to form, at last, the perfect couple whom everyone envies. As in the best tradition of sensational novels, the reader learns only in the final pages that Lore's father, hitherto unknown, is none other than Sturt. In short, the plots which constitute the main action of the novel have somehow had the effect of making it founder in triviality.

In spite of its defects, *Sphinx* is not as insignificant as it might appear. This double life, to which allusion is often made, lies at the very core of the dialectic of appearance and reality, so dear to Lindsay. Clothes do not make the man, especially not the clothes of an actor as in the case of Sturt. Behind the fine manners of this social milieu, there are hidden intrigues, and a vulgarity which Lindsay never ceases to denounce.

At the beginning of the year 1922, Lindsay was so little satisfied with *Sphinx* that he undertook, simultaneously, the writing of a work of a very different kind, *The Adventures of Monsieur de Mailly*, whose connection with the rest of his work is slender. The action takes place in France, in the reign of Louis XIV. Count Jambac comes to complain to a Parisian lawyer of being pursued by a woman, whose age is equalled only by her ugliness, and who, by means of smiles and an excess of attentions, schemes to compel the Count to marry her. Horrified at this idea, and treated with derision by the King's courtiers, Count Jambac seeks some means of keeping this tenacious Amazon away from him. De Mailly, who is with the lawyer when Count Jambac reveals his misfortune, suggests that he should intervene in the rôle of what we call a private detective.

This brief description of the opening of the novel should be enough to convey the tone and style of the whole book, so that there is no necessity to enumerate in detail the adventures, however racy and complicated. De Mailly's way of life isolates him very sharply from Lindsay's other heroes. Questioned about his tastes, he replies 'My amusements are simple, for I lead a quiet life. As long as women, wine and cards are close at hand, I do not look much further.'[11]

Notwithstanding the thoughtlessness which characterises him, de Mailly possesses an essence of pessimism that enables Lindsay to fire a few broadsides at the society of the period, and, by implication, at all society. Without being a rogue, De Mailly has no illusions about human nature. This private detective knows human passions better than how to use the sword. His interventions always rely upon the weaknesses and vices of mankind: the vengeance of this haughty character, the affectation of that beautiful woman, the fear of scandal of some statesman. He defines his method of working in these terms; namely, 'Men and women are always to be moved by what they desire, but do not possess. One has therefore but to hold before their nose the object of their desire, and they will instantly follow one with the utmost docility!' (page 98.)

The reader who does not know the author of *The Adventures of Monsieur de Mailly* will assuredly gain a very false impression. However, one finds certain remarks about women that give a hint of the author of *Sphinx*. One reads, in fact, this definition which might have had its place in *Philosophical Notes*. 'Where women are concerned, there is no certitude of anything, their wits strike at random like the lightning' (page 140). These few remarks so characteristic of their author, however, are quite rare, and this book must be regarded, above all, as an amusing diversion.

When he wrote *The Adventures of Monsieur de Mailly*, Lindsay had just finished two novels, and written a third. Literature which, when viewed from the outside, had exercised an irresistible fascination for him, proved to be a most arduous occupation, for which he was ill prepared. The writing of a novel demands months and months of effort, particularly testing for the writer's psychological balance. This effort increases when the writer lacks lucidity, as was the case with Lindsay. If Lindsay often compared literary creation to a woman's pregnancy[12], it is also true that, psychologically, these two gestations are identical. It could be added that it is not certain that the birth process can be repeated without risk. Hence, *The Adventures of Monsieur de Mailly* must be regarded as an interlude, intended to relieve the author's tensions, after the writing of the sterile *A Voyage to Arcturus*. There lies the explanation of this absurd humour which, admittedly, acts as a solace, coming as it does from a writer whose austerity has so often been emphasised, in spite of a very sharp sense of humour that he freely revealed throughout his life.

It is also probable that *The Adventures of Monsieur de Mailly* was as much the work of Jacqueline as of David Lindsay. We know that she took a very close interest in the writing of her husband's novels. Moreover, being of French origin on her mother's side, she was well qualified to provide all the relevant information on the background of the plot, while David's knowledge of France, and especially the France of Louis XIV, was doubtless very limited.

There is one further reason, by no means insignificant, to account for the writing of this book that was so little representative of its author's talent. The two earlier novels by Lindsay had suffered commercial setbacks. Now, after these three years of unrewarded effort, the family resources had been rapidly exhausted. The birth of two daughters, Diana in 1919, and then Helen in 1921, and the poor sales of his books, compelled Lindsay to reduce his standard of living, and to consider new ways to earn money. *The Adventures of*

*Monsieur de Mailly* was written partly with the object of resolving these financial problems. Unfortunately, once again, this attempt failed, since the book, completed in May 1923, was rejected by several publishers, not being published until 1926.

It turned out, moreover, that to the commercial setback there was soon added a problem of conscience that had been quite unforeseen at the start of the writing. Should a serious writer allow his integrity to become degraded, in order to cope with the pressures of external factors on his art? Was it not dishonourable to write just for money? *Sphinx*, which Lindsay wrote in a parallel direction to *The Adventures of Monsieur de Mailly*, contained, in essence, all the author's doubts about this problem of conscience. Hence, Lore Jensen, the musician, is accused by her friends of having degraded her art in stooping to write worthless popular songs aimed at the general public. Between Lore and Lindsay, the parallel suggests itself so strongly that it cannot be a matter of mere coincidence. It is the author of *The Adventures of Monsieur de Mailly* himself who seems to speak when criticism is made of this undignified compromise between art and money. 'It's all very well for superior persons to insist on pure art, as opposed to money-making, but, in the meantime, who is to provide the artist's bread and butter? The exalted few who know all about it, or the crowd who know nothing whatever about it, but are quite prepared and willing to put their hands in their pockets if they see what they want in the shop window? ... You don't for one moment imagine that anyone with brains – or without brains, for that matter! – writes everlastingly-round roses, and nightingales, and thatched cottages, and convent-windows, for the sheer love of the thing! Of *course* it's done for money! Of *course* it's pot-boiling! But if I don't boil my own pot, are you going to boil it for me?' (*Sphinx*, pages 71–72.)

The next novel, *Devil's Tor*, provides us with further evidence of this agony of mind. In circumstances that are broadly similar, Uncle Colborne is accused of having compromised his idealism by speculating on the Stock Exchange. Once again, Lindsay seems to intervene through the mouth of Helga, in defending the accused. 'But money is so necessary, and he was thoroughly upset by the poor reception of intellectual works that had cost him years and years of thought. That estate agency business, too, it wasn't sought, but was practically thrust under his nose' (page 47).

He also had cause to regret the setback in the negotiations that had taken place since 1924 between himself and the publisher, Jonathan Cape. Yet again, Lindsay proved to be unlucky. An earlier agreement with John Long, the publisher of *Sphinx*, prevented him from proceeding with the offer made by Cape, who had declared himself ready to purchase all rights of publication in his future work, and to publish immediately an anthology of short stories which Cape would commission. It seems likely that, guided by a publisher of Cape's ability, Lindsay's career could have been completely different.[13] Very strict discipline would have been necessary, and Lindsay did not seem inclined to yield. However, the contract offered to him by Cape certainly fulfilled the requirements that Lindsay had enumerated. 'What I really want is a publisher who will say to me "You write a book and we will do the rest!"'[14]

This rôle of 'guide' eventually fell upon the publisher, Victor Gollancz, to whom Lindsay was introduced in September 1929, through the good offices of Harold Visiak, who was about to publish his own novel, *Medusa*, with this firm. The welcome offered to Lindsay was encouraging, but Gollancz's caution as a businessman prevented the unreserved support that Lindsay so needed. It was not until 1946 that Gollancz agreed to republish *A Voyage to Arcturus* and *The Haunted Woman*.

As in the case of his contacts with Cape, Lindsay's destiny was not to be transformed. Gollancz never concealed his admiration for Lindsay. This affection, however, was probably more for the man than for the writer. From their few encounters, Gollancz gained the impression of having dealt with an exceptional man, albeit a pitiful writer. He was to say later of Lindsay that he was 'a remarkable man' who had always fascinated him. The originality of thought, applied by a powerful imagination and very sharp sensibility, were the real qualities that Gollancz recognised in Lindsay when he declared, 'In my view, he thought and felt and imagined superbly, but wrote abominably.'

Lindsay's beginning as a writer, in spite of commercial setbacks, had been relatively encouraging, to the extent that, without too much difficulty, he had succeeded in getting his books published. Between 1919, when he first started to write, and 1926, Lindsay published four novels. Moreover, he had scarcely expected to be a commercial success. He knew full well that he was running counter to public ideas and taste. He said, for example, of *A Voyage to Arcturus*, that the book 'was written in rather an unpopular style'. In

1929, when he went to see Gollancz to try to persuade him to republish his novel, he made this remark which showed very clearly his complete lack of illusions, 'Only a very few people will ever read *Arcturus*; but as long as even two or three people will listen to Beethoven, two or three people will read it.'[15]

In spite of his setbacks, Lindsay continued writing, faithful to his own concept of literature, rejecting any concession to public taste. It was thus that he undertook the writing of a book of which he said, even before it was published, 'No book *anything like* it has ever seen the light of day, but it may impose too many demands on readers.' This rather unusual book was *Devil's Tor*.

Soon after settling in Cornwall, Lindsay had started to interest himself in the prehistoric age. The countryside around Dartmoor had had a disturbing effect upon him, as if these sprawling heathlands hid some secret. Facing the hills, he found it difficult not to ponder upon human destiny, as if the answer awaited him there. Could it be that the ancients had a way of life and beliefs more consistent with a magical conception of the universe? His intuitions, the interest he felt in Scandinavian tales, his questions about the nature of women, were all going to find themselves amalgamated in this book to which he would be particularly attached.[16] It was perhaps because he wanted to include his entire philosophy that the book proved very difficult to revise. A rough draft, started in 1923, was completed within a few months, and entitled *The Ancient Tragedy*. In 1928, Lindsay went back to it, and revised it. He gave it a new title, *Devil's Tor*. This second version was sent to the publisher, Victor Gollancz, in 1929, at the suggestion of Harold Visiak. The book was rejected. Lindsay quickly set to work again, as he was not completely satisfied himself with this version. For nearly two more years, he spent long, laborious hours, striving to improve this book which had already become a 'monster'.[17] In spite of all this work, however, the message always seemed to swamp the framework of the book. Moreover, these constant revisions, instead of helping Lindsay to discipline his art, had the effect of making the book still more laboured in style. He had to wait until 1932 for the book to be published at last. When it came out, reviews appeared in most of the papers of the period, over the names of some of the greatest in the literary world, such as J. B. Priestley, H. E. Bates, Rebecca West, Hugh L'Ansson Fausset, L. P. Hartley, and others. In spite of the fairly favourable comments,[18] this presented a new setback. No book would henceforth be published during the author's lifetime by publishers now made cautious by the failure of this attempt. The setback to *Devil's Tor* prevented, in particular, any new edition of *A Voyage to Arcturus*, long unavailable, and which, in esoteric circles, continued to attract new readers. Even if one should not belittle the efforts made by the publishers to launch *Devil's Tor*, it is nevertheless regrettable that these efforts were made on behalf of so difficult a work, whereas, properly supported by a publicity campaign, *A Voyage to Arcturus* would quickly have established itself as a novel of great originality.

As in all Lindsay's writing, there is, at the root of the novel, a supernatural basis; here, a piece of magic stone that a character, Hugh Drapier, brings back from India, after it has been entrusted to him by two explorers met on the way, Arsinal and Saltfleet. Once back in England, Hugh Drapier stays with his parents, whose house is built near a hill, Devil's Tor, towards which Hugh feels irresistibly drawn. A first exploration, made with his cousin, Ingrid Colborne, reveals to him that this hill hides, in reality, a very ancient tomb. The next day, alone, he goes into the inside of the tomb, where he discovers the second piece of the magic stone that he possesses. Inside the tomb, he witnesses an apparition of a majestic woman, clearly some queen or ancient goddess buried there for a long time. The two explorers then arrive on the scene, to reclaim the stone entrusted to Drapier. Saltfleet, going in search of the latter, finds him at the foot of Devil's Tor, crushed by a rock that has become dislodged. In his turn, Saltfleet sees, in phantom form, a woman who resembles the Great Mother of primitive religions, whose coming signifies the rebirth of the world. Gradually, he becomes convinced that Ingrid is the reincarnation of this Great Mother. At the end of the novel, while the two pieces of the magic stone come together, to regain their primitive unity, the two young people, Saltfleet and Ingrid, unite to form the couple destined to redeem the world.

This very brief survey of the plot does not do justice to a novel of some five hundred pages, which abounds in ideas, but, in fact, the plot matters little here, since, as in *A Voyage to Arcturus*, it comprises merely a succession of new characters. What really counts is the philosophy that each defends, and, in this respect, *A Voyage to Arcturus*, like *Devil's Tor*, can be classified as a 'philosophical novel'. In *Devil's Tor*, the author succeeds in omitting all plausibility, in order to lead to its conclusion a very personal quest for the nature of the universe, its creation and its survival. Here, this universe is presented in parallel with mankind until it appears that the bonds between human and natural phenomena are more and more tight. We can be sceptical, the tortuousness and verbiage of the author may bore or irritate us, but could it be otherwise with a work which resolutely eschews the depiction of stereotypes in order to try to convey in words deep intuitions that are almost intangible.

## LIFE OF THE WRITER

Throughout these years, from 1919, Lindsay devoted himself to his new profession as a writer. He did so with a fervour that justified the years of waiting and patience that he had gone through before being able to realise his dream of escape. The publication of *A Voyage to Arcturus* in 1920, even if it failed to convince the literary world of Lindsay's worth, nevertheless enabled him to become known in the small village of St Columb Minor, in Cornwall, to which he had just moved. Hence, he entered the kind of rural circles described in *Sphinx*. In return, he organised parties, especially on the initiative of his wife, who liked to be surrounded by people, and whom her husband's austerity eventually wearied. She was young and lively, while David Lindsay could not stand the polite, trivial discussions of the drawing-room. He had a superiority complex that made him shun the platitudes of topical conversation. With him, the impression of unreality that he felt towards existence coloured his own life to the extent of making almost impossible any kind of human contact. To go to tea with neighbours accordingly became an ordeal. Nicholas Cabot, the character who resembled Lindsay like a younger brother, congratulated himself upon not being welcomed at the station by his hosts, as he was thus relieved of the obligation of talking platitudes on the way.

It is easy to see just how unbearable such an intransigent attitude must have been. His wife was obliged many times to reproach him about it. He must have been perfectly well aware himself of this characteristic when he wrote of Judge's wife 'She was one for society, while the master likes no one's company so much as his own' (*The Haunted Woman*, page 30).[19]

Under pressure from his wife, this finicky puritan ended by submitting himself to the company of people less concerned with virtue, saying 'to a man of active intelligence, *ennui* is so real an evil that he will prefer the society of those with intellect, but not morality, to that of those others with morality, but not intellect; this even if he is moral himself' (*Philosophical Notes*, Number 103).

So, boredom overtook Lindsay throughout this period. After the euphoria of settling into a new environment, after the excitement of writing *A Voyage to Arcturus*, and the joy that followed the almost immediate publication of the book, Lindsay discovered that the life that he had chosen threatened to be more difficult than he had anticipated a few months earlier. Cornwall certainly offered the three 'essentials for the production of a work of art; leisure, solitude and nature' (*Philosophical Notes*, Number 124). Each of these conditions brought its own disadvantages, however. To fill his leisure, he needed to be surrounded by books or friends. Now, friends were rare, or not very interesting. As for books, they were non-existent. Lindsay found himself completely isolated from the London literary world that he had previously frequented. Not one single literary magazine was available. Solitude may have stimulated creation, but it led a man to fall back on himself, and eventually could involve a degeneration of the mental faculties. Lindsay reflected 'The best artists love solitude' (*Philosophical Notes*, Number 138). He extolled the benefits of solitude, but, at the same time, he recognised its dangers. Carried to excess, asceticism, spirituality and austerity ended by damaging the mental faculties. A full and active life was the source of health, and the best antidote to depression. It was impossible, moreover, to isolate oneself from the world, without, at the same time, depriving oneself of the tools with which one worked, as the richness of experience and emotion that an artist requires can only be encountered in contact with the world.

Lindsay's daughter, Diana, remembers those sad winter evenings spent at the fireside. 'When I was a child, we lived in the country, there was no radio, we had no money. All the winter was spent reading; my father would read on one side of the fire, my mother on the other, and she would always read out to him passages from whatever she was reading, and they used to discuss whatever they read.'

During the early years of his writing career, Lindsay worked with a will in writing his novels. He preferred to get up early, often even before his wife and children, and even making these early mornings an indispensable condition of his work. He would then write throughout the morning and, usually, for a good part of the afternoon, writing his books directly onto the typewriter until reaching the final version, when he would type once again with very great care, starting each page again at the slightest erasure. Then he liked to go for a walk in the country, and the evenings would be devoted to reading. During the last ten years of his life, however, in view of the setback to his books, and his difficulty in finding a publisher, Lindsay worked in a much less regular fashion, getting up later, and resting during the afternoon. In spite of everything, he continued writing with exemplary determination.

After spending some hours writing, it was his practice to seek the necessary relaxation in the surrounding hills. The few visits that he had made to Dartmoor had become a kind of communion with Nature for him. He considered Dartmoor to be the perfect setting for metaphysical meditation. In front of these hills he felt a sort of terror, as if, fully aware of the age of the world, he was investigating the mystery of mankind. We know that *Devil's Tor* was set on Dartmoor; the Gaelic name, Tor, moreover, is still much used in this region for hills. The influence that the countryside exercised upon Lindsay is described at length in the novel. 'I think that there may be the slow accumulation through the ages of a chemico-physical secretion, our invisible contact with the fine emanations from which may produce in us the mental atmosphere of an awful antiquity' (page 35).

The coast of Cornwall and these hills of Dartmoor provided another interest from Lindsay's point of view; bad weather. We have already mentioned the ailment which impelled him to avoid sunshine. The writer discovered quickly enough that a climate of rain and storms agreed far better with his tortured spirit. 'The lovely weather makes everything exquisite, but it is my worst condition for writing; gloom and rain suit me far better', he wrote, soon after settling in Cornwall.[20] Elsewhere, we find frequent references to this preference of his for storms. His notebooks are full of remarks such as 'Darkness and gloom breed romance, mystery and philosophy.'[21] For him, bad weather alone could compensate for the insipid vulgarity of a landscape (*Philosophical Notes*, Number 136). Cornwall, and more especially Dartmoor, was a convenient substitute for distant Scandinavia, that he had learned to love through his stories, and which inspired him throughout his work.

The successive setbacks to his work left their mark on Lindsay, as might have been expected, and served only to increase his pessimism. On the financial plane, they had the foreseeable consequence of leading the family to the brink of ruin. It was partly for this reason that Lindsay decided to leave Cornwall, in order to settle, in October 1929, at Ferring, a small village in Sussex, four miles from Worthing.

Lindsay had invested a little money on the Stock Exchange, but this was soon spent. Over a period of twenty years, the family survived in a miraculous fashion, thanks to a legacy left by Lindsay's aunt, but especially thanks to the privations of all kinds that the family was compelled to accept. The move to Ferring, to a more modest house, was just one example of this decline in living standards. Unfortunately, this lowering of standards was to take full effect throughout the years spent at Ferring.

This change of setting occurred in the nick of time. At Ferring, in spite of the financial difficulties, ever more pressing, life was much more relaxed. Nearly ten years after having described them, Lindsay found the Sussex Downs.[22] He also found a gentler climate. Jacqueline looked after a kitchen-garden, which extended from the rear of the house, and she made jam. David, for his part, devoted himself to one of his favourite pastimes; the maintenance of his flower-beds. He loved roses, pansies and lupins, and took no small pride in showing visitors the wonders of his garden.

From now on, there were many of these visitors, coming from London, or even spending a few days at the Ferring house. Walks would be taken during the day, and the evening devoted to discussions, which often continued until well into the night. One of these visitors was the painter, Robert Barnes, a friend of long standing, since he had met Lindsay for the first time in 1921, when he was a young man of only twenty-one. Both were passionately fond of music and were in close touch until the Second World War.

In 1938, after spending nine years at Ferring, the Lindsay family moved once more, at the instigation of Jacqueline Lindsay. She complained bitterly of loneliness, and would have liked to be surrounded by more people. The bungalow that they occupied at Ferring seemed to her to be small. Above all, however, the family's financial resources had been exhausted for a considerable time. It was in this frame of mind that the Lindsays bought a large house in a residential district of Hove, not far from Brighton. To do this it was necessary to borrow money, as the Ferring house did not immediately find a buyer, and remained unoccupied for several months.

Settling at Hove was, indeed, the initiative of Mrs Lindsay, who had conceived the idea of running a family boarding-house, in the hope of resolving their financial problems. David Lindsay, for his part, scarcely approved of this plan. He had shown, in the past, that he would sooner barricade his door against strangers than open it wide. In *Sphinx*, he had described a family boarding-house with a critical pen. Was the spectre of 'Mereway' about to be reborn under his own roof? If he ended by accepting the change of residence, he did so without pleasure, the more so because he dreaded the nearness to Brighton, the fashionable seaside resort, invaded throughout the year by hordes of tourists. He agreed to go to Brighton only on exceptional occasions. The proximity of the beach held no attraction for him; he went there only rarely. This settling at Hove was a concession that he made to his wife, since he realised that he was largely responsible for the situation in which the family found itself through the failure of his books.

Soon after moving in, they started to welcome paying guests, and in particular French students who came to spend several months in England with the object of perfecting their English. Was it anti-Latin prejudice or for the good of the students that Lindsay would not tolerate hearing a single word of French spoken? 'They are here to learn English', he would say. 'They must speak English.' The coming of French students was interrupted, however, by the outbreak of the Second World War. It was accordingly necessary to replace them, and what was done was to make a lodging-house for young naval officers. Here again, Lindsay showed himself to be unenthusiastic. He had not forgiven the military for having called him to fight in 1916. He did not look kindly on his house being invaded by so many young men at a time when his two daughters, Diana and Helen, were of marriageable age. Nevertheless, in time, his hostility disappeared, or at least lessened. It even happened that Lindsay agreed to play chess with one of these naval officers.

## LITERARY FRIENDS

Settling in Hove brought at least one compensation. Henceforward, Lindsay found himself near to his friend, Harold Visiak, who lived in this same town. One has to go back quite a long way to trace the beginning of this relationship. It was in September 1921 that Visiak read, in *The Daily News*, Lindsay's novel, *The Haunted Woman*, which appeared there in serial form. Fascinated by the strangeness of the story, Visiak wrote at once to its author. It was in this way that a friendship began which would end only with Lindsay's death. If, however, the correspondence between the two men was prolific from the very outset, they had to wait for nearly eight years before they met, at the time of a trip to London made by Lindsay in 1929. Even if it occurred to Lindsay, sometimes, in the course of this relationship, to judge Visiak a shade too loquacious, he never forgot that this was, in fact, his first admirer; moreover, a not insignificant admirer, since Visiak was himself a writer, and one who was soon to become known, notably for his works on Milton.[23]

This long relationship, however, was not due to chance. Lindsay was quick to notice this, since, only a few months after his discovery of this admirer, he was writing to him in the following terms: 'I feel with you that, however different the *form* of our work may be, we have essentially a great deal in common.'[24] Both possessed, in fact, this temperament of the recluse, which distinguished them from all other current literary figures. Their respective efforts brought little enough reward, and, in this respect, their correspondence and friendship are those of two unlucky writers mutually comforting one another. Both were interested in the supernatural. Visiak recounted, in his autobiography, unexplained happenings and visions that Lindsay would not have scorned.[25] It was also this interest in mystery and the supernatural that made Lindsay say that he admired in his friend 'the living creed of the essential unreality of reality'. Let it be added that both regarded women with fascination and anxiety. While Lindsay very nearly never married, Visiak, for his part, remained a bachelor, living always with his mother. Visiak's description of his attitude towards women could equally be applied to that of Lindsay. 'A Zulu tyrant or sanguinary pirate I could romanticise, but not a seductive maid; my idealised abstractions belonged entirely to the masculine gender. They were expressed; the feminine leaven was repressed.'[26]

The second important literary friend of whom we know was the novelist, L. H. Myers, author of *The Root and the Flower*, a novel later unobtainable, and which few people knew, in spite of the eulogies heaped upon it. In September 1925, Lindsay received from Myers the following letter. 'About six months ago, I read *A Voyage to*

*Arcturus* for the first time. I have read it again since, and was still more impressed by it on a second reading. I don't, as a rule, care much about books of that kind, for the reason that, to create a successful fantasy, one must possess, first, a strong, deep, personal intuition, and, secondly, a very powerful imagination, and these qualities are, of course, rare, but your intuition was, I am convinced, strong and urgent, and your imagination seems to me to have been quite equal to its task. I am therefore full of admiration and curiosity. These are sentiments which prompt me, and, I hope, excuse the letter. There are many questions which I should like to put to you, and I should very much like to meet you. If you live in London, and feel, on your side, sufficiently good-natured, or flattered, to accept an invitation to lunch with me one day at my Club, I should be very pleased.'[27]

The club that Myers mentioned was none other than the Cranium, which then comprised a number of intellectuals from Chelsea and Bloomsbury, including such figures as Leonard Woolf, Lytton Strachey and John Maynard Keynes. There was also Myers, who would not have been slow to dissociate himself from this circle, but who, for the moment, felt at ease in these surroundings of which his aristocratic social background made him a part. It is not difficult to imagine the effect produced by this restricted circle upon Lindsay, who had just made his base in Cornwall, to be thus confronted by the élite of London; an élite which never neglected to proclaim its own superiority, to the extent of soon becoming the target of numerous caricatures, including those of Myers himself.[28] His background made Myers the very opposite of Lindsay. Born into a well-known family, educated at Eton and Cambridge, Myers was an aristocrat who 'had money enough not to work, except for a brief period at the Board of Trade during the First World War.'[29]

Between these two men, there was certainly a class antagonism, mitigated only by the fact that, even within his own social class, Myers was himself very isolated. This aristocrat was also a member of the Communist Party.

Fortunately, their friendship did not rest upon their social connections, but upon their writing talent. In Myers, Lindsay recognised a writer whose seriousness contrasted sharply with the aestheticism, or 'taste for the trivial', of his contemporaries. Myers, the writer, was intensely serious, even if the circles in which he lived were mediocre and empty. In reality, he was a man of harassed temperament. Disillusioned by social and human relationships, he immersed himself more and more in solitude, until finally killing himself in 1944, a year before Lindsay died. Myers felt a fundamental discontent with contemporary reality, which impelled him to seek the answer to his anguish elsewhere. He shared with Lindsay this belief in a transcendent world. If he turned towards Oriental religion and philosophy, it was to nourish a growing mysticism. 'I believe myself to have a very strong feeling of the numinous', he said.[30] Like Lindsay, Myers never succeeded in relating his religious need to established sectarian denominations.

From 1926 onwards, the relationship between the two writers was uninterrupted until the death of Myers. Moreover, it was greatly facilitated by Lindsay's move. In fact, after leaving the environment of Bloomsbury, Myers settled in Sussex, at East Grinstead. It was there that he undertook the writing of *The Root and the Flower*. Quite soon afterwards, Lindsay himself settled in this area, so that one wonders whether his choice of Ferring was perhaps dictated by the fact that his two friends, Visiak and Myers, already lived in Sussex.

Lindsay and Myers never ceased to interest themselves in one another's work. Hence, Myers was one of the first to read *Devil's Tor* in typescript, and even helped to get it published. Lindsay, in return, received *The Root and the Flower*, the first part of *The Near and the Far*, the week that it was published, in 1929. Perhaps Lindsay recognised in it certain of his own ideas, since *The Near and the Far* and *A Voyage to Arcturus* show several points in common, as a shrewd critic has already emphasised. 'Gangnet–Crystalman is Daniyal, ten years or so before Daniyal was conceived.'[31] In the novel by Myers, Daniyal is the chief of a clan of aesthetes, who are idle, frivolous and self-admiring. What could be no more than a harmless pastime, however, is presented to us as being one of the manifestations of Evil. By this yardstick, Daniyal, like Crystalman, is an incarnation of the Devil. Both are sophisticated and effeminate. In the two novels, the atmosphere of corruption and vulgarity is identical.

Certain passages in the two works seem to strike the same echo. 'It was by no means easy, in the Pleasance of the Arts, to escape from the sound of music, just as, on certain days, you could not escape from a sweet, sickly smell that hung over the whole place.'[32] The reader of *A Voyage to Arcturus* will find there the same symptoms of corruption. When he arrives at the top of the tower, in the last chapter of the book, Maskull finally recognises around him the atmosphere of Crystalman. He is equally assailed by 'the sweet smell emanating from it . . . strong, loathsome and terrible; it seemed to spring from a sort of loose, mocking slime, inexpressibly vulgar and ignorant' (page 246). Crystalman, like Daniyal, behind his good manners and attractive appearance, conceals a fundamental treachery and corruption. Myers and Lindsay put us on our guard against dangers which surround us. It is in contact with treacherous reality that the heroes, Jali and Maskull, succeed in thinking for themselves, and in distinguishing between Good and Evil.

Myers and Visiak seemed to be the only two writers with whom Lindsay maintained any relationship.[33] It is possible, however, that, through these two men, Lindsay was able to meet other writers, such as Walter de la Mare or Olaf Stapledon. Myers expressed great admiration for the work of Stapledon, and it seems probable that he tried to share this with Lindsay, especially as the latter did not scorn, on occasions, science-fiction novels such as those which Stapledon had made his speciality. As for Walter de la Mare, Visiak knew him sufficiently well to get him to read Lindsay's *Philosophical Notes*. Consequently, Lindsay could have read certain of de la Mare's novels, in which, as we know, the supernatural played a most important part.[34]

## THE END OF A CAREER

Contemporaneously with *The Ancient Tragedy*, which later became *Devil's Tor*, Lindsay had been writing another novel, entitled *The Violet Apple*. As soon as *Devil's Tor* was published, in 1932, he started work on a new book, *The Witch*, which also remained unpublished. The writing of *The Witch* proved to be no less laborious than that of *Devil's Tor*. Started in 1932, a first draft was completed two years later, only to be rejected by the publisher, Victor Gollancz. From that time onwards, Lindsay never ceased to write, and re-write, this novel, which seemed to elude him more and more. Throughout the writing he had before him a plaster effigy of a witch, sculpted for Lindsay's benefit by his friend, Robert Barnes, in order to inspire him.[35] Four years after beginning the writing, Lindsay said that he still worked each day on *The Witch*, with an unusual intensity. In 1939, the book was almost completed, but Lindsay no longer expected to get it published, and left the typescript in that condition.

The Second World War, which then broke out, did not surprise him, even though it affected him deeply. For a long time, he had not had any illusions about his contemporaries. For twenty years, he had witnessed, each day, an 'assassination of nature', knowing that, logically, the destruction of plants and animals led to the extermination of the 'human biped'. The war was now the culmination of this 'civilisation of decadence'. In spite of the high regard he felt for German culture, he was deeply shocked by the atrocities of which Germany had shown herself capable. Ever since 1933, Lindsay had seen through Hitler, as early as the occasion when one of his daughters had just made a trip to Germany. She had brought back with her a miniature soldier whose bellicose attitude revolted him. He lost no time in seizing this toy, and throwing it on the fire, thinking that it was made of lead that would immediately melt. Unfortunately, the toy was made of plastic, and started to burn with a nauseating smell. Lindsay, whose sense of smell was always most acute, took advantage of this to assert that this stench and treachery were completely characteristic of Nazism. He found Hitler's pretensions ridiculous, and used to say that he did not know what was meant by the Aryan race.

The last six years of his life passed quietly. In spite of worrying financial difficulties, Lindsay seemed to have achieved a kind of serenity of spirit. If he complained very little, this was partly because fortitude had always been for him the great lesson to learn from philosophy. In his detachment, he noticed that, in spite of the failures with the public, the difficult experience he had been through had enriched him on a personal level. It had allowed him to embark on an internal quest that inspired his idealism. The serenity that he demonstrated was that of the Stoic, as summarised by a remark that he recorded in his notebook; 'To find oneself in opposition to a few people is worrying and disturbing; but to set oneself in deliberate opposition to the whole world has a calming and ennobling effect upon the character' (*Philosophical Notes*, Number 389).

To be alone against everyone seems, in fact, to be the best proof of being in error. Yet, who can assert that, in 1940, it was not the world that was wrong, and that the truth was not in Lindsay's message? Already, in 1918, Oswald Spengler had proclaimed the 'decline of the West'. A few years later, Sigmund Freud had diagnosed 'discontents of civilisation'. At the same time, *A Voyage to Arcturus* passed unnoticed. Then, twenty years later, the wheel of

Fortune seemed to return to its starting-point, apparently reaching its nadir. Throughout those inter-War years, mankind had continued to cherish illusions. In the United States, the 'Jazz Age' was born, while 'a whole race was going hedonistic, deciding on pleasure'.[36] In this exaltation, *A Voyage to Arcturus* continued to pass unnoticed. Nevertheless, at the moment when war broke out, it would have been good to remember this obscure book, *A Voyage to Arcturus*. Lindsay's characters, too, are drawn towards death, as though to the tune of an irresistible waltz, while humanity continues to 'kill, dance and love'. When war broke out, Maskull had reached the last journey of the circle. The morning mist cleared, revealing the spectacle of 'millions and millions of individuals, grotesque, vulgar, ridiculous and corrupted by pleasure', and who, in their despair, called for help to him, the sole survivor, surviving against everything.

David Lindsay died with the War on 16 July 1945. During these final years, he had suffered from anaemia, aggravated by the hardships that he had endured for so long, and by the poor quality of the food then available. Already stricken with this anaemia, he lost blood on several occasions. The first time, while he was taking a bath one morning, a bomb was dropped near to the house. In the explosion, the bathroom window was broken, and a splinter of glass seriously injured him, causing much loss of blood. A short time later, after he had recovered, he was knocked down by a child on a bicycle, and lost more blood. Finally, during the month of June 1945, he had an abscess on a tooth, which infected him very quickly. Detesting doctors as he did, and always refusing to be treated by them, he did not say a word to his wife. By the time it was noticed, it was too late. The whole of one side of his jaw had been destroyed by the abscess. All that remained was an enormous, painful hole. This abscess swiftly contaminated the blood. David Lindsay died of 'haemorrhage due to erosion of vessels, and carcinoma of the mouth, with gangrene of lower lip', to quote directly from the Death Certificate.

## THE MAN

We must now try to evaluate further the personality of this exceptional man, whose life we now know. What manner of man was he? What were his tastes? Throughout the main events of his life, we have already outlined his personality.

Physically, Lindsay was of medium height, rather thin, and giving an impression less of weakness than of reserved strength. Different pictures that have survived show a man with an oval face, and hair cut short, parted on the side. The most noticeable feature is unquestionably the clearness of his grey-blue eyes, admirably penetrating, and testifying to an intense inner life. Of all his characters, it is Nicholas Cabot who seems to correspond most closely to the physique of the author. 'He was a pale, lean, shortish, inconspicuous young fellow, in the middle twenties, with rather delicate upper features, but with strong-looking eyes, a determined jaw, and the full thrust-out lips belonging to an audacious mind, as distinguished from an audacious temperament' (*Sphinx*, page 7).

More interesting is the psychological portrait. All those who knew Lindsay recognised in him a very attractive man, and, at the same time, a very unhappy one. To cast the author among the eccentrics, as there was no reluctance to do when his books came out, is to be particularly unjust to him. This would be to believe that he sought this singularity, when in fact, he was doing no more than to declare the deep disagreement that existed between himself and those around him.

At the root of this reaction, there was unquestionably a very deep sensitivity, that he often sought to cloak beneath an appearance of hardness. Added to that, there was a great shyness that prevented him from being completely at his ease in the company of others. Here is how Visiak described their first meeting. 'On the evening when he came to see me at Brondesbury, he was at first formal, stiff, inhibited; but he soon relaxed, and then spoke in his normal, somewhat stilted manner . . .'[37].

Lindsay found the necessary solace in music and solitude, but, when these tensions were not liberated, he experienced abominable bouts of pessimism, which led him to shut himself in his room for several days. With him, tragedy was not a vague doctrine or theory, but a painful fact of life. The frequent quarrels between husband and wife invariably ended with his withdrawing to his room, which he would not agree to leave until he had brooded on his rancour for several hours. He was not a man who could confide in anyone, preferring to hide his grief, notwithstanding the disastrous consequences that such an attitude could not fail to entail. His philosophy of fortitude derived, in part, from this inability to pour out his misery. 'In times of great emotional disturbance, the first essential is concealment of the emotion, whether it be anger, remorse, love or fear. The natural desire to somehow express the feelings, and so relieve oneself by action, if acted upon, is certain to be afterwards regretted. The only wise course is to endure and wait' (*Philosophical Notes*, Number 331).

Jacqueline Lindsay had a habit of telling her husband that he was inhuman, but perhaps he was too human, seeking to hide the weaknesses of his suffering nature behind a mask of hardness. It was because he felt so vulnerable to emotion that he made of emotion the supreme enemy. During his life, Lindsay always forced himself to subjugate his true nature to one that was superimposed. Since he felt rather lazy, he forced himself towards certain activities, such as rising early to compel himself to work. In all things, moreover, he made himself take meticulous care. His determination to dig up the weeds in his garden went far beyond a simple love of flowers. He also made it a point of honour never to send off any typescript containing the slightest erasure. He took punctilious care of his clothes, and ensured that he never appeared untidy.

This rigour was not, however, one of his façades, since all those who knew him are unanimous in praising his charm.[38] Surrounded by his family or friends, he was a polite, affable man, whom Visiak has described in these terms; 'In fact, he was apparently one of the most equable and placable of men. He lived normally in a state of settled, and sometimes it seemed almost phlegmatic, good humour; a genial, comfortable presence, whether seated squarely and comfortably in his chair, or forging heftily along in a country walk. He enjoyed life; relished his food, his drink – especially ale in an inn – and his pipe.'[39]

Lindsay's temperament was not always so placid. There is no doubt, however, that this portrait of him is true. As Visiak told me shortly before he died, it is difficult to imagine that such an attractive character could possibly be hidden behind the author of *A Voyage to Arcturus*. To Visiak's portrait should be added the fact that Lindsay liked not only beer, but also whisky, the effect of which can scarcely have helped to cure his liver complaint. As regards home comforts, his marriage, from this point of view, was very disappointing. He left his sister and aunt without finding in his wife the skill of these two excellent cooks.

Lindsay was, in fact, a much more tormented character than Visiak's portrait suggests. He did not feel very much at ease in the

company of others, unless he knew them well. For one thing, he
hated the triviality of normal conversation, but, at the same time,
hesitated to broach important topics, or to embark upon philosophical discussion. In fact, he lived a little apart, deep in speculation,
and not appearing to notice those around him very much. He never
paid much attention to the presence of his children, for example,
which delighted the latter, as they were accordingly left at complete
liberty to play. For the children, to be left alone with him was like a
short stay in paradise, so tolerant was he. All the practical organisation of the family life rested, in fact, with his wife, leaving him to
live in his intellectual world, without caring too much about those
around him. He was another example of the 'outsider', 'a man who
cannot live in the comfortable, insulated world of the bourgeois,
accepting what he sees and touches as reality'.[40] It is even possible to
say that he was the typical 'outsider', as defined by Colin Wilson,
because he could not accept the values of others, and because life
was nothing more than 'one long discomfort' (*A Voyage to Arcturus*,
page 40).

One wonders whether this feeling of being different, of being an
'outsider', is not the sign of a personality flaw. It is certainly difficult
to speculate upon the personality of someone whom one has not
known. Prudence asserts itself. It need only be said that Lindsay's
life and writings are full of indications which compel one to ponder
upon the stability of his character. The first of these nervous, or at
least depressive, syndromes is the uneasiness about contact with
other human beings. Lindsay was a restless, irritated individual.
There was, especially in his relationships with strangers, a tension
which appeared through strained attitudes and a language that was
sometimes affected. It was, to a large degree, in order to escape the
embarrassment he felt in such circumstances that he made solitude
one of his sacred values. This tendency towards isolation brought
with it a propensity to withdraw within himself; for example, to
repress his instincts and hide his emotions. These are the characteristics of the schizophrenic personality, rooted back, by definition, to
an inability to face reality. The forms of the escape, in addition to
the falling back upon oneself, are the flight into dreams and,
especially in the case of Lindsay, unadulterated speculation, leading
to sheer philosophical fantasies. These often took the form of
prophecies, visions, even cosmic anguish, and explanations of the
nature of the universe. One can speculate as to the attraction

exercised by fantastic literature upon temperaments that are sometimes depressive, and sometimes clearly pathological. With Poe, Maupassant, Machen, Hoffmann, and many others, one wonders whether the fantastic in literature is not a sign of the author's neurosis.[41]

The personality is assailed by various discomforts, amounting to anxiety, obscure anguish or, quite simply, tiredness and headaches. These discomforts manifest themselves by a disgust with life, which, in certain cases, can lead to suicide. Disgust with life, as we shall see, is a recurring theme with Lindsay. As for suicide, it is not absent from his works; Lore Jensen's suicide in *Sphinx*, and, in *A Voyage to Arcturus*, suicides disguised under the name of 'sacrifices', even though Lindsay's characters normally give evidence of such capacity for endurance that suicide never comes about. This latter symptom is arguably the most disquieting; a fragment of the personality between the demands of reality and the lure of the beyond. This division corresponds, in fact, to the dissociation between the part that is well-adjusted and the part that is failing, and which can end, in the case of certain sufferers, in a real fragmentation of the body, in which some limbs seem to be gifted with a life of their own.

All these elements dovetail too closely for the evidence to be denied, that there was a psychic weakness in Lindsay, although this was as nothing beside the force of which he gave proof in overcoming his more unstable tendencies. The imbalance was there, even if it is difficult to assess the gravity of it, and to establish its origin.[42] In some cases, the neurosis is barely noticeable. It co-exists with an amiability and politeness that make the individuals particularly attractive. Modern psychology teaches that there are no clear boundaries between mental health and sickness. We are all sick, concluded Freud, after considering the case of Leonardo da Vinci. Only the strongest, or the luckiest, succeed in sublimating their impulses in a satisfactory manner. Between mild passing depression, or melancholy, as it is sometimes termed, and acute schizophrenic disorders, there are many degrees. Neurotic elements, hidden or revealed, moreover, are nothing beside the value of Lindsay's work. The important factor remains the creative power of the artist, the power to harness his neurosis and to work on a material level.[43]

Given this tendency to retire within himself, it was almost inevitable that Lindsay would be the main character of his work.

Certainly, this autobiography is never open, but, of all his principal characters, there exists scarcely one who has not inherited some characteristic of his author. Although this resemblance is always kept discreet, a character such as Nicholas Cabot, in *Sphinx*, would easily pass for a young counterpart. Like Lindsay at that age, Cabot knew very little about women, had made a reputation as a misogynist, disliked futile conversation, detested modern literature and read only philosophical, historical or scientific works. We shall still have the opportunity of citing several examples of these portraits through which, at the same time, the author looks at himself. There is scarcely a single character in *Devil's Tor* who is not, in varying degrees, the counterpart of the author. Peter Copping, for example, is young and lacks maturity, but, like Lindsay, he is an artist. Ingrid is a woman, but she shares with Lindsay his taste for 'walking, reading and dreaming'. If the author never gives us a character who is completely himself, he takes pleasure in studying his own personality from the angle of several characters, as if there were, at the root of all these pieces, an intimate crack that he sought to repair. Hence, this vicarious introspection springs from a judgment that he makes on each of these parts of himself. When Isbel rejects her fiancé, Marshall, it is Lindsay, too, who roundly condemns one aspect of himself, the businessman.

Nature, music and books were the great passions of Lindsay. We shall have the chance to study in detail the feelings that united the author with Nature. Hence, it is towards music that we must now turn. It was not as a dilettante that he appreciated music, but as an enlightened amateur capable of understanding it with discernment. This attraction was such that it has been said of Lindsay that he was more of a musician than a writer.[44] Sunday mornings, at the hour of Divine worship, he would organise improvised concerts at home, to which all the family had to listen in a state of peaceful contemplation that was almost religious, and woe betide the children who, by accident, disturbed this ceremony! During the whole period of his life spent in London, he went frequently to concerts. The period spent in Cornwall was, for this reason, bitterly resented, as it deprived him of his favourite diversion. He put concerts at the top of the list of performances, above both the cinema and the theatre. Such music programmes as were broadcast on the radio, moreover, seemed to him to be vastly inferior to concert music. He did not take kindly to the fact that one could not choose the music one wished to hear, and he was, throughout his life, hostile to this idea of the popularisation of music by radio.

Lindsay's musical tastes are revealed by the fact that he was opposed to the concept of music as a simple diversion, in the same way that Lindsay, the writer, scorned what he termed 'The Sentimental School' in literature.

Of all composers, the undisputed master was Beethoven. Lindsay knew by heart all of Beethoven's symphonies, which he had himself re-named. For him, the Third was 'the Historic', the Fifth was 'the Autobiographical', the Seventh was 'the Sensational', and the Ninth was 'the Psychic' (*Philosophical Notes*, Number 102). His notebooks were full of comments on the Beethoven symphonies, for which he felt unbounded admiration, particularly for the Seventh and Ninth. His next preference was for the *Andante favori in F*, and for the 'Coriolan' Overture, 'the two noblest musical works'. In his view, Beethoven had led the alchemy of sound to its very limits, as far as the quintessence of music. Lindsay recognised in no other writer the equivalent of Beethoven. It seemed to him that, after Beethoven, everything had been said. 'One element remained to be explored after Beethoven; viz. the sweet freshness of nature. This is found in Tchaikovsky.'

Nevertheless, tempting though it might be, the freshness never succeeded in fascinating him. Lindsay would always prefer a kind of passionate violence, such as in the music of Beethoven and Brahms. In Mozart, he was also able to appreciate a certain majesty. In *A Voyage to Arcturus*, it was not Beethoven who was entrusted to introduce the theme of the work, but Mozart, the Mozart of *The Magic Flute*. 'To consider Mozart as a gay, delicate childlike composer is wrong. The best, and most representative, of his music is powerful, stern and austere' (*Philosophical Notes*, Number 431). In spite of this leaning towards solemn music, he did not disdain listening, from time to time, to the operas of Gilbert and Sullivan, which he found very witty.

As a general rule, however, Lindsay hated opera. Music should be sufficient in itself. To need to resort to a text was to confess an inability to use music, and to pervert the spirit of music. The only operas that he liked were Beethoven's *Fidelio* and a few of Wagner's operas, such as *The Flying Dutchman* and *The Ring of the Nibelung*. As for Italian opera, he thought that this form had no connection with true music, being comical farce that could scarcely be taken seriously.

Music never ceased to be important to him. His novels are full of this sense of music, and anyone who will not let himself be transported by their rhythm and movement will remain unaware of their very nature. He shared the view of Beethoven and Schopenhauer that music was a greater revelation than all philosophy. All found in music a revelation of the inexpressible, in which they immersed themselves to saturation point. 'Music is the experience of a supernatural world. The attempt to identify it with world-experience is a proof of the practical, utilitarian nature of man, which always tries to change the wild into the domestic' (*Philosophical Notes*, Number 490).

What attracted Lindsay towards music was the escape that it was able to offer to him; not the kind of escape that relieved anxiety, but the essentially tragic Bacchus-like art which was a fathoming of the mystery of life. It was not concerned with expressing life in terms of anecdotes, women, love, destiny or death. Music was superior to the world, just as, for Schopenhauer, it ranked outside the hierarchy of the arts. Music did not express the world's phenomena, since music *was* the world. Music was metaphysics. More than just an escape, it must be seen as uplifting. Hence, in Lindsay's view, it became the privileged instrument of the Sublime.

After music, books were another of Lindsay's passions. Books were everywhere in the house, and his study walls were lined with them. Lindsay's favourite books testified to the very special tastes of the author of *A Voyage to Arcturus*. One category comprised adventure novels as if of an adolescent who had grown up too quickly. On these shelves, Jules Verne's novels rubbed shoulders with those of Robert Louis Stevenson and Rider Haggard. Perhaps one should mention two titles in particular that Lindsay regarded as masterpieces of their kind; Rider Haggard's *She*, and *The Wrecker* by Robert Louis Stevenson. Was it as with that other admirer of Jules Verne, 'to rummage amongst the scanty remains of the painful body'[45] of the child, that the adult so leant towards his past? Or was it, indeed, to seek in adventure novels that which life had denied him? He revelled in these wonderful tales. Equally, this tendency impelled him towards an interest in old German literature, especially in Scandinavian stories, full of legendary exploits. He was never closer to his children than when telling them, on their return from school, of the adventures of Grettir the Strong, or of Odin in the Land of the Giants. He remembered them all his life, and did not hesitate to introduce trolls into the mists that were already a Scandinavian feature of his books. In *A Voyage to Arcturus*, the Christian concept of Hell as eternal damnation is amended by Nordic mythology. The flames are replaced by the Hell of ice, Niflheim, the world of mists. The Paradise towards which Maskull strives is identifiable. It is Muspellsheim, the realm of fire in Nordic mythology. Similarly, *Devil's Tor* opens with a great clap of thunder, an echo of the hammer blow of the god, Thor.

Another favourite author was George MacDonald, whose influence upon all English fantasy literature has been considerable.[46] MacDonald was a close friend of Lewis Carroll, who entrusted him with the typescript of *Alice's Adventures In Wonderland*. C. S. Lewis also acknowledged his debt to MacDonald.[47] This Scottish Calvinist appealed as much to Lindsay as he did to his contemporaries from Dickens to Wells. The mysticism of this man, already considered by his schoolfellows to be a visionary, the recall of Scottish superstitions, and the symbolic approach of the author, a disciple of Swedenborg, all attracted Lindsay, even if one should not exaggerate the influence of MacDonald.[48] MacDonald's moralising must have been as insufferable to Lindsay as was his basically optimistic temperament. Whatever his influence may have been, Lindsay felt that he had found, in Crystalman, a worthy successor to Lilith, the Devil's wife, sinner and rebel.

After these adventure novels, it is in Germany that we must seek further affinities. Germany was one of Lindsay's passions, which he discovered through its literature and musicians. This feeling must have begun at quite an early stage, since he learnt the German language whilst still young. His knowledge of German literature was extensive, embracing its philosophers no less than its novelists. He had read, and loved, the German Romanticists whom he quoted in his correspondence. He did not conceal, for example, his admiration for the novels of Tieck. 'In general, the works of the early German Romanticists are like *spring songs*; how different from the prosaic drawing-room stuff turned out by the thousand to-day!'[49]

Lindsay had read all the great German authors, Hegel, Schiller and Goethe in particular, but also the more obscure writers, such as Jacob Boehme. It is difficult to appreciate the extent of the influence of 'Teutonic philosophy' upon Lindsay, because, after all, Boehme was the basis of the whole idealistic stream from Hegel to Nietzsche. Boehme, like Lindsay, was a rebel who sought, in mystical re-

velation, a solution to the ills of the world. For Boehme, and for
Nietzsche after him, the tangible world was a fraud; it contained an
interior, fascinating reality of which we were unaware. 'The visible
world is a manifestation of the interior, and spiritual, world', wrote
Boehme. The majority of us are misled by external appearances,
and have no suspicion of the existence of this interior reality. The
mystic, for his part, has learned to 'open the doors of perception'.
Beyond the greyness of existence, he sees, as in *The Haunted Woman*,
the sunlight penetrating the clouds, and he hears the singing of
birds. Separated by four centuries, Boehme and Lindsay fought the
same fight; the fight to preserve the human spirit ceaselessly
threatened by a corrupting environment.

It merely remains to mention two more eminent Germans whose
influence upon Lindsay was certainly more important;
Schopenhauer and Nietzsche. From Schopenhauer, first of all,
Lindsay borrowed the essential element of his philosophy: the Will,
seen as the amalgam of all power, conscious and unconscious. All
was derived from the Will; love, egotism, will to live. To these,
Lindsay added the idea of a transcendent world, Muspel, which did
not depend upon Will. This new world was governed by a new law,
of which the Will of Schopenhauer was no more than a corrupt
likeness.

Lindsay, however, was perhaps interested still more in the aes-
thetics of Schopenhauer, and in particular in his definition of the
Sublime. Lindsay borrowed this term from him, which, however, he
used in a very different sense. The aesthetic theories of Edmund
Burke are familiar, inasmuch as they were developed in England
during the course of the eighteenth century.[50] Schopenhauer returned to Burke's theories of the Sublime, as opposed to the
Beautiful. According to these theories, the Beautiful was based upon
pleasure, depending on the delicacy of the object in contemplation,
while the Sublime was linked to a vast, sombre, disturbing world.
Instead of feeling pleasure, the spectator experienced anxiety.

Lindsay totally disagreed with this definition of the Sublime. He
contrasted it not only with the Beautiful, but also with the Vulgar.
With him, the Sublime lost its aesthetic sense to become a metaphysical fact; the experience of transcendence, at the moment
when man lost his individuality to make himself part of the Whole.

The second German author was, quite naturally, Nietzsche, who
himself owed so much to Schopenhauer. In Nietzsche, Lindsay

recognised the classic example of 'the outsider', misunderstood in a decadent world. Nietzsche taught Lindsay the nihilism and the prophetic tone, and also the dialectic of appearance and reality, the calumny of the senses and the sensibility, the moral of the harshness and the conception of an aristocracy of spirit looking down contemptuously on the crowd of barbarians and slaves.

We shall have occasion to return more fully to the influence of these philosophers when we come to study the works of Lindsay. The mere fact of naming them demonstrates that Lindsay was no mere science-fiction author, working as a dilettante. His work is eminently serious, too serious perhaps, since it sought, quite frankly, to be the explanation of the world. Should one refuse to listen just because the explanation seems too preposterous? Is it not a question of the non-scientific reflex of the man of theory, the descendant of Socrates, whose activities even Nietzsche has condemned? Has not Nietzsche become one of our current philosophers?

The few names already quoted indicate that Lindsay's tastes were quite well defined. He scarcely appreciated poetry, for example, and was hardly a great reader of novels. On the contrary, his tastes were towards historical works, mythology, and idealistic philosophy from Plato to Nietzsche. As regards contemporary literature, Lindsay did not conceal the gaps in his knowledge of this period, but he hastened to justify this by the futility which, according to him, was the hallmark of many modern authors. Galsworthy, Richard Jefferies, and even Stevenson, were all classed in the ranks of 'the Sentimental School'. Nothing exasperated him more than the dialogue of these novels, 'with their little exclamations of wonder, admiration, pleasure'. The pantheism of Jefferies, for instance, seemed to him to be completely pretentious, and characteristic of this school, which, in its 'mysticism', could not succeed in giving divinity any appearance but that of man. There is no evidence that he read, or was interested in, the more experimental fiction of James Joyce, Virginia Woolf or D. H. Lawrence. Only his wife, who did not share his literary tastes, tried to make him read, and appreciate, novels that were less austere or reputedly difficult. She introduced him, for example, to Thomas Hardy's novels, for which she felt a great admiration. She also introduced him to the latest French literature, and in particular to the books of Proust and Anatole France.

The attraction of Russian literature was unquestionably very strong. In his correspondence, as in the *Philosophical Notes*, there

appeared the names of Tolstoy, Turgenev, 'a great man, but an
Artist – that is, not quite sincere' (Number 200), and especially that
of Dostoievsky, 'perhaps the greatest of all writers' (Number 352).

Without going so far as to despise the novel as a literary form, as
a critic has stated,[51] Lindsay, as a disciple of Schopenhauer, certainly regarded it as limited by its very nature. Compared with the
sublime universe, the transcendent world, in fact, the novelist's
world lost any value that might be found in it. The novel stayed too
attached to the world down here, since the object of any novelist is
to portray mankind. Now, according to Lindsay, the Sublime Ideal
was not human at all. Everything that concerned individuality,
either closely or remotely, was limited, being nothing more than
imperfection, caricature, failure and vulgarity. Of all the literary
arts, tragedy seemed to him to be the most interesting, and so he felt
obliged to depict the world of tragedy in his novels. Yet, Lindsay's
attraction itself is limited, for, although tragedy can provide a stage
for the possibility of man surrendering his will, there still exists an
art situated above will. This art was music. Lindsay tells us that
Dostoievsky is perhaps the greatest of writers, but 'up to the present,
there is no Beethoven of literature' (*Philosophical Notes*, Number
357).

The tragedy of Lindsay, and it was indeed a tragedy, was that he
was not a born writer. In his case, creation resembled more an
interior necessity, a personal redemption, than a fruitful dialogue of
a writer with his public. He became a writer not by chance, but by
luck. Had he not met his wife, it seems likely that he would always
have remained an insurance broker. He possessed all the necessary
elements for literary creation, the temperament, the culture, the
ideas, but it was his wife who constituted the catalyst for all these
elements. He himself had the sharp awareness of belonging to a
cultivated, not to say literary, environment. A few years before
David had started to write, his brother, Alexander, had set him an
example, with ambitions and preoccupations vastly different from
David's. The genealogical research of which David Lindsay was so
fond also allowed him to discover, in the family's past, other writers
more or less known; Lady Anne Lindsay (1750–1825), the author of
*Auld Robin Gray*, and especially the Scottish sixteenth-century poet,
Sir David Lindsay, who, in his time, became famous for his savage
satires.

In spite of these ancestral influences, David Lindsay always lacked that facility that is recognisable in the best writers. His clumsy style of writing has frequently been stressed. A recent article summarised quite well the opinion of many critics when it described Lindsay's novels as being 'sublimities in a blotting-paper style'.[52] Another reviewer depicts Lindsay as 'a victim of Mark Twain's shoddy style'. Jacqueline Lindsay, too, when wishing to ridicule her husband, was in the habit of saying that he tried to copy the style of Carlyle.

It must be said, however, that Lindsay approached literature in a very particular way. We have seen his attitude towards contemporary literature. For him, the majority of the writers of the past were distinguished by one sole characteristic: their taste for the trivial. He wished not only to avoid what he considered to be the errors of his predecessors, but also to write books which were revelatory by virtue of their manner of understanding the world. In spite of the gaps in his knowledge already mentioned, it would be a mistake to regard Lindsay as an opportunist writer, whose failures were due to an inadequacy of education. His education was inadequate only to the extent that he scarcely recognised any teacher. To read his *Philosophical Notes* is, in this respect, highly instructive. The number of comments upon literature to be found recorded there cannot fail to impress one, proving that the author had formulated his own rules as regards writing. Moreover, to seek to apply to him the criteria prescribed by other critics would be dangerous, and likely to serve little useful purpose.

## THE FATE OF THE WORK

Lindsay died a few months too early to realise one of his fondest hopes; namely, to see *A Voyage to Arcturus* republished. His death was the signal for an astonishing resurge of interest in the whole of his work, which would doubtless have surprised no one more than the author himself, so little could this have been foreseen in 1945. A year after his death, the standing of this writer, who had seemed decidedly forgotten, as much by the public as by the publishers, was to be abruptly changed by the appearance of a new edition of *A Voyage to Arcturus*.[53] Simultaneously with this publication, a discussion programme was broadcast by the B.B.C. This programme, in the opinion of Jacqueline Lindsay, was hardly a success.[54] Ten years later, the B.B.C. tried to redeem itself with a new broadcast.[55]

It consisted, this time, in the reading of extracts from *A Voyage to Arcturus*. The effort of imagination demanded of the listener by the medium of radio exactly suited this kind of work. In the transmission, the mellowed words of Crystalman came across better than would have been possible with a silent reading to oneself.

This republication of *A Voyage to Arcturus* came in time to satisfy the requests of admirers, more and more numerous, who despaired of ever finding the book, already unobtainable for fifteen years. Several friends of Lindsay mounted a campaign to have the book broadcast: Gollancz, the publisher, Visiak, who, as early as 1962, decided to write a biography of his friend, and John Pick, whose work over twenty years has been considerable. In 1963, *A Voyage to Arcturus* was published yet again in England, and also appeared, for the first time, in the United States. The American publisher tried to contact both Bertrand Russell and T. S. Eliot, with the intention of inviting them to write the preface. William Holloway, in turn, considered the idea of making a film of *A Voyage to Arcturus*. At the same time, developments occurred in France, where the publisher, Christian Marin, declared himself ready to publish *A Voyage to Arcturus* and *The Haunted Woman*. This publication project came to nothing, even though the contract had been signed. At the beginning of the 'Sixties, something seemed to have changed. An author who had died in complete obscurity was reborn, and one witnessed a literary discovery of what had scarcely existed. Simultaneously with this interest on the part of publishers, the critics took up the current trend. *The Times Literary Supplement* at last judged the book to be 'tonic and terrible'.[56] The critic of *The Sunday Telegraph* went still further in his praise of *A Voyage to Arcturus*. 'It must be counted one of the strongest, and in some ways most powerful, books of our time. Undoubtedly a work of genius, invested with a sweeping imagination that can only be compared to Blake's. One of the profoundest, and most awe-inspiring, enquiries into the problem of evil ever written, and one hopes that this edition will confirm it in its place.'[57]

It is also noticeable that the trend of the English fantasy novel bypasses David Lindsay. One knows the influence that William Morris and George MacDonald have exercised upon writers such as C. S. Lewis or Tolkien. What is more often not known is that, between them and MacDonald, there was David Lindsay. C. S. Lewis and Tolkien were both Oxford professors, and were joined, in

September 1939, by Charles Williams, then the representative of the Oxford University Press, who accompanied his firm to Oxford, when they moved there at the beginning of the Second World War. Thereafter, these three men met frequently, to the extent of forming a literary coterie. It was also in that period that Lewis wrote *Perelandra* and *Out of the Silent Planet*, two books in which he owed much to Lindsay, as he confessed unequivocally. Hence he wrote, to a researcher who had just published a study of his works, 'Morris and MacDonald were more or less given to you ... The real father of my planet books is David Lindsay's *A Voyage to Arcturus*, which you will also revel in if you don't know it. I had grown up on Wells's stories of that kind; it was Lindsay who first gave me the idea that the "scientifiction" appeal could be combined with the "supernatural" appeal ...'.[58] It is worth adding that *A Voyage to Venus*, the new, more commercial, title which has just been given to *Perelandra*, comes a little closer still to this last-named work of its 'real father'.

The trend which manifested itself in the early 'Sixties has been rapidly confirmed, since *The Haunted Woman* was republished in 1964, forty-two years after its first appearance! A few years later, *A Voyage to Arcturus* was published for the fourth time; this book which, during the lifetime of the author, had simply had the reputation of being unsaleable! Since that time, nothing has been able to stop the dissemination of Lindsay's books. The work of these latter years, since 1968, has even overtaken all the accumulated efforts of forty years. *A Voyage to Arcturus* was revised in 1968, and, since then, a new edition in a pocket collection has also seen the light of day, thus allowing a wider distribution.[59] A French translation has also been published. Finally, Lindsay's hitherto-unpublished books, *The Violet Apple* and *The Witch*, have just appeared in print.

Alongside this distribution of Lindsay's books, these last few years have seen the appearance of several critical studies, which confirm the author's originality of thought, and contribute to a better understanding of his work, which, if not difficult, at least demands an effort of sustained thought on the part of the reader. Nevertheless, the essence of the interpretation remains to be made, as the research so far available, notwithstanding its immense interest, is mostly confined to the presentation of an unknown author. Everything points, however, to the fact that this initial phase is now complete, and more penetrating studies are already appearing.[60]

Admittedly, *A Voyage to Arcturus* has not yet become a classic, even if, in the United States, the book is already on the syllabus of certain Universities, with a number of theses devoted to it. Does this mean that, since his death, Lindsay's audience is limited? This must, in fact, be feared, when one considers the strangeness of these works. The advent of this 'superior race' of readers, anxious to go beyond the plot, is doubtless something for to-morrow. The average, sensual reader is in serious danger of being disappointed in Lindsay, but it would be a mistake to suppose that the success currently being enjoyed by Lindsay's books is due to chance. It is not an irrational infatuation provoked by the exaggerated interest now being created by whimsical literature, whether it be fantastic or supernatural. Never before has there been such passion for mystery. From now on, every publisher has his shelves of science-fiction and strange adventures. Even if Lindsay's work undoubtedly benefits from this general infatuation, the slow revival of this author is the best proof that his emergence is not entirely due to a passing fancy.

# 2

## BACKGROUNDS, SETTINGS
## AND PLACES

We now know what kind of man David Lindsay was. His entire personality is a microcosm of his work. It has been seen that his career as a writer was, to a large degree, an escape from an environment that he found far from agreeable. Accordingly, it is both tempting and logical to begin any study of Lindsay's work with a detailed consideration of the settings he chose for his novels; what they are, how he presents them to us, and how, as a writer, he relates them to reality.

### NATURE

Far from being just a prop for the action, Nature plays an important rôle in Lindsay's work. The background of his novels is Nature, and, between the human world and Nature, strange relationships appear. This presence of Nature has a definite purpose. Behind it can be seen the author's love of Nature. Lindsay loved plants, and was passionately fond of gardening. He adored walking over the Sussex Downs or the Cornish hills. In London, the author felt unhappy, and, whenever he could, he isolated himself in the country, making only rare trips into town. Nature, along with its corollary, solitude, was, in his case, an essential condition for artistic creation, and it was to the hills of Dartmoor that he went to seek inspiration for one of his novels, *Devil's Tor*. His wife shared his admiration for the work of the naturalist, W. H. Hudson, and especially for his novel, *Green Mansions*. Lindsay's Scottish origins determined his parallel interest in natural phenomena, like so many of his compatriots from Sir Walter Scott to J. M. Barrie. Lindsay's career, too, was linked to Nature, since his first writings corresponded, in the event, with his move to Cornwall, to the country.

One might well have supposed that this writer, who spent the first forty years of his life in London, would have chosen that city as the background of his novels. This, however, was not the case, and all his books are set in the provinces, with, admittedly, the single exception of *A Voyage to Arcturus*, which differs from the rest of his work in more than one respect. Newleigh, the village in *Sphinx*, is situated in the county of Hampshire, near Southampton. The action of *The Haunted Woman* unfolds in the Brighton area. In this novel, Runhill Court is precisely situated at some eight miles to the north-west of Brighton, and 'three miles north-west of Steyning'. Finally, the background of *Devil's Tor* is the vastness of Dartmoor. The village of Belhill referred to therein does not actually exist, as far as we know.

In spite of this, these places correspond more to a region considered in its entirety than to places that are faithfully described, partly because, in the author's view, each of these regions possessed a value of its own. For the austere philosophy of *Devil's Tor*, the solitude and desolation of Dartmoor were essential, while the New Forest area readily lent itself as a paradise for tourists and second homes. In stark contrast to the antiquity of Dartmoor, the New Forest could only be artificial, just as the village which served as a microcosm of the affluent society, right down to its name and its modernity, 'Newleigh'.

Not only are these places located in the provinces, but they are to be found at the extreme end of the provinces, almost isolated from the outside world, lost in Nature. Runhill Court is so inaccessible that Isbel and her aunt lose their way on the occasion of their first visit. It takes them several hours to cover the eight-odd miles between Brighton and Runhill, after having been lost in 'a labyrinth of minor roads'. Isbel is so disenchanted with the remoteness of the place that she accuses her aunt of wishing, at any price, 'to bury herself in the back of beyond'. The Court is surrounded by a wall, and screened by the trees of a large park. In another book, Lindsay places 'Whitestone' on Dartmoor; that is to say, an area sparsely inhabited and seldom visited. As if this were not enough in itself, the house is not even part of a village. The nearest dwelling is a quarter of a mile away. All around 'Whitestone', moorland extends as far as the eye can see.

If all the characters turn towards the woods, rather than to the country roads, this is assuredly because the author always preferred Nature in the raw to Nature that had been tamed by man. The freshness and attraction of Nature certainly exist in his work, but the author often describes it in order to be able to show more clearly that which is lacking or corrupt, by comparison with the grandiose, and untamed, wildness of Nature. Rather than the plains, which he found too monotonous, he preferred the hills, or, better still, the mountains of Scotland or the Himalayas. There are few cultivated fields to be found in his work. From the area around Brighton, he particularly remembered the fields that were almost grassless. This remained true in the case of the imaginary background of the star, Arcturus, where there was almost no grass at all. There were only rocks, or sand formed from disintegrated rocks. This predilection for the wildness of Nature explains the fact that Lindsay found his most moving, and remarkable, powers as a writer in describing it; for example, when the storm strikes Devil's Tor, and the very ground trembles. His most colourful descriptions in *A Voyage to Arcturus* are those of the fragmented heights that Maskull crosses over. As the hero himself points out, 'those mountains have most extraordinary shapes. All the lines are straight and perpendicular – no shapes or curves' (page 82). Any list of all the precipices met in this book would be a long one, beginning with that 'Gap of Sorgie', in the North of Scotland, which afforded to Maskull and Nightspore a foretaste of the Arcturus landscape.

Oddly enough, although his house at Porth was situated only a few steps from the sea, Lindsay was never very attracted towards the ocean. His favourite walks were those which led him in the direction of the hills and woodlands, far from the sea. In his writing, the sea scarcely exists at all. When he does refer to it, he does so in grandiose terms. Hence, at the beginning of *A Voyage to Arcturus*, the observatory of Starkness is situated at the edge of a cliff on the North Sea coast. An initial walk along this cliff takes place at night, in order to make the landscape seem even more alarming. The sea itself is invisible, only the cries of the gulls and the sound of the waves on the rocks making one aware of its proximity. Even though several scenes of *The Haunted Woman* are set in Brighton, the sea held no interest for Lindsay. The house that Mrs Moor wished to buy was not one with a sea view, but an old manor house, buried in the woods. One need only compare *The Haunted Woman* with Graham Greene's novel, *Brighton Rock*, to notice the difference in the attitude of the two writers towards the sea. Both novels are set in Brighton, but, whilst the latter is inextricably involved with the sea, the former ignores it completely. For Lindsay, a rock was nothing to do with the coast, but a stone set at the top of a hill. Isbel Loment spent a good half-hour walking along the Brighton promenade, beside the sea, without there being the slightest reference to it (page 103). The distant views in Lindsay's writing are always of hills. 'The landscape seen from the top of Cader Idris', Lindsay tells us, 'is poetic, wild and beautiful-looking inland, but, where it includes the sea, it is commonplace' (*Philosophical Notes*, Number 31).

Rather than the expanse of the sea, Lindsay preferred a closed-in countryside, a lake or a pool. He replaced the 'deep blue' by water that was oppressive and melancholy.[1] His pool in the forest has a dismal aura, in spite of the sunshine from outside. Its water, Lindsay tells us, has 'a muddy opacity' (*Sphinx*, page 37). Lore Jensen commits suicide by throwing herself into water, but is this really suicide? This dark, still water is seductive in its stability and inscrutability. Lore Jensen, so the author suggests to us, did not seek death; it was the water that tempted her. 'I think that this water has *tempted* her. She has not sought it; it has come in her way' (*Sphinx*, page 282). The North Sea, seen from the top of a cliff, in the gloom of the night, is no less dismal.

Lindsay's feeling for Nature is intimately linked to an acute sensibility for climate and season. He sets a good number of his novels in summer. The action of *Devil's Tor* takes place in the month of August, while, in *Sphinx*, Cabot's arrival at 'Mereway' coincides, as if by chance, with 'the first really-hot day of the summer'. As for *The Haunted Woman*, the plot begins on a sunny September day, one of the last days of summer. These coincidences would lead one to believe that summer was Lindsay's favourite season, if we did not already know that he hated the sun. For him, seasons were not a convenient back-cloth that was virtually interchangeable, but a natural fact of fundamental importance. Each season is linked to a climate, and each kind of weather corresponds to a certain attitude towards life. 'Man as an organism responds to weather' (*Philosophical Notes*, Number 445). Lindsay himself complained of being often compelled to seek a new subject for a novel during the summer, whilst the winter was his favourite season for work. Like so many thinkers before him, Lindsay explained the great doctrines of mankind by the climate of the regions from which they emerged. Islam could only apparently have appeared in the hot desert and under the starlit sky of Arabia. The cult of Aphrodite, on the other hand, was linked to the blue seas and scents of the Greek islands. Finally, that of Thor needed the grey, cold skies of Scandinavia in order to flourish (*Devil's Tor*, page 272).

Lindsay knew how to describe those summer days when a storm

threatens. The atmosphere is strained, charged with electricity. The
sweltering atmosphere invites the walker to seek refuge in the woods.
The road is covered by a fine, white dust that is raised by each
vehicle that passes. Lindsay, however, pauses more readily to describe the mysterious shapes of the trees in the haze, weighed down
with drops of water, or the ground saturated with humidity, or else
the long crest of Dartmoor visible against a clouded sky. Inter-
rupting the symphony of colour that constitutes *A Voyage to Arcturus*,
Lindsay also excels in painting the countryside in tones of grey,
when the colours of granite, sky, fog and trees merge.

The description of the elements offers more than just documen-
tary interest. Country scenery and fogs are not back-cloths that are
interchangeable at the whim of the writer. Between the background
of Nature, in particular, and the characters, there exists a kind of
affinity. The pale complexion of several of Lindsay's heroines is
explained by this predilection for clouded skies. As regards Ingrid,
he comments 'Ingrid's race was in her complexion ... certainly the
moist, cool, fragrant Dartmoor winds and mists must have been
kind to it ...'. It is in contact with Nature that the human spirit
attains its full magnitude, away from the trivialities of the modern
world. For Lindsay, these realities of Nature are invariably those of
unleashed elements and a grim landscape. 'The long black winter
nights, ... the impassable forests filled with imagined shapes of awe
and panic terror, the bogs, rains, damps, chills and fogs, making of
life one long misery and struggle ...' (*Devil's Tor*, page 333). It was
in this Scandinavian countryside, so dear to the author, that he set his
New Jerusalem, in a kingdom of perpetual fog where the characters imagine the ghosts of dead friends appearing at every step.

Winter became Lindsay's favourite season. A sad winter's day
constituted the ideal background for meditation. For the writer, it
was the best season of the year. For the man, it was the season in
which he felt closest to Nature. 'A rainy relaxing day, like a relaxing
illness, acts upon the nervous system, and produces vivid and
delicate mental impressions' (*Philosophical Notes*, Number 445).

On the metaphorical level, the world is nothing but an immense
fog which conceals from mankind the splendour of divinity, the
quest for which can only be pursued in this surrounding mist. In *A
Voyage to Arcturus*, Crystalman's body is portrayed as 'a bright mist'.
Little by little, Maskull becomes aware of being engulfed. Whereas,
at the time of his arrival on the new planet the sky is perfectly

transparent, it is not long before the formation of fog indicates Crystalman's presence. 'The sun was obscured by masses of cloud which filled the whole sky. This vapour was in violent and almost living motion' (page 171).

The sun is certainly not absent from Lindsay's work. We have already noted that the plots of his novels generally unfold in summer. Lindsay even had a tendency to accord an almost exceptional place to sunshine. In the case of *Sphinx*, for instance, we notice that each house described, each room, and every landscape, is defined in relation to this criterion: the sun. From the fourth line of the novel, we know that 'the day was gloriously fine, without a cloud in the sky, but with a crisp breeze tempering the otherwise overpowering sun'. On page 10, the house entered by Cabot is one in which 'the sunlight streamed in'. Again, on page 35, the day following his arrival is 'the first really-hot day of the summer'. On page 37, we learn that 'five minutes later he had left the blazing sunshine for the deep shade of the straight, slender, red-boiled pines'. By page 55, he has returned to 'the room streaming with sunlight, the open window with its blind half-lowered'. Finally, on page 69, Cabot and Sturt, at the end of the afternoon, visit a neighbour, Lore Jensen, in her 'untidy room, illuminated by the rays of the late afternoon sun'. Many more examples from the same book could be added to this list, all confirming the important rôle played by the sun in Lindsay's work. Apart from that, it reveals an autobiographical trait of the author, bearing in mind the jaundice which prevented the author from remaining in the sun.

This would suffice to explain the negative value that he attached to the sun, which was not, for him, 'the glorious planet Sol' of Shakespeare, nor the star of life of the Mediterranean civilisations. Northern man, with whom Lindsay identified himself, made of the sun, by contrast, a disastrous star belonging to the tropics, from which one sought protection behind drawn blinds, or in the freshness of the woods. It should be stressed that there is very little temperate sunshine, however, with this author, even though he was more familiar with a gentle climate than with the dog-days. The sun on the planet Arcturus was so intense that it was impossible to travel by day, and necessary to wait until nightfall to move around. Even the England of *Sphinx* is depicted to us as 'a drowsy country', so hot is it there.

Lindsay's sun is, above all, a destructive sun which makes plants die, and plunges mankind into a state of lethargy. The star Arcturus has two suns, we are told, Alppain and Branchspell, whose combined effect is destructive. In contemplating the spectacle of these two suns, Maskull feels his entire being disintegrating in the face of such beauty (page 159). This disintegration, however, is not the loss of consciousness of the mystic's transcendental meditation. If it is the abnegation of free will, in Schopenhauer's sense of the term, it is also, more dangerously, the destruction of the entire personality. One has to await the final pages for the truth to come out; namely, that the sun is the instrument of Satan, the trap and 'Crystalman's trump-card'. It is the sun which has corrupted the blood of the Scandinavian races, adds Lindsay (*Devil's Tor*, page 273).

In this respect, if Lindsay's novels are a quest for Light, they are also a flight far away from light. Behind the use he makes of the sun, there lies this ambiguity; the Truth, to become Light, can be discovered only in the shadows. Moreover, one sees Lindsay fleeing from the midday light, in preference for gentler atmospheres, often those of dawn or twilight, or even of night. He expresses this clearly through one of his characters. 'I have wished to believe that the vulgar noon was preceded by a wild dawn' (*Devil's Tor*, page 228). Of all these moments of light, it is the dawn which fascinates him with its colours, and especially, perhaps, with the promise that it contains. Of all the spectacles offered by Nature, sunrise on the mountain is the most impressive, appropriate for inciting man to silence and to prayer.

Often, too, the starlit sky attracts him. For Lindsay, night is not the time of cruelty, but of meditation. Night calms the spirit, and encourages metaphysical contemplation. It is while looking at the night-sky that Nicholas Cabot becomes aware of the vanity of human effort, and the insignificance of man in the face of Nature. Here, the starlit sky is the cue for reflection upon human destiny (*Sphinx*, pages 182–183). To the vulgar clamour of noon, Lindsay opposes the mysterious softness of the night. In his world, it is the night-people who are the more worthy. It is by night that Cabot works at his invention, and the goddess of night, Nyx, is Ingrid's favourite mythological figure. Above all, night presents a problem. It is mysterious, and seems to hide some secret. Twice in his work, Lindsay equates the epithet 'hieroglyphical' to the starlit sky,[2] as if to stress the secret that it conceals; no doubt, the existence of another world of unsuspected beauty.

He belonged to a generation which, although it had seen important scientific discoveries, still knew nothing about the conquest of
space. He may possibly have regarded recent scientific developments
as representing the loss of a sense of the sacred. In this connection,
he said that 'the vile intrusion of a machine ... in this mystic sky
was unthinkable' (*Devil's Tor*, page 300). It is no less significant
that, in the only book in which he lets his imagination dwell upon a
conquest of space, that of the star, Arcturus, the author carefully
avoids the technicalities of science-fiction. Admittedly, there is an
air-ship in *A Voyage to Arcturus*, but this machine works without any
motor, thanks to an attractive force of luminous rays.

The moon hardly ever appears in his work. Perhaps it was too
romantic for his taste. He was content, apparently, to use it as a
symbol. It was of the moon that he thought when he wanted to
make a comparison with the complexion of the Great Goddess, as it
appeared to several of the characters in *Devil's Tor*.[3] The pale
reflection of the moon suggested spirituality and depth to him, a
purity and mystery that he contrasted with the crude glare of the
sun.[4] Light was splendour, and splendour was emptiness. If it was
not to be hostile, this Light must come from the stars, across millions
of miles, filtered by the immensity of space.

What linked Lindsay to darkness was a semi-mystical Nature.
Dark places often serve as refuges for his heroes. The half-light in
the undergrowth of woods calms troubled temperaments. Nicholas
Cabot likes to stay in his room in the evenings, with all the lights
out, looking at the sky. Just as in the case of Pascal meditating upon
the night sky, darkness is synonymous with depth. With Lindsay, as
also with the Romantics, this resemblance is accompanied by a
reappraisal of darkness and night. Lindsay was very familiar with
the German Romantics, and had certainly read *Hymns to the Night*
by Novalis, so deeply imbued with this intimacy of darkness. One
also finds in Lindsay this dialectic between darkness and brilliance,
night and light, even going far beyond the background of Nature.
With him, darkness and holiness are intrinsically interwoven with
one another. It is the 'sacred darkness' of the Romantic poets.
Hence, the tomb of the Great Goddess is one of the sacred places of
the kingdom of the night. When Hugh Drapier tries to penetrate it,
he learns, to his cost, that the darkness of the tomb will not suffer
the crude intrusion of his electric torch, which slips from his hands
and breaks (*Devil's Tor*, page 86). 'The Mother could only have

created herself in the human intelligence in some physical region of gloom, silence and impenetrable forest . . .'

Lindsay was often inclined to prefer the simple dialectic of light and shade to the full variety of colour. He did not ignore colour. On the contrary, indeed, a novel like *A Voyage to Arcturus* is astonishing in its blaze of colour. Nevertheless, Lindsay particularly liked pallor. He depicted the tangible world as he saw it, 'the solid, coloured universe', but knowing that the grandeur of the intangible world surpassed colour. This explains a statement such as 'The stern, clear-cut purity of this half-stormy silver dawn was worth many coloured sunrises. All was black and white (*Devil's Tor*, page 67). For him, brilliant was gaudy, and he preferred the word 'dark', with its strong emotional appeal. One need only read again the description of Runhill Court to notice this love of darkness, and the care with which he describes the dark wainscotting of the old Elizabethan dwelling, and the half-light through the windows, contrasting with the modernised part of the building, a façade of 'dazzling white stucco' and glistening copper.

It seemed that Lindsay's preference was towards a landscape that was rather austere and grandiose, reminiscent, in certain aspects, of that described by numerous Romantic writers. The love of the Romantics for mountains, for instance, is well-known. Quite often, too, Lindsay would try to enhance the description of a landscape that was too commonplace. The peaceful, idyllic charm of the green English countryside never managed to fascinate him completely. Rather than this peace, he was inclined to prefer a Nature that was more rugged, born of storms, darkness and jagged landscapes. In his eyes, Dartmoor was a small mountain which could not begin to compare with the higher summits of the Alps, but which, by English standards, managed to satisfy his strong emotional needs, just as the modest English peaks offered Wordsworth perspectives not far short of sublimity. It might be added that Lindsay's predilection for darkness, and unrestrained elements, reverted to the Romantic literary trend, of which Byron was unquestionably the most famous exponent, and which embraced Macpherson, with his Nordic landscapes shrouded in fog, the night poetry of Novalis and Young, and the winter poems of Burns.

Nevertheless, it would be an exaggeration to regard Lindsay as a great painter of nature, in view of the absence of detailed description, the comparative rarity of such notation, and his very fragmentary presentation, even if his feeling for Nature does deserve our attention.

Having regard for these limitations, it must be said that Lindsay never sought just to depict Nature. His real interest lay elsewhere. If he confined himself to the natural background, he was happy to describe successfully imaginary landscapes. What lent force and beauty to the Arcturus landscapes was certainly the fact that the author's imagination could, at will, give itself free rein. Freed from the constraint of having to render a servile description of reality, with which he was never at ease, Lindsay delighted himself in invention. This was true, of course, with *A Voyage to Arcturus*, but also, in an even more revealing way, in the case of the novels having the everyday world as their main background. It should not be overlooked that, in *Sphinx*, *The Haunted Woman* and *Devil's Tor*, the best descriptions of Nature are those which come to us through visions or dreams. For ordinary Nature there is substituted a Nature fired by the imagination, a kind of spiritual landscape that the writer evokes with great flair. In *The Haunted Woman*, this unreal landscape takes the form of the enchanted garden of the haunted room, impregnated with the scent of spring, and bathed in sunlight. Another example is provided by the landscape of *Sphinx*, in which Nature is transformed into brilliance by the dream. 'On the shore itself were only the delicately-coloured fantastic-shaped rocks, the pools of sea-water left by the ebb, and the gleaming, wet sands, reflecting the tints of the sky, and disappearing at each end into obscurity; while the visibility of the landward side was bounded by low-lying marshes, the bright green hues of which appeared in the twilight as metallic and luminous, as though their slime were exhaling gases. The sea was a vast, swelling, blue-green surface, and enormous white-crested waves continually came tumbling in, breaking with periodic thunder, like the regular breathing of some mighty monster. A strong, rough salt breeze was blowing off the sea, and each impregnated gust seemed to bring her another message from the dawn.'

Certainly, Nature was, firstly, a background, even when it was essential to the plot. It is equally true that this natural background often does not appear by chance. It is all needed as much by the author as by his characters. In at least two of the books, this orientation, this deliberate choice of Nature, is made obvious. In *Sphinx*, Nicholas Cabot comes from London to spend his holiday *in the country*. In the same way, in *The Haunted Woman*, the move to Runhill Court is destined to bring to an end the life led by Mrs Moor and Isbel, wandering from town to town, which no longer satisfies them.

Far from the drabness of human relations, Nature is a safe refuge for the discontented, such as Lore Jensen, Nicholas Cabot and Hugh Drapier. For Cabot, it is a haven of peace, where he can stay for hours on end, without being bored, since it is the only place for walking likely to soothe his nerves. Similarly, it is towards the silence of the forest that Lore Jensen goes to escape the noise and frenzy of the human merry-go-round.

In spite of the delights bestowed by Nature, it often happens that the enthusiasm and sensual pleasure of the discovery give way to a deeper feeling that subconsciously transforms one in meditation. Nature's influence on man disturbs the walker as it had over-whelmed with panic the heart of the young Wordsworth, in dis-covering those 'presences of Nature in the sky and on the earth'. All told, there are few enough pleasant reveries in Lindsay's work. It is not Nature's rôle to soothe, but rather to awaken man to a meditation on the meaning of his own life. It compels the lone walker to reflect as much on his work (*Sphinx*, page 37) as on the mystery of human destiny (pages 182–183).

Sometimes, even meditation assumes the complexion of a confus-ing feeling of communion with Nature, as if the grandeur of the latter awakens aspirations in man towards the hereafter. More than this, Nature then becomes the witness of a transcendent world, and a creation of God (see Chapter 5 herein). Nature thus serves to remind mankind of the existence of another world that is more grandiose than the surrounding tangible world, and towards which a whole part of his being, his soul, feels irresistibly drawn. Reverting to the very basis of Platonic philosophy, Lindsay joins Nature and the soul in the world of Ideas. To commune with Nature is to begin the rediscovery of the dignity of life. It is also to learn how to die, since Nature teaches disdain for the earthly world, by revealing to mankind the wonders of this spiritual world. As with Plato, this communion with Nature is, in reality, a reminiscence of an earlier life. 'The mood was familiar, and since he could not understand it, he had long ago invented a formula for it. The mysterious hour and dusk, the aloneness of his being, the dark friendly trees, the intimate

wind, and breaking sky; it, as its equivalent of sombre enchantment experienced elsewhere on earth, he recognised to be the right
element of his eternal part. Yet it was all no more than a hint. It
stood for nothing of itself, but was the faint imperfect copy of
heaven; the proof being that, though it might call, it could not
satisfy, but on the contrary produced in him such states as disturbance, sullenness, infinite longing, sadness, despair. Thus he was
inevitably reminded by it of some grander world not present'
(*Devil's Tor*, pages 67–68). In spite of the rather tortuous style, the
language of Platonic philosophy is easily recognisable. It is the
splendour of the Ideas of the intelligible world which appears here
confusingly to man, in the form of nostalgia and vague recollection.
In the whole of the tangible world, it is Nature that provides the
best evidence of something else. In the same passage, Lindsay ends
by asserting that this beauty of Nature is nothing more than a
deformation, a reflection of the Idea of Beauty. The Sublime, he
says, is 'the shadow of the beauty of another world'.

It is to the extent that this Idea of Beauty is identical to God, that
Nature, in which it is reflected, is divine,[5] and not because it is the
creation of a God who built the universe. References to the sacred
character of Nature are rare, but it is an aspect of the presentation
that cannot be ignored. One can take as proof the feelings experienced by Mrs Moor, at the time of a car drive in the countryside just
outside Brighton. 'Her aunt viewed the changing landscape sternly.
These trees, these fields, and meads, but, above all, those bare
Downs of grass-covered chalk in the background, were to her *sacred*'
(*The Haunted Woman*, page 20. The italics are Lindsay's).

Being a reflection of another world that is more genuine than the
tangible world, Nature thus lends itself to become a substitute for
ultimate reality. This identification appears several times in
Lindsay's work. Nature is the reality beside which the greater part
of human activity is secondary and insignificant. Moreover, Lindsay
often compares scornfully the cares of everyday life with the much
more substantial truths of Nature. 'The lightning flashes, the thunder is rising, the wind is moaning – and you ask if a strange and
unpardonable romance is on its way!' protests Saltfleet (*Devil's
Tor*, page 371). Nature is a school of truth which shapes, as
nothing else can, man's temperament, as it stamps itself on his
physiognomy. Saltfleet surely owes his intransigent attitude to this
constant confrontation with Nature. 'No doubt it arose from the
striving with realities – the realities of Nature. Instead of figures,

markets, competitors, and labour troubles; things like precipices, storms and floods!' (*Devil's Tor*, page 172.) It would be futile to add that, as between Nature and the artificial world of business, Lindsay made a choice, and one which led him to sever all contact with the London business environment, in order to devote himself to writing in the solitude of the English provinces.

Nature, therefore, occupies in Lindsay's work a much more important place than the frequency of his references, or his descriptive ability, might suggest. If it provided a background for the novels, its function did not end there. Nature finally became the prop of metaphysical meditation, integrating itself in the author's own philosophy. The procedure by which the tangible world becomes the exponent of a system of thought is so typical of Lindsay that it is going to reveal itself again in the second vital element of the background; the home.

## THE DOMESTIC BACKGROUND

First of all, when we analyse Lindsay's novels, what do we find? The immediate answer is provided by the period in which the author sets his plots. If the unfolding of the action is, in general, rigorously detailed, it is not the same as regards the overall setting. Only rarely does the author specify precisely the year in which the events he describes take place. The greater part of *A Voyage to Arcturus* takes place against the background of a distant star, quite imaginary, so we are scarcely surprised that the introductory chapters prior to the pilgrimage are not set in any specific time. The author is no more generous with information in *Sphinx*. Only a brief reference to 'the war'[6] enables us to place this novel as being post-World War I. *The Haunted Woman* and *Devil's Tor* are fixed with rather greater precision, though only indirectly.

The general atmosphere allows them to be easily placed in the social context of the period. The environments described are invariably those of the wealthier middle-class of business and commerce. It is, in a sense, the whole of this limited society that Lindsay gathers together in the first chapter of *A Voyage to Arcturus*. In the drawing-room of the merchant, Montague Faull, are assembled a stockbroker, a coffee importer, a lawyer, etc. In *The Haunted Woman*, Mrs Moor's fortune comes to her from her husband, a stockbroker, who had known how to invest his money skilfully in the rubber business. Lindsay was very familiar with this environment, through having frequented it prior to becoming a writer. These were the times which Ramsay MacDonald had called 'The Age of the Financier'.

Following the rapid development of industry throughout the Victorian epoch, the old hereditary aristocracy had been replaced by a new élite which derived its power from commerce, business and speculation on the Stock Exchange. The First World War was perhaps the catalyst of a new spirit, made both of carelessness and revolt, but it was also the ratification of a trend of cynicism already established, and hostile to spiritual values. From this point of view, Lindsay's novels are not so far removed from the books that E. M. Forster had written some ten years previously, dramatising the rivalry between the Wilcoxes and the Schlegels, the former family deeply attached to material values, and the other one to spiritual values. The departure for Arcturus can be construed as the rejection of the society of the period.

In Lindsay's case, there also appears this picture of a society that is easy and stable, delighting in its comfort and leisure. In spite of the recent war, the period remained, to all intents and purposes, close to the Edwardian era, 'the halcyon period before the storm'. Symbols of this gracious living, week-ends away and holidays, were henceforward to become fashionable necessities. Accordingly, at the end of each week, thousands of Londoners would leave the capital, like Marshall Stokes, to go to Brighton.[7] The period also saw the appearance of the first 'second homes' hastily erected by un-scrupulous speculative builders, with contempt for the countryside, for the benefit of wealthy people wishing to spend the summer there.

It should be added, however, that the historical context remains vague. One need only refer to the books of Evelyn Waugh and Aldous Huxley for a true, precise picture of the post-World War I English scene. One often looks in vain for the solid detail that would have set the plot in a definite period of history. Apart from the question of clothes,[8] Lindsay's novels contain scant information on the evolution taking place in English society at that time. It needs an attentive reader to detect a few characteristics of the period, such as the use of make-up by women, which did not really develop in England until after World War I. High heels also appeared, impor-ted from the Parisian cabaret scene. As for dresses, they became much shorter, and, especially, more low-cut. Isbel's dress[9] makes

her a good witness of this period of history, that has been called 'the
Dorsal Period'.[10] If Lindsay's heroes often seem sadly old-fashioned,
under the burden of their chivalrous code and inhibitions, the
women, on the other hand, never fail to flaunt the self-assurance,
indeed, the boldness, that the feminist movement was in process of
justifying and encouraging. Isbel does not offer herself to her fiancé
as a submissive woman. She warns that she will not tolerate being
treated as a female chattel, and strongly emphasises that it is
scarcely agreeable for a woman to continue to live with a man if the
only bond keeping them together is the husband's money. It is here
that a new language is found in the mouth of several of Lindsay's
characters, such as Isbel, Tydomin in *A Voyage to Arcturus*, and also,
most certainly, Lore Jensen, whose everyday demeanour is a chal-
lenge to the Victorian image of the submissive, virtuous woman.
Lore is typical of the new woman, independent even in the choice of
her lovers, indulging in both the pleasure of tobacco and alcoholic
intoxication.

The importance of the means of locomotion, train and car
especially, becomes more relevant when one considers the places
where Lindsay situated his plots. It is rare for the background
setting to be a place that is easily accessible; instead, it is the semi-
deserted Dartmoor plains in *Devil's Tor*, the countryside around
Brighton in *The Haunted Woman*, or the New Forest of Hampshire in
*Sphinx*. Train and car are not just features, nor, indeed, fascinating
novelties of the period, but absolute necessities. It is no mere chance
that two of the novels describe, on the very first page, an arrival or a
journey; Nicholas Cabot's arrival at the small station at Newleigh,
and that of Marshall Stokes coming from London, by car, to
Brighton. These districts are only rarely the places where one lives.
One arrives, one penetrates, often for the first time. The train
becomes the tool of the twentieth-century adventurer.

The action takes place at the farthest end of the country. With no
air-ship, there could have been no voyage to Arcturus. With no
train, there could have been no journey from London to Scotland,
whence the air-ship took off, unless, of course, made on foot, on
horseback or by car. The adventure really begins well before the
signal that marks its start; in the labyrinth of railway-lines, stations,
main roads and secondary roads which lead to the assembly-point.
To proceed from Oxford to 'Whitestone', it is necessary to take the
car as far as Swindon, a train to Plymouth, and then a second train

to climb northwards to plunge into the solid mass of Dartmoor. Even on leaving the train, the journey is not yet completed. It is necessary to cover by foot the remaining half-mile separating the village from the house (*Devil's Tor*, page 258). The road leading to Runhill, or to Newleigh, is no easier.

At the end of this labyrinth, we know, there is a small, sharply-defined place that will serve as the background to the plot; a house with a name like 'Mereway', 'Runhill' or 'Whitestone', each with quite distinct architectural features, just as, at the beginning of the 'Gothic novels', the reader is almost invariably confronted with the structure of the castle. Situated apart from the whole village, amidst Nature, this house is much more than a simple dwelling, chosen at random. Its name isolates it, just as its geographical situation separates it from the village, in order to emphasise its uniqueness.

The importance of this kind of house in Lindsay's work never wavers. To be convinced of this, one has only to recall the themes of his books. In *The Haunted Woman*, it is the purchase of an old manor house, Runhill Court, by Mrs Moor and her niece, Isbel Loment. The plot consists, in essence, of visits made there by these two characters, prior to buying the property. In *Sphinx*, there is also a house with an important rôle. 'Mereway' is a modern bungalow, adapted as a family boarding-house to welcome Nicholas Cabot, the novel's hero, who comes to spend a month's holiday as a paying-guest. We find, yet again, a house in *Devil's Tor* called 'Whitestone', an old dwelling built on the heights of Dartmoor, drawing towards it, as if by some magnetic force, the destiny of several characters otherwise never likely to have met. Its location, close to a haunted place, Devil's Tor, immediately makes it a point of contact and observation, towards which different aspects of the novel's plot converge. *A Voyage to Arcturus* is located on a distant planet, upon which there exist, in fact, no houses at all. This, however, does not make this novel an exception in Lindsay's work, since the earlier chapters, before the journey into space, confirm the characteristic structure of the whole of his work. More than this, the structure appears from the book's very first sentence, and hence from the first line that Lindsay ever wrote. 'On a March evening, at eight o'clock, Backhouse, the medium – a fast-rising star in the psychic world – was ushered into the study at Prolands, the Hampstead residence of Montague Faull' (page 15). Here, from the first line of the book, from the first sentence of the entire work, there appears the funda-

mental orientation. Two worlds meet; that of the medium and that of
the merchant, Backhouse and Faull.

### The town

The background of Lindsay's novels begins with the house and
finishes with nature. Between these two realities, there scarcely exists
room for anything else. The house is rural, isolated and solitary. It
accordingly takes up a position of contrast. As a country house, it is
polarised from the town. There is nothing remarkable in this. A love
of nature would be enough to explain it, if the town did not shine so
brightly by its absence, and if the silence, like all the silence in the
work, were not so charged with meaning. In making a frequent use of
the country-house setting, Lindsay *deliberately* excluded the town, in
order to indulge in a very precise type of novel.

The plots of his books have retained an archaic aspect that is
reminiscent of the tradition of the eighteenth-century novel. Lindsay
would go even farther than Jane Austen, when she said 'three or
four families in a country village is the very thing to work on'.

With Lindsay, matters get under way before the real action
begins.[11] Everything beyond the limited confines of the house is
presented to us in the form of flash-backs and recollections.[12] In the
rare passages where it appears, the street becomes the opposite of
the house, and defined in relation to it. 'The three men gathered in
the street outside the house', to quote from the chapter in *A Voyage to
Arcturus* (page 25) entitled 'In the street'. This proves particularly
disappointing to the reader in its lack of description. Night has
removed all trace of the town. The main interest is elsewhere, and
attention turns to the starlit sky. This street leads to Starkness
Observatory, in Scotland, where the telescope is directed, once
again, towards the sky. When, as in *The Haunted Woman*, the plot of
the novel has, in effect, the background of a town, the latter seems
to shrink to the dimensions of an hotel with a revealing name, such
as 'the Metropole Hotel' (p. 7). *The Haunted Woman* is distressingly
bereft of firm details about Brighton life. There appear only brief
references to places, like the Baths (page 99), the seaside promenade
(page 94), the pier (page 36). The description is then limited to a
few comments on the crowd of walkers (page 19), a small orchestra
playing every Sunday morning in one of the town's bandstands
(page 36), a hurdy-gurdy grinding out a popular tune in an alley
(page 13). More often, Lindsay confines himself to psychological

comments. Isbel can wait an hour on the promenade for someone, without there being the slightest reference to the place itself. The entire passage is devoted to a description of the character, her shame at having been badly dressed the preceding day, her fear of having missed her appointment, her disappointment and her impatience. In every case, she seems to pass through the town with closed eyes. 'At the top of Preston Street, she caught a bus to Hove Station, and, on arriving there, purchased a ticket to Worthing' (page 94). In *Sphinx*, Lindsay shows great skill in obliterating any description of London, when Celia and Nicholas Cabot go there for shopping. From one paragraph to the next, the town has been forgotten. 'A more introspective nature than his might have been hard put to it to analyse with exactitude the curious feelings that passed through his mind during the seven-mile drive to Southampton.' This is immediately followed by 'They arrived back at Newleigh Station the same evening, as it was growing quite dark' (page 182).

Quite often, Lindsay justifies the paucity of description in a still more skilful manner. There is nothing to report, he seems to say to the reader, as when he writes 'The life of the street was quiet and normal' (*Devil's Tor*, page 235). From one novel to the next, the town appears to be nothing but an enormous desert. By what curious chance are his characters always alone in such public places as the street, the station and the train? 'There was little to see, for the platform was nearly deserted; no one else appeared to have got down' (*Sphinx*, page 7). The village through which Cabot passes, after leaving the station, is itself also deserted.[13] There is never anything to report. In another novel, Isbel takes the train, where she has an entire compartment at her disposal.[14] Reaching Brighton, she walks along the famous sea-front promenade, frequented only by a few exceptional people, in spite of the time and the season.[15]

For what reason did this writer, who had some forty-odd years behind him of existence that had been almost exclusively urban, very carefully erase all reference to the city, and to the environment that he knew best? His powers of observation were certainly limited, but, if Lindsay sought so much to exclude the town from his scenes, it was also because it was too closely linked to his personal setbacks. The problems of his business career, that he tried to forget, were compounded by his difficulty in living amongst others. London was synonymous with the financial circles that he had been compelled to frequent throughout the whole of the first part of his life, in spite of his deep antipathy. Literature presented itself to him as a dream of escape. No doubt, to describe these environments would have been, in his case, to attack them, but it would also have involved rediscovering them, rather than keeping them at a distance. Apart from this, the town, a public place above all, was a continuing invitation to make contacts, set up meetings and discover others. Surrealist poets delighted in these furtive encounters, and even the erotic images of the town. This was an aspect to which Lindsay remained immune. Austere and puritanical, he judged the throng of townspeople without complacency.[16] He preferred to keep himself at a distance from the town, as he did from women, and to roam alone amongst the hills. The return to nature concealed a double flight, from the town and from women. In his eyes, the town was always the 'swarming city' of the poet, Baudelaire, but the laudatory epithet in the mouth of the one became a deeply pejorative term in the mouth of the other. Referring to one of his characters, Lindsay makes a remark which could well be applied to himself. 'The business of all those swarming, crawling day-labourers was not his, nor his theirs' (*Devil's Tor*, page 209). In the same novel, he adds 'The towns are abominably stuffy and overthronged' (page 20).

If the town had no body, it certainly had a soul, which combined within it all the horrors of modern times. Progress was no more than a return to barbarism. In this universe, all was bad, and 'distorted'.[17] The suburbs were dismal and dirty, 'unfit to live in', while 'flats are prisons', and hotels monotonous and tiring.[18] One could easily recognise the townsman by his pallid complexion (*Devil's Tor*, page 95), as well as by his prejudices (*Sphinx*, page 7). It was difficult to approach a large town without experiencing a feeling of disgust.[19] Only a few neurotics were attracted by towns. On the pretext of finding stimulation there, they sought to conceal the emptiness of their lives, and the gravity of their psychological problems. 'Streets, shops, crowds, any form of human activity, enabled her to forget herself, but natural surroundings threw her back on her own mental resources, and then the whole emptiness and want of purpose of her own life loomed up in front of her ...' (*The Haunted Woman*, page 20). Criticism of the town mounted to such a point that, quite suddenly, the town, formless, like a ghost, reappeared in a vision of the Apocalypse, on the Dartmoor hills. 'All over England and Europe, and gradually all over the world, the houses, pavements, factories, mines, quarries, cuttings, bridges, railways, cars, engines and machinery, slag-heaps, gas-works, roads, stagnant canals, the grime of unreckonable chimneys, the grit and dust of a hell-maze of thoroughfares; and the slums, and backyards, and hidden corners of filth and shame' (*Devil's Tor*, page 68).

As always with Lindsay, the criticism was not limited to a simple statement. The corruption was not a natural excrescence. Mankind was responsible for it, and so should be crucified. According to the poetics of the visible and the invisible, 'I was by now surfeited with the eternal daily spectacle of mean modern city faces, the indices of meaner souls' (*Devil's Tor*, page 115).

It is not surprising, therefore, to meet several characters who seek in the country an antidote for the town. The direction of the work is always from the town towards the country. Hence, Uncle Colborne, in *Devil's Tor*, moves to 'Whitestone' through disgust with the town. Lore Jensen, Isbel Loment, Nicholas Cabot, and certainly others, come from the town, but, unlike the townspeople of to-day, find that a week-end in the country, or even a month's holiday in the provinces, offer no solution. To be of any value at all, the return to nature must be a permanent one. There is quickly established a sharp distinction between those who come from the town to seek a temporary haven in the country, and those who come on a different basis. In the first category are townspeople who are frustrated, in the manner of Mrs Moor, Isbel Loment, Nicholas Cabot and Lore Jensen. Their quest generally ends in a setback. The second group is that of the hunters and the adventurers, such as Saltfleet, Hugh Drapier, and also, to a certain extent, Maskull.

### Finding the house

The converging point of all routes, starting sometimes from America (*The Haunted Woman*) or Asia (*Devil's Tor*), is the house, which is clearly something very much more than a mere structure of bricks and mortar. The theme of the house appears for the first time at the beginning of *A Voyage to Arcturus*, in the shape of the residence of the merchant, Montague Faull. We know it only from the inside. Every detail suggests a wealthy dwelling. In the second novel, the description is more searching, since Runhill Court is at the very heart of the plot. The book is ostensibly about the purchase of this manor-house. In *Sphinx*, the bungalow, 'Mereway', plays a rôle that is no less important, since the book's hero, Nicholas Cabot, goes there to spend his holiday, as a paying-guest. We find the same kind of house again in *Devil's Tor*, with the dwelling, 'Whitestone'.

Externally, Lindsay's prototype house has scarcely any aspect worthy of our attention, at least at first sight, since it resembles all other English houses. It is also true that it evolves from one novel to the next, in an architectural sense. Runhill Court is a large, three-storeyed building which, in spite of frequent renovations, has retained some of the extravagant features of its Elizabethan origins, with its pointed roofs and multifarious gables. 'Whitestone' dates from the early nineteenth century, and is distinguishable by its age and architecture. In contrast to the flamboyance and medley of styles of Runhill Court, 'Whitestone' offers an appearance that is remarkably austere, relieved only by two pillars on either side of the entrance, and by a profusion of jasmine and roses (*Devil's Tor*, page 38). 'Mereway', in short, is a modern bungalow. In spite of an architectural style that is surprising on first sight, this turns out to be no more than part of the decoration, like the garden and the tennis-court (*Sphinx*, pages 8–9).

The furniture confirms the overall impression made on the spectator by the façade. There is nothing remarkable about it, any more than there is in the architecture just mentioned. The houses, however, are not completely identical, one to the other, any more than they resemble the first house chosen by chance in the English countryside. Each is distinguishable from its neighbour in one way or another. Its age, its style, its architecture, its furniture, its environment, all contribute to separate it, and to describe it. Each element stands out enough to create a genuine identity for the house.

Superimposing itself, therefore, on the description that is real and factual, there exists an unravelling of atmosphere. To the very down-to-earth argument of 'I suppose that a house cannot be more than a house' (*The Haunted Woman*, page 31), there is a magical counter-conception which makes the dwelling into a veritable private world. 'It certainly has an atmosphere of its own, this house', says one of the characters (page 27), thus confirming a sense of atmosphere. The background assumes a psychological depth which appears very clearly in the majority of his novels. It is one of the most characteristic features of his work always to return the reader to a code of moral values or psychological notation which embellishes the factual presentation, investing both house and décor with a much deeper significance than was apparent at first sight.

In most cases, the house is not a place of permanent residence, but somewhere one penetrates, often for the first time. It is this act of entering, this discovery of the house, that allows Lindsay to describe so carefully the impression felt standing in front of it. Before turning out to be a haunted house, Runhill Court is striking in its architecture and atmosphere. Soon, it seems to affect the visitor's nerves, then it soothes him by its prevailing peace, the gentleness of its light, and the shades of its wainscotting. The threshold of the house marks out the gateway to 'a new and marvellous world'. Strange music is heard which does not seem to come from a piano situated in any definite room, but rather to emerge from the entire house, as if it were its very embodiment. The doors are not just ordinary wooden panels, but become threatening, as if to warn young girls against the danger of amorous passion (page 49). 'This house ain't going to be played with. Perhaps it'll bite back and bite hard.' Is it because it suggests so many dangers that it has such an irresistible attraction? 'Something called her, and that silent voice was irresistible. It was something in *that house* ... It was like the call of a drug; she was a drug-maniac ...' (page 152; see also page 83). The menacing features culminate in the assertion 'The house is alive (page 41).

Sometimes, the background seems to precipitate the plot. It is because Devil's Tor is 'a hill unlike the others' that Uncle Colborne cannot resist the urge to buy a nearby house, for want of being able to purchase the hill itself. Devil's Tor, like Runhill Court, is a *living* place, we are told.[20] To penetrate a place is, therefore, to a very large extent, to be confronted by an organism gifted with a kind of interior life, a soul. In all Lindsay's novels, there is no presentation of a background which is not, at the same time, a thorough investigation of the soul of the place. The condition of a house tells us something about its owner even before we have had the opportunity of meeting him. For example, the high moral tone of Judge reveals itself behind the order and neatness of his house (*The Haunted Woman*, page 24).

## Appraisal of the house

In the first place, the modern house relates to a scale of values that Lindsay rejects. 'Mereway', for example, is distinguishable from some thirty neighbouring properties only by its name. All are identical, being 'high-class residences in the bungalow style for that numerous class of leisured people who delight in sunshine, nature, pseudo-solitude, and new art' (*Sphinx*, page 9). Separated one from the other by about a hundred yards, all the dwellings are identical, being the work of the same architect. Each has a bizarre name, the same lawn, the same tennis-court, the same garden. To call them ugly would doubtless be untrue, since, in their own style, they are not lacking in attraction. In Lindsay's eyes, however, they are grotesque. They have been tastelessly built. 'Mereway', like the surrounding bungalows, corresponds to no real need. It is more of a symbol; the dream home amidst grass and trees, which has been elaborated to satisfy secondary needs; comfort and leisure. Everything is clean and scented. Everything harmonises to the point of perfection; the drive, the garden and the curtains (page 67). This house seems to be the perfect image offered to us in the brochures of estate agents. The new orientation is no longer religious or symbolic, but hygienic; health, sport and sunshine. A country-house, 'Mereway' is primarily a holiday home, seemingly far removed from the cares of everyday life. It has a tennis-court and a croquet-lawn, in conformity with the fashion of the period. The young Sturt girls, Lindsay tells us, 'live for tennis'. Could there be a more candid admission of the new ideal of modern times, of which the country-house is the embodiment?

This soulless dwelling is also a house without roots. Lindsay presents it to us as being situated outside time. On the Newleigh estate, each bungalow seems to have no age. 'The house, from its appearance, might have been put up yesterday, yet, actually, it had been standing for more than twenty years' (page 9). Runhill Court provides the same example of the prostitution of values demonstrated throughout the restoration of the manor. The original dwelling dates back to the sixth century, but only the famous 'East Room', known to be haunted, has survived. The hall is from the fifteenth century. Finally, the greater part of the building has been renovated. The overall effect is not of the best, but rather 'a veritable *pot-pourri* of styles and centuries'. The original manor has been so renovated that it resembles 'a modern erection'.

Hence, the proprietorial instinct becomes associated with contempt for the past. The first anxiety of every purchaser is to renovate. The log-fire must be supplemented by central heating.[21] In all this debasement, no transformation is more evident, and more significant, than that of the roof. With the roof, one recognises not

only the house but the owner, so true is it that the roof is often a
symbol of the home. Language teaches us that the man without a
dwelling is a 'man without a roof', truly without a home. Lindsay's
heroes are often men without a roof. Legend had it that, to punish
the first owner of Runhill Court for not believing in the supernatural, and for defying it by building the house on sacred ground,
the trolls, those goblins of Scandinavian tales, carried off the roof
(*The Haunted Woman*, page 43). Symbolically, it was enough to destroy
the roof in order to demolish the entire house. As soon as possible after
the purchase of his country-flat, Peter Copping, in order to announce
his arrival more clearly, replaced the old thatched roof with red tiles
(*Devil's Tor*, page 373). In Lindsay's mythology, the renovation was
inevitably accompanied by debasement. The thatch on the roof is the
link between earth and sky. Being a vegetable material, it stretches
towards the sky. In this encroachment by red tile, he sees a clear
sign of the decadence of modern times. That the industrial tile in
discordant red should replace the dark thatch, and indeed the slate,
was an affront that Lindsay could not tolerate. Henceforward, he
would measure the extent of the ravages by the number of tiled roofs
at Newleigh,[22] at 'Mereway' (*Sphinx*, page 9), and, finally, at
Runhill Court. 'The irregular, many-gabled roof was bright with
new red tiles, the facing of red bricks on the ground storey had been
pointed recently, while the two upper storeys were plastered with
dazzling white stucco' (*The Haunted Woman*, pages 21–22). Under
this double layer of plaster and brick, there was discernible the
likeness of twentieth-century man, the idol of all that seemed false.
Everyone has the house that he deserves.

The metaphor of plaster completes that of tile, with which it is
often associated. Plaster, like tile or brick, is the quintessence of
modern material. Because it is essentially a coating, plaster easily
becomes a symbol of disguise, an object of façade. It is underneath
this layer of plaster that the true nature of Runhill Court lies
concealed. The modern edifice hides a very ancient house, a haunted dwelling. Behind this thin layer of stucco, there begins the more
profound world. The plaster, moreover, is an artificial material,
lacking the solidity and noble origin of stone and wood. In Lindsay's
eyes, the true house, free of all artifice, could only be built with
wood or stone. It is doubtless no mere chance that the dwelling best
preserved from the outrages of modern civilisation affirms, even by
its name, this attachment to stone, 'Whitestone'. It is Runhill

Court, however, which offers the most striking contrast between plaster and wood. The modern renovated part is made of stucco, while the Elizabethan hall is in wood, as is the haunted room, naturally. The author makes frequent reference to the manor's ancient wainscotting, contrasting the simplicity of the rough wood with the gaudiness of the copper and the gilded façade.[23]

The renovation, far from being a step towards the future, is a return to barbarism. Deprived of its roof by the trolls, Ulf's house had become a deformed monster. Each wing added to the original house is a graft. Normally, all habitation expresses, by its form, a direction of the spirit. The mandala of the Buddhists, in India, is one of the best known of these symbolic places, being a union of three basic figures; the circle, the square and the cross. The mandala is interpreted as a return to unity through a representation of the cosmos. The modern, or renovated, house, on the other hand, is an assembly of bastard forms, breaking primordial harmony. Behind the extravagance of the architecture of 'Mereway', Lindsay recognises an absence of direction, and then an absence of significance. 'It had the same queer, unmeaning gables, chimneys and window-bays, stretching out at all sorts of angles' (*Sphinx*, page 9). Therein lies an architecture that is evidence of bankruptcy. The plaster, the multifarious gables, the painted façade of vivid colour, the tiles and the red brick, are as many of the elements that Lindsay assembles to constitute the image of the modern house. We can take, as evidence, his description of what was, in the sixth century, the first Runhill Court. In a dream, it appears through the mist, and, significantly, the ancient dwelling is exactly the opposite of the modern restored manor. 'It was a different building. As well as could be distinguished through the mist, it was constructed entirely of unpainted timber, from top to bottom; the roof was flat, without gables, and there appeared to be four storeys' (*The Haunted Woman*, page 166). Contrasting with all these examples of modern dwellings already mentioned, this is the old abode which is Lindsay's ideal, austere, having neither paint nor gables, and built exclusively of wood. It is more a construction of the spirit than the work of an architect.[24]

### The garden

This quasi-symbolic house with neither roof nor basement, all corners and in plaster, this skeleton lacking flesh and soul, is

paradoxically embellished with a lavish garden. Throughout
Lindsay's writing, there is scarcely a single house without a garden.
The façade of 'Whitestone' is decorated with a profusion of roses
and jasmine. It is in *Sphinx* in particular, however, that the garden
becomes a vital feature of the décor. At Newleigh, each bungalow
has a garden, with attractive beds of roses. The visit to the house
often begins with the discovery of the garden. Sometimes the garden
is so indispensable that it constitutes an integral part of the house, in
the same way as the curtains with which it harmonises (pages 66–
67). It can even happen that the name of the house relates to the
garden, so closely are they linked, an example being Celia Hantish's
house, which is called 'The Arbour'.

The permanence of this theme is explicable, firstly, in autobiographical terms. A keen amateur flower-grower, Lindsay ended
in making gardening one of his favourite pastimes. His knowledge in
this field, and his love of flowers, were such that he could always
take pride in his magnificent flower-beds. Surprisingly, however,
Lindsay never conceived the garden as being a place where his
characters might develop. Here, there is an obvious contradiction
between the man and the thinker. The thinker judges such in-
dulgences severely.

Nowadays, our ideal house, the kind of which we dream, is
inconceivable without a garden. 'The garden is part of our house
within, and everywhere to-day its absence is felt as a deficiency',
wrote Olivier Marc.[25] To judge from his writing, however, Lindsay
ran counter to this psychological trend. Far from being felt to be the
expression of fullness and harmony, the existence of the garden
seemed, on the contrary, to be evidence of the owner's psychological
bankruptcy. In nearly all the cases encountered, the metaphor of
the garden is synonymous with negative values. If it does sometimes
happen that a guest begins a visit to the house with a tour of the
garden, Lindsay hastens to stress the fact that this is an obligation,
with the real interest elsewhere. 'The afternoon was as delightful as
possible, but Mrs Sturt at once perceived that the interest of her
guest was not in her rose-buds and perennials. He kept looking at
the distant trees' (*Sphinx*, page 21).

Several times, Lindsay associates the garden with negative values.
An agreeable background for relaxation, the garden contrasts with
his ideal of anguish, renunciation and self-transcendence. To deserve
the attention of a visitor, the garden must be a vale of tears, and not

a sunlit meadow. As Lindsay presents it to us, the garden is the place for insipid love-affairs. It is in the garden that Peter Copping declares his love for Ingrid (*Devil's Tor*, page 123). In *The Haunted Woman*, the awakening of the love between Judge and Isbel occurs against a changing background. The Runhill Court property gives way to the new setting of a sunlit garden, impregnated with the scent of spring, and strewn with primroses and violets. For all the idealists in Lindsay's novels, the garden is the trap to avoid at all costs, largely because it is the favourite field of action for women. Nicholas Cabot is well aware of this on the way to Celia Hantish's house. 'He felt that he, too, ought to be at work, instead of sauntering past flower-gardens, on his way to an appointment with a pretty woman' (*Sphinx*, page 169). The risks incurred do not prevent Cabot, on the occasion of his next visit, from allowing himself to be led into Celia's garden, and then into a kind of wilderness extending to the rear, access to which the mistress of the house reserves strictly for her male guests.[26] As anticipated, Cabot forgets his fears and his work, stammers a proposal of marriage, and ends in Celia's arms somewhere at the bottom of the garden. The trap is sprung. Nicholas Cabot is as much the prisoner of the woman as of the garden.

The garden is, at best, the waste-land which is the heritage of Original Sin, a field of limitations. The artistic disintegration of the musician, Lore Jensen, can be perceived in the titles of her compositions. Her latest piece is called 'Pamela in the Rose Garden'. To the inspired art of her period of glory, represented by the work, 'Sphinx', Lindsay compares the decadent realism of her current work. While the music inspired by the Sphinx leads man to reflect upon his destiny, that of the rose-garden can be nothing but 'a delightful little fancy'. The garden, therefore, is not the glory of the house, but merely its mediocre extension. For Lindsay, the sunlit flower-bed becomes the symbol of triviality. The real values lie elsewhere, in the woodland that extends beyond the garden. The garden, in terms of human achievement, cannot pretend to replace Nature. It is Nature that is distorted, and can satisfy only the tastes of those townspeople temporarily exiled in their second homes. To the question 'You are not a flower-lover?', Cabot replies 'I prefer nature' (page 21). Hence, the garden is to Nature what the house is to the temple; namely, a poor substitute with which certain people are content.

*The hotel*

The hotel is the final link in the chain of soulless houses, as soulless man also becomes man without a house. We know that 'Mereway' was not exactly the model of the idyllic house. Its owner, however, does not hesitate to extol its attractions. 'For the sum you are willing to pay, you may live at any good hotel, with luxuries possibly superior to those we shall offer you, but ... in a hotel, you will not meet solid, family people, established in their own homes. You will enjoy no privacy. You will be a solitary stranger among strangers. You will have no delightful home life ... and you will scarcely find a hotel where you will be able to step out of the back door, as it were, into the very heart of the pine woods' (*Sphinx*, page 13). Once again, the house tries to crystallise around it dreams of intimacy and security, and the promise of a better life. We have said that, in many cases, the house would not offer the refuge so much desired. In the author's scale of values, however, it shows itself as being superior to the hotel, which is the perfect dwelling for townspeople, and the anti-Nature symbol of anonymity. In contrast to the cottage, the hotel is the degraded image of the town-house, so we are scarcely surprised to discover that Lindsay gives his hotel the name 'Metropole', thereby symbolising the connection between the hotel and the town. It is not enough that Mrs Moor's basically masculine tastes make her the opposite of the indoor woman.[27] She scarcely has the spirit of adventure, since her discoveries and acquisitions are limited to the hotels she frequents in the four corners of the globe.

We have seen the different types of dwelling one meets in Lindsay's books. In spite of certain superficial attractions, Lindsay presents these décors as limited, and essentially devoid of meaning. This criticism is directed particularly at a certain type of modern dwelling which, in its architecture, furniture and general appearance, is the reflection of those who live in it. The degradation of the house corresponds to the loss of something sacred. The town ends by becoming the symbol of the modern world, and the hotel as the perfect dwelling for townspeople.

The criticism, however, is not simply directed at the background of the modern house, but extends to encompass all forms of artificial dwelling. It is here that we reach the ultimate point in the author's internal itinerary, to which all earlier accusations lead. Everything concerned, directly or indirectly, with the house is mediocre and insipid. It is always at a great distance from it and its world that man achieves his true stature. The house is certainly the place that Bachelard has made one of the symbols of intimacy and security.[28] It is precisely this that Lindsay condemns in this habitation. Of one of his characters, for example, he writes 'Peter was sound, small, domestic and good, like a sweet apple' (*Devil's Tor*, page 106). There scarcely exists a more severe condemnation than 'domestic'. The word recurs endlessly from the author's pen, sometimes even in the most surprising contexts. The domestic nature of Peter Copping reappears in the mouth of another character. 'For this young man, perhaps, was neither a fool nor a weakling, though he was obviously rather pulled down by an indoor existence' (page 252). Invariably, the daily routine is associated with the world of the house. When Ingrid returns home, after having seen the storm strike Devil's Tor, she gets the feeling of having left 'a high-seat of grandeur, in order to re-seek dullness, meanness and common-place' (page 32). The opposite of the grandiose is the narrow world of the house, whether it be ancient or modern. The ideal is always associated with the liberty of great open spaces, in contrast to the restraints of the house. How, otherwise, can one understand such an assertion as 'Without savagery, a book must have a more or less domestic character'? (*Philosophical Notes*, Number 544, paragraph 24.) Here again, there appear the basic orientations. On the one hand, there is the wild, the grandiose, and, hence, the Sublime, and, on the other, the assimilated mediocrity of the domestic.

Is it, then, purely by chance that two of Lindsay's characters are in the business of estate agency? Cabot sells houses, which is certainly an honourable vocation, but one which does not escape Lindsay's biting irony. 'One has not the same prejudice against the trade of estate agent as against certain others. If it is not quite a profession, it is almost an art, for, after all, a fine mansion is a distinct advance upon a consignment of coal, or bricks, or coffee' (*Sphinx*, pages 11–12). Uncle Colborne, in *Devil's Tor*, is the second of these 'artists', intellectuals but also estate agents,[29] able to combine the highest idealism with the most shameless business sense. In all the books, there scarcely exists a single false note. The four walls of the house invariably serve to mark out the inadequacies of everyday life. For the man eager for the ideal, the house soon becomes a 'prison of unutterable boredom'.[30] Thus entombed in the prison of the senses and the tangible world, 'We are like domestic fowls, picking up crumbs amid glorious scenery' (*Devil's Tor*, page

228), unaware of the surrounding beauty. Again, elsewhere, the house has been so renovated that it has lost its magical orientation, and the ties that bind it to cosmic forces. It no longer has meaning. Caught in the trap of his own making, twentieth-century man, domesticated and effeminate, can no longer distinguish between God and the architect of his house. 'Who except the troglodytes can worship to-day?' asks Lindsay (*Devil's Tor*, page 396). Hence, the flight from the house-trap begins, towards a magical place inherited from the past, such as the temple, the church, the cave, the troglodyte's home, but never the modern bungalow.

### Destruction of the house-trap

If the first movement in the books is from the hotel, or the London flat, to the country-house, the fixation with this location might equally be considered by idealists as representing stagnation, and, indeed, reaction. The road leading to the house also leads to disappointment. This feeling is inescapable in *The Haunted Woman*. The enchanted house is a trap, a creation of the Devil, that he makes and destroys to mislead mankind. If this house resembles Paradise, then it is a Paradise that is purely artificial.

Hence, Lindsay's ambiguities begin at the very threshold of the house. At first a refuge for Cabot, wanting peace and quiet in which to continue his experiments on the functioning of the unconscious, 'Mereway' shows itself to be a trap for him. 'In staying as a paying-guest in a house containing young girls of marriageable age, he had acted like a thoughtless idiot.' The house, a symbol of social conventions, becomes a prison for all those in search of an ideal. Paradise for some, it is a hell for the man who is a rebel, for whom the anguish is so much more painful to bear that very often rebellion does not go beyond the realisation of his own damnation. No character expresses this better than Lore Jensen. Lore, like so many of Lindsay's heroes and heroines, has come to the country to seek peace and quiet, and essentially peace of mind. She finds herself, however, shut up all day long in a solitary, small, dark room, contemplating the sunshine outside, as if she were in a box at the theatre. As for the enigmatic Mrs Brion, Lore's lady companion, she could equally pass for Cerberus, with her 'snake-like eyes ... impassive, unsmiling and inscrutable ...' (*Sphinx*, page 279). In Evelyn's dream, Lore walks in the forest, bearing an expression 'as a woman might wear who is being removed from a torture-chamber, knowing that she is to return there a few hours later, when her strength has been sufficiently restored' (page 159). Lore goes to the village fair, not by choice, but because she seeks, at the fête, a means of escape from the house-prison. 'I loathe that house I live in!' she says.

Admittedly, the prison is often no more than the equivalent of the psychological confinement of the individual. The wall is not just that of the house, but also the barrier against which man knocks himself in pursuit of the ideal. In order to succeed, he must leave the house, or, better still, destroy it. The house which, seen from London, could pass for an enchanted isle, is revealed as being only a 'waste-land', the narrow world of the rural middle-class, a land of false values and social conventions. Henceforward, the house will be the enemy. The more one seeks to attain it, the more one ends by fleeing from it, or, even better, destroying it. Hence, to the domestic background, whose inadequacies we have shown, there is substituted another background, much more satisfying. If the quest passes by the house, it can only end beyond it. Nearly all Lindsay's novels return to this theme most specifically. In *A Voyage to Arcturus*, Maskull penetrates, first of all, the home of the merchant, Montague Faull, before departing, in preference to this environment, for the freedom of inter-planetary space. The plot of *The Haunted Woman* oscillates between the hotel and the haunted room at Runhill Court, the secret place and Ali Baba's cave, to enter which one has to possess the 'open-sesame'. Finally, in *Devil's Tor*, the quest begins from the house, 'Whitestone', to lead towards the sanctuary of the Great Mother. In each case, we discover two parallel worlds, the first being only the conventional, limited world of the house, but the second being magical, the supernatural world in the case of *Devil's Tor* and *The Haunted Woman*, and the unconscious world of *Sphinx*, and also, to some extent, *The Haunted Woman*.

In both *The Haunted Woman* and *Devil's Tor*, the plot lies almost entirely in the progression between two places, from the hotel to the haunted room in the former case, and from the house to the hill in the latter, as if both haunted room and sacred hill were magnets, drawing the characters towards them. The plot progresses only because of unexpected events that occur to disturb or provoke these movements. The intermediate chapters often serve merely to explain these comings and goings, and the discoveries which accompany them.

The juxtaposition of these two places is far from being involuntary. It serves to enhance the mediocrity of the domestic background, as compared with the grandeur of the magical background. The stability of the small, closed world of the house lends itself so well to analysis that the slightest crack is capable of having far-reaching consequences. It is certainly Lindsay's intention to paint the wall so as to be better able to spotlight the crack. If he builds house after house, it is in order more easily to destroy them.

Each study consists of the definition of the conventional environment of the house, in order, afterwards, to hurl a 'bomb', and await the reactions of the characters. In *A Voyage to Arcturus*, this 'bomb' is none other than the arrival of Krag, erupting into the home of Montague Faull, in order to scare the middle-class circle there assembled. In two other books, the disruptive element is more an object than the character who introduces it. In *Sphinx*, for example, Nicholas Cabot carries in his luggage a machine of his own invention, intended to record, and unravel, dreams. This machine brings into the open certain secrets that are as shameful as they are unexpected about characters who, otherwise, pass as models of respectability. Finally, in *Devil's Tor*, the magic stone, brought from Asia by Hugh Drapier, conforms to the same rule. It upsets daily life, revealing the existence, just a few steps from the house, of a tomb, the discovery of which is destined to be very important.

The machine to record dreams very nearly becomes an infernal machine. This point is repeatedly stressed by Lindsay. Soon after the arrival of her lodger, Mrs Sturt, curious to know the contents of the packages that he brings, worries to discover if there is any risk of an explosion.[31] The explosion certainly occurs, at least metaphorically, since two characters meet their deaths, and the identity of Lore's father is revealed. At the root of these upheavals lies Cabot, and his infernal machine. His arrival at Newleigh heralds, for the family into which he comes, the beginning of all these complications.

This theme is found again in *Devil's Tor*. The discovery of the magic stone, the arrival of Hugh Drapier, then that of Saltfleet, are all elements which come to disturb the normal course of events. Henceforward, nothing will be quite the same again. The home will be irrevocably transformed. Once, more, it is the entire house that collapses, and there recurs this metaphor of the infernal machine. Referring to the arrival of Saltfleet, Lindsay writes, of Helga, 'She only of those in the house knew of this awful shell about to explode within it' (page 239). Saltfleet himself, the intruder, is seen as 'an element of disintegration'.

These few references to magic stones and machines for recording dreams are undeniably part of the vocabulary of fantasy. For this reason, Lindsay should be able to figure most worthily amongst the pillars of fantasy literature, such as Lovecraft, Machen, Edgar Allan Poe and so many others. The time has not yet come to assess the fantasy work of Lindsay. Suffice it to say that it is firmly placed in the purest tradition of the genre, 'the irruption of the inadmissible in the midst of the unalterable everyday legality', according to the definition of Roger Caillois. Now, if the house occupies such an important place in Lindsay's work, is it not perhaps also because it epitomises to perfection 'the unalterable everyday legality', here blasted to smithereens by supernatural elements?

Lindsay's novels, however, are distinguishable from all these tales that have made of the house 'the perfect fantasy place',[32] such as *House of the Sorcerer* by Lovecraft, *The Fall of the House of Usher*, or indeed *The House on the Borderland* by W. H. Hodgson. In contrast to other fantasy spaces, the house, with Lindsay, has nothing horrible in itself. Having neither cracked walls nor bad sanitation, it is in no sense an environment of unwholesome experiences. It is quite fitting to find, in *The Haunted Woman*, an Elizabethan dwelling, with irregular gables, to remind us of Lovecraft and the Gothic novel. In general, this house is as respectable as it is solid. It does not impress the reader by the mystery that it hides, but by the serenity that it suggests. In itself, the house is the very opposite of fantastic. It becomes a fantastic place only on contact with the supernatural.

Just as the call of the ideal corresponds, in Lindsay's novels, to the necessity to escape from the house-prison, so the intrusion of the hereafter is accompanied by the collapse of domestic values, or, to put it metaphorically, by the collapse of the house. The metaphor, however, duplicates itself, and feeds upon reality. It is by no means rare to find examples where the discovery of the transcendent world is accompanied, in effect, by the destruction of the house. In *The Haunted Woman*, the legend went that, in order to punish the first owner of Runhill Court for not believing in the supernatural, spirits had carried off the top storey of his house. One also remembers that, in the very earliest pages of *A Voyage to Arcturus*, the irruption of the supernatural is accompanied by the sound of falling masonry. The metaphor, in this case, has a personal origin, and dates back to an incident in his own life of which Lindsay made use in the example just quoted. 'A few weeks before the death of my only brother, some years back, I was awakened in the middle of the night by a tremendous crash, as though a chimney-stack had crashed through the roof overhead. That it was not imagination in my case is proved by the fact that my aunt, who slept in the room above, came flying downstairs for help – she also had heard the noise, and was frightened nearly out of her senses ...'[33]

### The temple

For want of finding, in his own life, the ideal house, Lindsay imagined it in his novels, and especially in *The Haunted Woman* and *Devil's Tor*. Paradoxically, Runhill Court is at once the ideal and its very opposite, the temple and the 'domestic house'. From her first visit, Isbel notices a discordant note that she cannot exactly define; in fact, it is the juxtaposition of different styles of architecture. Even if the greater part of the building has been restored, and scarcely differs from any other modern structure, one entire wing remains untouched. This part includes a thirteenth-century hall and a storey designated 'the East Room', which dates back to the sixth century, a unique trace of the first house at Runhill. Parallel to the restored house, there exists, then, a structure inherited from the past. With undeniable skill, Lindsay assembles, under the same roof, at once the temple and the 'domestic house', which is the reason why this dwelling does not have the same value for each of the characters. What attracts Mrs Moor to 'Runhill', for example, is the renovated part, comprising the gleaming kitchen, the central heating and the electric light. Isbel, on the other hand, finds this mixture of ancient and modern to be in the worst possible taste. If the age of this dwelling frightens her on her first visit, she ends up by being fascinated by the dark, winding corridors of this old Elizabethan manor, to the point of being able to forget completely the existence of the renovated part.

With the renovated section of the building, Lindsay contrasts the famous thirteenth-century hall, which has preserved its wainscotting. This hall has also kept from the past 'its steeply-pointed roof ... covered with grey slates'. This pointed roof, stretching towards the sky as though in an effort to tear itself from the ground, already contains the Lindsay mystique. He recognises a trend which he contrasts with the shapeless mass of modern houses, with their 'queer, unmeaning gables, chimneys and window-bays, sticking out at all sorts of angles' (*Sphinx*, page 9). The dark shades of the wood and slate contrast with the brilliance of the new paint, the red tiles and copper in a dialectic of colour which animates the entire work.

The hall at 'Runhill', with its modern wainscotting, its carpets in restful colours, its massive oak beams, its pointed roof, the glass of its windows (page 23), is the image of the temple. Isbel says of this part of the building that it is like 'an ancient chapel'[34]. In fact, the hall of Runhill Court is only the entrance to the temple, the really sacred place being the haunted room, with which the hall is connected by a series of relationships. Firstly, access to the haunted room is by way of the hall. Secondly, in that room is to be found the dark wainscotting of the hall.

This image of the temple recurs in other novels of Lindsay. *A Voyage to Arcturus*, for example, opens with the décor of the temple. The spiritualistic séance in the opening chapter of the book has the improvised background of a theatre. 'A replica, or nearly so, of the Drury Lane presentation of the temple scene in *The Magic Flute* was then exposed to view.' This tall statue of a Pharaoh, placed in one corner of the stage, could not fail to remind one of another giant of the temple, Samson. The middle-class group assembled to witness the spectacle are certainly the merchants from the temple. Soon, with the arrival of Krag, the pillars crack with 'a loud and terrible crash of falling masonry', ready to fall down on the Philistines. Finally, in *Devil's Tor*, the temple is none other than the tomb of the Great Mother, situated near 'Whitestone', at the side of the house, on the hill which gives the novel its title, Devil's Tor. Between the 'chapel' at 'Runhill' and the tomb at Devil's Tor, there is more than a passing resemblance. In both books, the quest is directed from the house towards the sacred places; from the hotel towards the haunted room, in the case of *The Haunted Woman*, and from 'Whitestone' towards Devil's Tor, in the case of the second novel. In both cases, Lindsay stresses the sacred nature of these places. If 'Runhill' resembles a chapel, then Devil's Tor has the sinister profile of the gargoyles of our cathedrals, the guardians of the temples. Both seem to be the trustees of menacing secrets, and of places haunted by strange presences.

No one should enter lightly, and, to this end, there is a warning network of winding paths, accessible only to the initiated, the

difficulty of which is intended to discourage all but the most
determined. Runhill Court is situated at the farthest end of the
English countryside, on the edge of a labyrinth of small tracks. Once
one arrives there, it is necessary, in order to reach the haunted
room, to surmount a succession of staircases and dark corridors.
'Parallel with, and overlooking, the stairs, was another little corridor, stretching to the front of the house, and lighted by a dormer-
window at the end. Along this, Mrs Priday conducted them. When
they could nearly touch the sloping roof, the corridor turned sharply
to the left, and became a sort of tunnel . . . After twenty paces or so,
there came another twist. A couple of shallow stairs brought them
up into a widening of the passage, which might almost be described
as a room . . . The second section of unlighted passage led to another
gable-roof, and this, in turn, was succeeded by a third, but shorter,
tunnel. The passage was terminated by a plain oak door' (pages
32–33). Thus, at last, the visitor reaches the threshold of the
haunted room, but does not get *into* the room, since it is kept locked.
In face of this literature of underground vaults, it is difficult not to
evoke memories of the *Mysteries of Udolfo*, and so many other 'Gothic
novels', in which the adventures of the heroes are so closely linked to
journeys through labyrinths, corridors, galleries and rooms.

The essential point, however, is not so much the mystery and the
terror created by the investigation of these dark, narrow places, but
the initiation. This long march is, in fact, a procession, the ritual
that must be observed before penetrating the temple. One enters the
'domestic house' unannounced, indeed unwelcomed, in a manner
quite different from when one enters the temple. In order that the
spiritualistic séance, along with the Temple scene from *The Magic
Flute*, can begin, the High Priest must make his speech against a
background of Mozart's music.[35] The exploration of the tomb of the
Great Mother is particularly revealing in this respect. It is necessary, first of all, to travel across several miles of difficult paths, in
order to reach the hillock underneath which is hidden the tomb.
Then comes the initiation, as in *The Haunted Woman*, with the
underground experience, first a spiral pit, and then a tunnel. In
addition, the descent compels Hugh Drapier to sit down, so that he
can then slip, one step at a time, in a parody of pilgrimage. As in
the case of numerous legends, the cave is the home of Divinity.
Access is not only difficult, or forbidden, but, once having entered,
the visitor must submit to the laws that are in force. 'This buried

crypt was holy with antiquity and mystery and night, so that to
have one undedicated step into it would be like profanation. The
hard, white, modern glare from his torch was already a profanation,
but look he must' (*Devil's Tor*, page 84). Happily, a clumsy gesture
breaks the torch! At last, Drapier can enter the tomb, from which
'he stole, bare-headed, forth, as from the celebration of a
sacrament'.

It is equally worthy of notice that, if the architecture of the house
develops along a horizontal plane (ground floor, garden, lawn,
tennis-court), that of the temple is vertical. The ancient part of
Runhill Court, the 'chapel', is distinguished by its pointed roof. As
Bachelard has emphasised, the ground floor corresponds to the
platitude of ordinary life.[36] With Lindsay, the ground floor is limited
almost exclusively to the living-room, a place devoid of any mystery.
A phantom was never seen in a living-room. Sunshine, however,
cannot be absent, any more than everything necessary for the
comfort of mankind. The living-room is the monotonous world,
calm and 'undramatised'.[37] Nothing surprising can happen there.
Hence, it corresponds perfectly to the image that Lindsay creates of
the 'domestic house', which is conventional and limited.

The temple, in contrast, is built in height, as if the sphere of
mystery, adventure and the unconscious can be either cave or attic,
vault or hill, low or high. The sanctuary of the Great Mother is
situated at the top of a hillock. At Runhill Court, it is not known
exactly at what floor the haunted room is located. Was it, quite
simply, this room which was formerly carried off by spirits, and
which reappeared at some time or other? The sanctuary is situated
on high. It is also underground, in the same sense that, on the third
storey at 'Runhill', one reaches the haunted room after having
passed through 'tunnels'. In *Sphinx*, Nicholas Cabot's experiments
with dreams are not conducted on the ground floor, but on the top
storey of the house. Hence, the architecture parallels the ambition of
the spirit to break away from everyday life, and expresses this flight
in symbolic form.

These two worlds, then, co-exist, each one having its own laws
and architecture. The temple does not exist merely as an ideal, but
rises up just a few steps from the house, and sometimes even inside
the house. Accordingly, the transition from the one place to the
other assumes the aspect of a procession. Each of Lindsay's novels
creates this impression of waiting, which is then followed by as-

tonishment at the discovery of the temple. In *A Voyage to Arcturus*, the domestic background of the house becomes suddenly transformed. The curtain rises upon a theatrical stage, having the décor of *The Magic Flute*, with pillars ranged against a background of sky. In *The Haunted Woman*, the music of Beethoven creates this atmosphere of waiting 'as if a curtain were about to be drawn up, revealing a new and marvellous world'.

At the same time, the juxtaposition of these two edifices creates uneasiness. The presence of the temple overwhelms the domestic world which belongs to the image of man. In at least two books, the temple is not situated to one side, but is actually found *within* the house. This is the case with the Mozart temple in *A Voyage to Arcturus*, and also with the haunted room at Runhill Court. In the former case, the spectators assembled to witness the spiritualistic séance lose all significance with the appearance of the grandiose décor of the temple. We enter a world of superhuman dimensions, represented on the stage by 'the gigantic seated statue of the Pharaoh' (page 19). The old scale of values, based upon material success, is superseded. Grandeur no longer relates to the importance of wealth, but to the degree of acceptance of the supernatural. The more grandiose the temple, the more limited the house. Two worlds exist side by side. On the one hand, there is the world of the giants, Maskull, the Pharaoh of Mozart, and the Samson of the Bible, and, on the other, that of mankind, spectators in search of sensation, or Philistines. Lindsay himself has summarised his meaning, in one of his *Philosophical Notes*, better than we could hope to do. 'Both words and men appear absolutely insignificant and meaningless beside the music and the solemn grandeur of the Temple' (Number 362). Can this not be seen as being almost a direct exposition of the novels, and a confirmation from the author's own pen of the opposition between house and temple? The music of Beethoven, which serves as an introduction to the visit to the haunted manor, is also presented to us as 'a fragment from giant-land'. Soon afterwards, the scales played by the pianist give rise, in Isbel's mind, to the vision of 'huge stairs', just the same as later appeared leading to the haunted room. In *Devil's Tor*, such colossal architecture is found yet again, in the shape of Devil's Tor itself, this enormous rock fashioned in the human image, like a second Pharaoh statue, which overwhelms Hugh Drapier and Ingrid, and seems to want to swallow them up. 'The black crag of the summit stood high above them, against an ugly lead-coloured background of sky. Its face was no longer recognisable, but the new towering elevation of the hill lent it a still more evil and menacing character. It looked as if it might fall and overwhelm them as soon as they should approach within practicable range' (page 20). Confronted by this enormous rock, the country-side in which stands the 'domestic house' shrinks to the dimension of 'a toy world, charming but churlish and unmeaning' (page 80).

# 3

## THE HUMAN WORLD

The human world of a novelist is, in varying degree, of necessity
linked with the author's own experiences. Scarcely any books exist
which do not contain pen-portraits inspired by the writer's circle of
friends. In Lindsay's case, this circle was a very limited one. At the
time of his death in 1945, very few could claim to have known him
at all well. He lived on the fringe of a society that he had rejected.
He had not made any effort to make friends. He never sought social,
or personal, relationships, preferring to withdraw himself within a
life of solitude which, it seemed to him, offered a protection against
the deceits and platitudes of social contacts. Both by nature and as a
matter of principle, Lindsay showed himself distrustful of this
human world, whose image, throughout his writing, is presented as
particularly negative. His attitude was critical, justifying solitude,
and, on the philosophical level, was a denunciation of all association
of individuals, which he regarded as being an attack upon the
Sublime. The attraction of the hereafter, the moral strictness, the
creation of characters in many respects out of the ordinary, all
explain why there will be no shortage of readers likely to find his
books inhuman.

### HUMAN RELATIONSHIPS
#### The theatre
Lindsay's first book begins with an account of a spiritualistic séance.
Some dozen people meet in the living-room of a wealthy London
merchant. These opening chapters, so different from the rest of the
book, and the voyage to Arcturus, certainly contain the germ of an
idea to feature in future books. Most notably, they reveal a
background that will recur each time the human world obtrudes.
This background is the theatre.

The spiritualistic séance does not take place around a table;
armchairs have been positioned facing a stage. There are pillars to

set the scene. A curtain rises upon a back-cloth of glowing sky. There is even an orchestra in the ensemble, to play the music from *The Magic Flute*. The medium protests, in vain, against such a setting, declaring that his art is being assimilated into a 'theatrical performance', and that nothing will come of it. There is the theatre, installed once and for all. There is no better background for the human comedy that will now follow. Once put in a theatre, man becomes an actor. He no longer watches, but participates. The spiritualistic séance becomes a pretext for the performance, creating the refinement of a so-called aesthetic pleasure, and the ambiguous looks that men and women exchange in the dark.

The background thus established in *A Voyage to Arcturus* reappears in *Sphinx*. Cabot has scarcely had time to put down his luggage in the family boarding-house where he is going to lodge, than the master of the house introduces himself, in the shape of Sturt, a professional actor, now in retirement after a 'brilliant' career interrupted by an accident sustained on the stage. This abrupt termination leaves him with only his memories, on which he is all too ready to harp. The daughters of such a father, Audrey, Evelyn and Katherine Sturt, soon attract attention on account of their own artificiality, and for their ability to dissemble. As one of the characters emphasises, 'All those girls have stage blood in them...' (page 114). One should not judge the members of the Sturt family too harshly; the other characters are not so very different from them. Nicholas Cabot's father was a musician in a *theatre orchestra* (page 19). The real father of Lore Jensen was none other than Sturt, a *professional actor*. Her mother was an *actress* whom Sturt had known in the past (page 206).

Genealogy plays an important part in Lindsay's novels. To be born the son of a musician, or of a merchant, is to have one's future already marked out. In the eyes of certain people, actors and musicians resemble one another, in the sense that they are all artists, accustomed to projecting themselves before the public. Nothing is less true, however, with Lindsay. Actors and musicians may be brethren, but they are warring brethren. All Lindsay's subtlety is required to unite these extremes. For example, there is the genealogy of Nicholas Cabot, whose father, a violinist, played in a theatre. The same contradiction is evident in the case of Lore Jensen, who was a professional musician, because, while the actor, Sturt, had pretensions towards music, with the piano the most prominent item of furniture in his living-room, Lore, on the other hand, allowed herself to be corrupted by the theatre, composing tunes for it.

At the end of *Sphinx*, all these actors, Sturt, Lore and Cabot, find themselves, in one way or another, on the stage. A woman neighbour invites them to take part in an open-air fête, of which the centre of attraction is a masked ball, itself another form of theatrical performance, revealing the dissimulation that is part of the true nature of the theatre. Earlier in the book, there is another theatrical performance, very subtly blending the techniques of theatre and music. On a stage, some of the guests perform a 'masque', or a kind of opera in traditional costume, the name of which best expresses the sense of the performance, which is, at once, an entertainment and a charade. It is Lore who has composed the music for the 'masque', thus entitling her to claim to be the creator of the charade, with all the implications that this involves. 'I say *my* masque because the music is mine' (page 243).

One looks in vain, in Lindsay's books, for characters without faults, created to perfection. With just a few exceptions, they do not exist. Actors, either by profession or as the occasion arises, they never cease to develop according to circumstances, changing their rôle, and indeed their personality, as readily as they change their clothes. The metaphor of the theatre, omnipresent throughout *Sphinx*, the book which features most noticeably human relationships, could scarcely expose more clearly the intrigues, lies and dissimulation so characteristic of these relationships. Celia Hantish says of Evelyn Sturt that, since her father was by profession an actor, she could scarcely be expected to be a model of sincerity.[1] The accusation levelled at the daughter is even more true of the father, and the point is very soon made. 'Mr Sturt's having been an actor will not assist the prevailing of the truth in the minds of certain simple people' (page 175).

### Clothes

Linked to the theatre, with which it tends to be confused, the metaphor of clothing is often used by Lindsay. This assimilation is scarcely surprising when one remembers that, in ancient Greece, for example, the masque was the principal method of theatrical performance, taking the place of the modern theatre. The 'masque' and the masked ball in *Sphinx* are performances in costume. When, at the height of the fête, in the thoughtlessness and gaiety of the charade, reality breaks through with the death of Lore Jensen, the dancers hasten to remove their costumes. The fête comes to an end with 'a tragic interruption', to quote the title of the chapter in question.

The affluent people depicted by Lindsay belong to a circle in which clothes are important, and this importance is accentuated by virtue of the number of female characters encountered. Is it through a regard for verisimilitude, or by personal taste, that Lindsay interests himself in clothes? He has described, with almost unusual care, the clothes of his characters. He can ignore the question of whether someone is tall or short, dark or fair, but one subject upon which Lindsay never fails to embark is their clothing.

If a man is almost invariably elegantly dressed, it is nevertheless the women who triumph in the art of clothing themselves. The careful description is still more striking when it is concerned with gowns and skirts. From all the evidence, a woman is never more at her ease than when enveloped in chiffon. Cabot only has to notice, at a first glance, a few fashion catalogues left on the armchairs to be able to guess that the house he has entered is one dominated by women.[2] He himself, through his mother, a dressmaker, had a good knowledge of the subject.

If Lindsay described male elegance with some interest, it was as nothing compared with the pleasure, tinged with irony, that he displayed in depicting women. He enjoyed seeing them change their clothes several times each day, studying the sky to see what the weather would be like, and hesitating in face of some dilemma such as whether to wear a fur coat, at the risk of seeing it ruined by a sudden downpour of rain, or a tweed dress, with the danger of passing unnoticed. A man had clothes for each day, but a woman clothes for each hour. Celia Hantish's wardrobe is of 'apparently-inexhaustible resources'. Her neighbours say that she changes her gown for each new emotion. She appears before the marvelling eyes of Cabot, wearing first a fur gown, and then a summer-dress, complete with parasol (pages 170, 179, 180), to say nothing of her dress for the gala. 'Every part of her attractive person was adorned for a visit of ceremony. The elaborate frock, which was to be studied as a work of art; the eccentric-looking shoes, with their prodigious high heels; the huge, dark, curving hat crowning her coal-black hair; Nicholas had seen none of this attire before, and it gave him an impressive notion of the apparently-inexhaustible resources of her wardrobe' (page 210). Sometimes, Lindsay could not resist the temptation to caricature. For example, there is his description of Mrs Richborough, one of the secondary characters in *The Haunted Woman*, whose body ended by losing its substance through being no more than 'a floating mass of soft furs'. Elsewhere, Lindsay compares her to 'a mannequin on holiday', adding that her heels were like stilts.

All this minutiae goes almost beyond the bounds of realism. Here, dress takes over completely. 'Study their clothes', Lindsay seems to whisper to us, 'and you will know all about my characters.' To find fashion magazines spread around a living-room is, at first sight, a confirmation of the kind of living-room this is, and of the character of the place and its people. Clothing reflects a code of values. Behind the elegant sophistication of Celia Hantish, there is discernible her affluence, her superiority, and also her frivolity. Throughout the pages, a sartorial philosophy emerges. Refinement overtakes the framework of ideas. One can be 'aristocratic from top to toe' (*Sphinx*). High society has its own ideas and manners, just as it has its sartorial elegance. The class struggle manifests itself in the manner of wearing clothes. The embarrassment felt by Nicholas Cabot, in the face of the wealth of Celia Hantish, expresses itself as a pang of conscience at his lack of elegance.

Lindsay was very familiar with the writings of his Scottish compatriot, Carlyle. Like Carlyle, Lindsay had read Swedenborg, and the German philosophers. He had adopted as his own the theories of Professor Teufelsdröckh. 'Society is founded upon Cloth'[3]. 'What is Man himself, and his whole terrestrial Life', asks Carlyle, 'but an Emblem; a Clothing or visible Garment for that divine me of his, cast hither, like a light-particle, drawn from Heaven?'[4] After Teufelsdröckh and Carlyle, Lindsay exposes, not the spirit of customs, but the 'philosophy of Costumes'.

Lindsay depicts inability to dress elegantly with the same insistence that, previously, he had exposed the refinement of certain attire. His heroes divide themselves into two recognisable groups. On the one hand, there are those who dress with studied elegance, whilst, on the other, there is the smaller number for whom clothes are of little importance. Isbel contrasts with her aunt in *The Haunted Woman*, Celia with Lore in *Sphinx*, and Peter with Ingrid in *Devil's Tor*, to make up a series of couples. Of all his principal heroines,

Isbel provides an exception, inasmuch as she is the only one who attaches little importance to dress. Some are in the height of fashion, whilst others mistrust it, preferring to wear invariably the same clothes, regardless of what may be said. Novelty holds no attraction for these exceptional beings, whose ideas are otherwise more solid than the superficial values respected by their contemporaries.

Hence, Ingrid is distinguishable from other modern young girls by her old dress and by the woollen socks she wears (*Devil's Tor*, pages 2, 42), just as much as by the originality of her ideas. Lore Jensen has no need of elegant gowns in order to charm music-lovers. She is always 'dressed in the dark colours which were the only ones she could wear' (*Sphinx*, pages 69, 171, 190, 242). This clothing scarcely enhances a body otherwise far from graceful. If it is assumed that Celia and Lore are 'sirens', as is asserted, it is clear that the musician attracts only by her singing, and most assuredly not, as in Celia's case, by her attire. Another example is provided by Evelyn, who has been accused of 'play-acting'. It does not prevent her, when the time comes for assuming a disguise for the masque, from being the only one of all the guests to refuse to dissimulate. 'As she continued trying to attract his attention, it occurred to him that hers was the only masquerade in the hall which appeared not to be a masquerade at all, but a personal dress. It was not that her Roman draperies approximated to modern fashions . . . but that she seemed totally unconscious of her apparel (*Sphinx*, page 261).

The austerity that Lindsay maintains is not limited to a spiritual exercise. It also shows itself as regards clothing. A gown in gaudy colours, a hat whose brim is too large, a fur coat that is too expensive are all enough to make men and women suspect. Rare indeed are the individuals who, on the spiritual level, do not reveal, ultimately, some fault more or less hidden by their attire. Sartorial elegance, in the majority of cases, is a form of dissimulation, a means of concealing the absence of all ideals, and, conversely, the exaggerated evaluation of occupations that are void of interest.

Hence, it is those who care little about their clothes who are preferred by Lindsay. The tendency of these individuals to despise the body in order to enhance the soul and the spirit is revealed by this rejection of finery. The most noble people are, in general, the characters who are most simply dressed. In refusing to disguise herself for the fancy-dress ball, Evelyn chooses a plain gown, worn in an old-fashioned style. When, at the end of *Sphinx*, Nicholas

Cabot joins Lore Jensen in death, Lindsay presents them to us dressed in the same clothes,[5] as if this moment of truth which is death could not tolerate the gowns, and other clothes, imposed by modern society. It was at about this same period that Isadora Duncan was using veils to revolutionise the dance, in much the same spirit as Lindsay was depicting draperies as a sign of truth and simplicity, and as being the dress of patricians of the soul.

For those lacking the boldness to dress in the style of the ancients, Lindsay recommends tweed which, in this scale of values, provides the best antidote to fur and velvet. To wear a tweed jacket is, in itself, a confirmation of one's independence of spirit, and scorn for fashion and tradition. It is no mere chance that the characters engaged in the quest for the Sublime, Maskull, Nightspore, Saltfleet and Isbel, all wear tweed clothes.[6]

The qualities of the tweed jacket can never be praised enough. This does not alter the fact that it remains a garment, however. It is not free from the suspicion that attaches itself to all clothing, which is synonymous with concealment. Carrying this to its extreme limit, there would be truth only in nudity. The ideals of the 'Shirtless Ones' are discernible in Lindsay's *Philosophical Notes*, when he writes 'Clothes as decoration are a survival of mediaevalism, that is, arbitrary, rigid and grotesque. Nakedness, on the other hand, is in conformity with science, freedom, and purity of the intellect' (Number 487).

Most assuredly, propriety, together with the strictness of his own puritanical moral code, made Lindsay ill-fitted to be the apostle of strip-tease, but that which would cause raising of the eyebrows in the society of *Sphinx* and *The Haunted Woman* would no longer be forbidden when the society in question was an imaginary one, as in *A Voyage to Arcturus*. Maskull would never have presented himself at Montague Faull's home in the nude! A few pages later, however, when he recovers consciousness on the soil of Arcturus, Maskull finds himself to be naked. Nobody knows what has become of the tweed suit he was wearing on Earth. A young woman comes to welcome him, scarcely blushing at all to find him nude. Why is there this difference in attitude? Between the home of Montague Faull and the star, Arcturus, there has been the imaginary voyage. Nudity, so recently improper, is now accepted. It is part of the conventions of the unknown. The exotic has its advantages!

The first gesture of Joiwind, who has come to welcome Maskull to this new star, is to offer him a garment similar to the one that she herself is wearing, a kind of sheepskin that is wrapped around the waist. The gesture is important, being a way of welcoming the new arrival. It is also a means of integrating him into the community. This garment offered to Maskull as soon as he arrives on Arcturus constitutes the initial act of indoctrination. The quest for the Sublime, having been commenced in the only possible manner, nudity, is thwarted, from the moment of arrival on Arcturus, by the gesture of Joiwind. *A Voyage to Arcturus* is not a leap into the future, but rather a return to the Middle Ages, from which clothes are a survival.

The grandeur of the Sublime has a basis in nudity. The real quest begins with the death of Maskull, when the clothes which have been imposed upon him have become useless. Everything indicates that Nightspore, the spiritual second self of Maskull, who takes up the task on his death, is naked, as was Maskull on his arrival. This interpretation is reinforced by the revelation that comes to Maskull from his mission to the Wombflash forest. A man appears to him, sitting against a tree, and he is 'nearly naked' (pages 134–136). This man is Krag in person, who, it is later learned, is the instigator of the quest. A second vision lends meaning to Maskull's adventure. He notices three men walking ahead of him, towards a goal that they alone know. These are Krag, Nightspore and Maskull himself, and *all three are naked*. Clothes are an obstacle to metaphysical quest. There can be no more categorical denunciation of the imposture that they symbolise.[7]

### Dissimulation

Both the theatre and clothes are metaphors of disguise. If Lindsay uses them with such predilection, it is because the human world of his novels appears, to a large degree, to be founded upon a lie. The heroes whom he admires are those who, perceiving the inherent falsity of human relationships, disengage themselves in preference for an unworldly contact with the hereafter.

Lindsay's novels often have actor-characters as their protagonists. They play a rôle which does not correspond to their true nature. Rare indeed are those who, in the image of Saltfleet and Ingrid, accept their lot as ordained by destiny. For these latter, truth has no need of justification; it is, first and foremost, truth in its own right, in contrast to the 'truth' of the actor, compelled to assume several rôles at the same time.

The most striking example of this kind of lie is provided by Sturt, the professional actor. Until the final pages of *Sphinx*, Sturt maintains that he is interested in Lore Jensen solely because she is the daughter of a former woman-friend. It transpires that, in fact, he is her father.

The dissimulation is seldom as extreme as this. Falsehood, Lindsay insists, is the foundation of all human and social relations. Moreover, his characters are experts on the subject. They know all the subtleties of the cruel pastime of secretly slandering one's fellow-beings. Women, in particular, strain Lindsay's indulgence. Most certainly, men and women quarrel, but their rivalries are as nothing compared with the intrigues that underlie the relations of women with one another. Jealousy, desire to be noticed, anxiety to please and seduce, are all incitements to intrigue. To a man, viewing them from outside, these rivalries are as incomprehensible as they are unjustified. It is admitted that, between women, there exists 'a natural antipathy' (*Sphinx*, page 167), against which the most cogent logic is unavailing. As one of the men in *Sphinx* puts it, 'Women are *spasmodic*. Always hang on quietly till the spasm's passed' (page 189). This is easily said, but, between the onset of the spasm and its end, much damage will have been done. A partner, neighbour or 'friend' will often have been severely judged, and quite unjustifiably. Lore sees Evelyn as being so cold 'that she wouldn't attract a Trappist monk' (page 196). This 'compliment' is one that Evelyn cannot allow to pass, and she riposts that Lore is a drug-addict, drinking to excess like a Pole, and that the innocence of which she boasts is simply a way of being better able to deceive the host of admirers of her mawkish music (page 62).

Certainly, Lindsay's characters are not very animated. They leave no memorable impression, as only the very great writers are capable of creating. In spite of these limitations, however, it would be quite wrong to deny them any complexity at all. The dialectic or Manichaeism of any author, such as Lindsay, intent upon getting a certain message across, simply does not exist. Even if, as in Lindsay's case, he is trying to divide his characters into two groups, good and bad, the ambiguity remains. The qualities of the former are not above some reproach, nor, indeed, free of some vices. There would only be Saltfleet, in *Devil's Tor*, who would ultimately be above all suspicion.

To know these characters, one must either look them in the eye or else hear them speak. Ingrid's personality, for example, seems to be entirely contained in her face. One sees there her astonishing passivity, and that availability which places her at the disposal of destiny.[8] Isbel's eyes, like those of Ingrid, are 'indecipherable' (*The Haunted Woman*, page 17), and reveal a complex nature. Finally, Lore's eyes betray the character's neurosis. Their continual movement is a pathological sign of nervousness, and certainly not of 'cynical energy', as Lindsay claims.

This importance of the look, and of the face in general, is scarcely surprising when one remembers Lindsay's interest in physiognomy. He extolled the force of character of a Sulla, and never wearied of admiring portraits of the Roman Emperor, so expressive are they. The study of physiognomy should be part of the education of every citizen, he said, just as botany and gardening constitute the main interests of country-people (*Philosophical Notes*, Number 435). Moreover, he had his own ideas upon the benefits of ugliness, which he presents in his new Gospel in the clearest terms. 'Blessed is he who looks in the hand-glass, and finds himself repulsive; for he shall thereby be driven to activity' (Number 276).

Whilst eyes are evidence of depth, and the pattern of the mouth shows the degree of sensibility and nobility (Number 398), it is the voice which better expresses the complexities of the human soul. The eye is seductive, and is also the organ for judging appearances. 'The ear is the sense-organ by which reality is grasped.' To understand anyone properly, one must hear him speak. The hypocrite knows how to conceal his face or veil his eyes. He cannot disguise his voice. Gangnet–Crystalman's voice, sickly and effeminate, expresses the falsity of the character. Maskull never perceives better the difference between the harshness of Oceaxe and the sweetness of her voice than when she speaks to him with her back turned, in the famous episode of the cavalcade of the 'shrowk' (*A Voyage to Arcturus*, page 88). Finally, in *Sphinx*, the compositions of the musician, Lore Jensen, do not betray the artist's interior 'flaw'. One must hear her speak, or, better still, sing, in order to discover the tormented being who hides behind an outward cynicism, and bring to light the complexities of her personality. 'She had, as it were, two voices, the one, which she chiefly used, was a little too sentimentally soft and honeyed, but every now and then the other made its appearance in a single tone, which affected Nicholas's nervous system as though a sweet, metallic string had been twanged;

the sound seemed to go in and in to his consciousness without reaching an end' (page 91). It is again the same metallic sound that Sherrup, a portrait painter, and hence a specialist in physiognomy, also recognises in Isbel's voice. 'Her character possessed an important quality which he was unable to locate on her features; it was contained only in that quiet, pleasant, yet metallic and foreign-toned, voice' (*The Haunted Woman*, page 39).

### Dual nature

The study of physiognomy, and of the voice, yields rewarding results. Lindsay's characters are restless. They have about them an instability and nervousness. On the surface, all is peaceful. The voices sound all right. The clothes are impressive. Beneath the outward signs, however, there are strong undercurrents. Rare indeed are the characters who are all of one piece. There are two Ingrid Colbornes. The first one is a shy young girl, living with her mother, and absorbed in domestic tasks. The second is reserved, living apart from her surroundings, in a private world consisting of intuitions and communications with the hereafter. The two suitors who want to marry her have no need to compete with one another, since each nurtures a different image of the loved one. If Peter ends by abandoning any idea of marriage, it is because he discovers in his fiancée a 'mystic' vein, hitherto unsuspected.[9]

There is often a co-existence of several facets of the same personality. Uncle Colborne combines idealism and pragmatism. He has gained a reputation as a misogynist, but suddenly begins, to the amazement of his relations and friends, to sing the praises of feminine virtues. An analysis of dreams shows that, in Lore Jensen, there exist three different personalities, or, more accurately, three levels of her existence. The first Lore, who appears in the final dream, has no reality outside the subconscious. Paradoxically, this one is the truest, and most real, of the three characters. It is the only one with awareness of a metaphysical goal, and the existence of the hereafter. The second Lore, a shadow of the first, so Lindsay tells us, is the restless, indeed depressed, character, who has been shown in an earlier dream, wandering in a Dantesque forest. Finally, the third character, 'shadow of a shadow', is the heroine of the book, as she is known to her friends. This is the face that shows us the clear conscience, or the Lore of the social conventions.

The theme of the split personality has often been used by writers, including Baudelaire, Poe, Lowry, and many others.[10] It lends itself to all manner of extensions and modifications, to say nothing of the reproduction of the complexities of introspection or the depiction of the difficulties of human relations. With Lindsay, too, the characters understand one another badly, because they do not know one another well. Frequently, they allow themselves to be carried away, at the first encounter, by unreasonable antipathy. Often, the real affinities manifest themselves later, when the hidden nature of each has been better understood.

This complexity could be a sign of inner riches, but this is not the case. It is rather a wound that proves slow to heal, or the 'flaw' of which Scott Fitzgerald wrote in *The Crack-Up*. This multiplication of the self is not an expansion, but a division. Divided so much more painfully than in the majority of cases, it passes unnoticed, not only in the eyes of others but also by the person concerned. There is some relief, and even deliverance, in this admission by Isbel to someone met by chance. 'I'm afraid I'm rather highly-strung by nature, although, oddly enough, not one of my friends appears to have any suspicion of the fact. I pass for being stolid, rather than otherwise. You are almost the first to give me credit for exceptional feelings' (*The Haunted Woman*, page 44).

The superimposing of these different layers of the personality poses psychological problems. A number of Lindsay's heroes come to terms with this division of their ego. Sometimes, however, it happens that the mirror cracks and splits.

Lore Jensen's neurosis has its origin in her split personality. Aware of the multiplicity of her different facets, she never succeeds in giving preference to this or that tendency. A situation so much more painful than the lucidity of conscience allows no respite for introspection. Lore agrees to go to the fête for which she has composed the music. 'I have a whim to hear the effect from a long way off, among the trees, out of sight of everyone' (*Sphinx*, page 191). She thus rejects an aspect of herself which revolts her. Unable to reconcile these contradictions, Lore Jensen ends by committing suicide. In *The Haunted Woman*, Isbel appears as a creature no less divided. Her first nature leads her towards material comfort, money, social conventions, sartorial finery and affectation. Her second nature shows her very differently, as being sensitive, passionate and attached to the truth.

For these divided characters, marriage is the supreme test, in the sense that it brings them face to face with the necessity of making a choice between tendencies that are sometimes contradictory. Quite often, it precipitates a crisis that has been simmering for a long time. Marriage poses the problem of division of self, to the extent that one is compelled to choose the aspect that one would most wish to find in one's partner. To each part of the personality there correspond different inclinations and affections. When the psychological dissociation occurs, affinities are found to be in question. Isbel forgets her fiancé, Marshall Stokes, and declares her love for Judge. The same kind of volte-face occurs in the case of Lore Jensen, when she announces her engagement to the composer, Dawson. Finally, Ingrid rejects the love of Peter, the family friend, in preference for that of Saltfleet, the unknown, intransigent adventurer.

This theme of split personality recurs with such insistence in Lindsay's writing that it is tempting to draw a parallel with the author's personal circumstances. Such a course is far from new. It has often occurred in literature, and more or less consciously in the psychological novel, as Freud has recalled. 'In a large number of so-called psychological novels, I have often been struck by the fact that one single character, always the hero, is described from within. It is in his soul, in a manner of speaking, that the author lives, and it is from there that he considers the other characters, or, in other words, from outside. All in all, the psychological novel owes its characteristics to the tendency of the modern author to divide his ego by auto-observation in "partial selves", which leads him to personify, in various heroes, the conflicting currents in his own psychic life.'[11]

This definition could equally be applied to Lindsay. His male characters are manifestly transpositions of his own personal case. There is scarcely any one of them who has not inherited a few characteristic traits of his creator, such as misogyny, love of philosophy and music, and disgust for the town and modern life. Even more interesting is the distribution of these characteristics between the various characters. The books contain a series of couples that are quite remarkable; namely, Krag and Crystalman, Nightspore and Maskull, Lore and Celia, Judge and Marshall, Mrs Moor and Isbel, Saltfleet and Arsinal. Of all these couples, only Krag and Crystalman are incompatible. The others are members of the same 'family'. Quite often, they appear to be twins, separated by the experiences of life; or even the same character seen at different ages.

The quarrels which divide them do not invalidate their affinities. Marshall and Judge, for example, contrast with one another in *The Haunted Woman*, and it is between the two of them that Isbel is compelled to choose. They differ from one another as regards age, fortune, experience and profession. Neither one nor the other, however, remains any less of a transposition of Lindsay himself. Marshall, the young insurance broker, likes his comfortable life, as was the case with Lindsay. Judge is the mature man, courteous almost to the point of excess, and quite incapable of committing even the smallest social error. He, too, is a businessman. It is only their different conceptions of love that really separate them. Marshall and Judge could be the same man depicted at different ages, which is to say Lindsay himself, at forty, looking back to what he had previously been at the age of twenty.[12]

It is as if Lindsay were trying to study the separate parts of his own self through interpolated characters, so ruthless are his analyses. To judge by his writings, these divergencies amount, in principle, to an incompatibility between, on the one hand, the needs of the individual, and, on the other hand, the compromises necessitated by life in society. The individual and society are in constant conflict. Between the two, man seems torn asunder, wounded by the compulsion to choose, and ill at ease when he ventures to reconcile the two extremes. With Isbel, this contrast presents itself in the form of a clash between the woman of the world and the amorous woman, or between social experience and private experience. In the case of Lore Jensen, the contest ranges the new idealism of the artist against the need to satisfy public taste. Quite often, it is simply a matter of choosing between a love of solitude and the company of others. Against the experience of solitude, such as the artist's profession, life with nature, and the discovery of the Sublime, there are all those aspects of group life; social events, fêtes, urban life, the vocation of business, and so on.

To some extent, literary creation constituted a cure for Lindsay. When, belatedly, he started to write, Lindsay took a considerable risk. He knew that fortune rarely smiled on writers. He also knew that success in literature could be particularly brittle. If he abruptly left the financial world of the City of London, it was to alleviate an internal suffering that he resented more and more acutely, being torn between his idealism and his work in the world of finance. Literature presented itself to him as a means of reconciling his life with his ideas. After that, it is scarcely surprising to find, in his writing, criticism of the circles he had just left. The criticism, however, is also self-destructive. When he condemns the financier, it is also a part of himself that is called into question. It is always easier to settle accounts with others than with oneself.

Lindsay strikes but, at the last moment, turns his head, hoping that the blow will miss its target. He criticises the businessman, but concludes that, in every writer, a businessman does exist, and that the best of musicians condemns himself to death by starvation if, at one time or another, he does not compose for the public at large, who understand nothing of music but have full pockets and are prepared to pay. The analysis of oneself can be painful, but it can be equally comforting to say that 'everyone possesses a dual nature' (*The Haunted Woman*, page 60).

### The big world

Lindsay set the majority of his plots in affluent, middle-class environments. As one might expect, his description of them is scarcely a favourable one. Moreover, the criticism goes beyond the mere framework of these surroundings. Basically, it is the life-style of the modern world that stands condemned. 'Where are the idealists of yesteryear?' asks Lindsay. 'The man and woman of to-day gave the reply by talking only of money, luxury, sport, amusement and sex' (*Devil's Tor*, page 69).

To start with the question of money, Lindsay's characters are sheltered from financial worries. They are possessed of means which would be a source of envy to many people. For them, work is not a way of enrichment since, in most cases, wealth seems to come to them naturally. Sturt remarks of Celia Hantish 'Nature has richly endowed her. Fortune has followed on the very heels of Nature, and education has accomplished the rest' (*Sphinx*, page 66). The pressure of work is negligible upon these habitually-idle people, usually depicted on holiday. This is true of the 'realistic' novels, but also of *A Voyage to Arcturus*, in which the only character obliged to work for his living, and to support his family, is Polecrab, the fisherman.

In the majority of cases, money is neither earned nor deserved. It is inherited. One learns on the first page of *The Haunted Woman* that Isbel has just inherited an estate worth about £20,000, left to her at the death of her brother. Nicholas Cabot possesses a fortune of £55,000, bequeathed by his uncle. Hugh Drapier has more than

£19,000. The significance of these fortunes can be better appreciated by bearing in mind that these people lived in the 1920's! It might well be added that they were very young indeed to be possessed of such riches!

Money determines their life-style. The majority have no need at all to follow any profession. Hugh Drapier and Saltfleet are adventurers who travel the world throughout the year. Mrs Moor and Isbel go from one hotel to another in search of worldly pleasures. Sturt is retired. Celia inherits a fortune from her husband, a wealthy tea planter from Ceylon, who has died a few years previously. For others, work is in a subordinate rôle, and they can take it or leave it.

Industrialists, merchants, estate agents, speculators, tea planters and coffee importers are typical of the professions encountered.[13] These people live in Chelsea and Hampstead, and other residential London suburbs. When outside the capital, they are to be found at their Hampshire property (*Sphinx*), or in the four-star hotels of Brighton (*The Haunted Woman*). Champagne is a daily drink for them (*Sphinx*, page 69). When they go out for a picnic, the traditional pheasant is on the menu (*The Haunted Woman*, page 72).

'Mrs Hantish's world is the big world, which includes all the little worlds . . .' (*Sphinx*, page 29). In this world, affluence is the norm, and politeness is indispensable. Life is just a fancy cake that promises to be all cream and sweetness. Gallantry is obligatory. Women delight in their rôle as parasites. The ultimate refinement is polite conversation over a cup of tea. This ritual of tea is part of the human comedy.

## WOMEN

One cannot fail to be struck by the importance of women in all Lindsay's writing. From one novel to the next, he manages to expose spheres that are almost exclusively feminine. Quite often, the principal character is a woman, such as Isbel in *The Haunted Woman*, Ingrid in *Devil's Tor*, and Lore in *Sphinx*. If male heroes are not absent, it is nevertheless noticeable that they often lack the complexity of their female counterparts. The men are much less animated, as if, to describe his heroines, Lindsay shows himself more subtly psychological, and more interested.

It is true that, as a bachelor until his 41st year, Lindsay had had time to judge, to some extent from the outside, this creature who was so different. In one sense, women were what Lindsay knew best. On leaving his office, he hastened to rejoin the family hearth, where his mother, aunt and sister awaited him, all three very attentive towards the one they considered to be 'the man of the house'. Moreover, Lindsay had scarcely any friends, and went out very little. It was in this environment, and in these conditions, that Lindsay's convictions about women were developed. One can be quite sure that Judge, in *The Haunted Woman*, spoke for the author when he declared '. . . men happen to be the best critics of feminine human nature' (page 62).

Lindsay proclaimed himself to be a judge of women, but it must certainly be admitted that his life had ill-prepared him for such a rôle. Lindsay knew *certain women*, but there was nothing of the seducer about him. He scarcely sought the company of women. By nature, he was far more likely to flee from them.

### Discovery of women

David Lindsay's first book, *A Voyage to Arcturus*, is manifestly, above all, a voyage in space, and the discovery of imaginary landscapes. The human element is far from being neglected, however. For Maskull, the bachelor, it involves the discovery of women, of which he is no doubt more conscious than of the metaphysical quest, which is the real object of the journey. The quest assumes the form of the metaphysics of women, or what John Donne conceived as 'the metaphysics of love'. Tormance, the real name of Arcturus, whose resonance suggests 'torment', but also 'romance', is the feminine world to perfection. The journey begins with meeting a woman, and it ends with encountering a 'man–woman'. In between, we have seen a procession of characters, some female, often some of indeterminate sex, combining both female and male characteristics. When, at the end of the book, Krag rebukes Maskull for having wasted his time in 'killing, dancing and loving', there can be recognised the three activities which, in Lindsay's mind, are associated with women. On the dry Arcturus roads, among the traps set for the traveller, nothing is more dangerous than the fascination of women.

If the hero happens not to fall into the trap, it is mainly because, in the presence of women, he stays on his guard. Between hero and heroine, there always exists a barrier. Lindsay's first hero, Maskull, already sets the pattern of future characters. He is a bachelor. He is certainly courageous, but his lack of experience ill prepares him for encounters with the women of space. When he is asked if he has already had any amorous experience, Maskull replies with a vague 'maybe', leaving one to guess his embarrassment (page 178). From one novel to the next, the hero's name changes but not his nature, nor his situation. The list of bachelors grows longer; all fearless, like Maskull, up to the moment when the scent of a woman's perfume disarms them, and puts them to flight. With Lindsay, celibacy is not the gateway to vice, nor the certainty of being able to abandon oneself with impunity to the pleasures of the flesh. Celibacy is an oath of abstinence. A woman is far too much of an encumbrance for whom to sacrifice one's work and career, as argued by more than one of Lindsay's characters. Young Nicholas Cabot declares 'An essential condition of my work is a celibate existence' (*Sphinx*, page 29). His fears become understandable when it transpires that the family guest-house chosen by him as a holiday base contains no fewer than three young girls of marriageable age, to say nothing of female neighbours still more seductive.

The innocence of Nicholas Cabot is the inexperience of the orphan, deprived of mother, aunt and sister. For him, women are one of nature's mysteries. This inexperience is involuntary, in contrast to that of the adventurer who, in his turn, also flees from women. Saltfleet and Hugh Drapier have been 'deprived ... of the necessary experience of women' (*Devil's Tor*, page 10), because they have chosen a life-style in which humanity has scarcely any place at all. The mountain-peaks of Asia are the sole consorts of these men. At 36 and 37 years of age respectively, Saltfleet and Drapier, like Maskull and Cabot before them, are both bachelors. They are members of the clan. They, too, have known hardly any women, nor do they seek their company.

This ignorance was, to a very large extent, that of Lindsay himself. Behind the embarrassment of his characters, their mistrust, and their accusations, lies revealed the personal case of the author. The age of the heroes is manifestly that of Lindsay at the time the books were written. He, too, had been a bachelor for some forty years, for reasons that can be assumed to have been similar to those of his heroes. His marriage came as a surprise to many of his relations. His choice of a young girl barely eighteen years of age, moreover, was an indication that the 'reconciliation' between David

Lindsay and women was perhaps not as satisfactory as might appear
to be the case. In choosing a wife so young, Lindsay asserted, in his
own way, his superiority. Jacqueline Lindsay's youth operated as a
kind of guarantee for this man who never ceased to denounce the
sophistication, and indeed the corruption, of women of his own age.

When they are characterised by distance or mistrust, relations
between men and women, according to Lindsay, are hardly ever
satisfactory. Before achieving a harmonious relationship, one must
first destroy the prejudices created by years of ignorance. Between
man and woman, there certainly exist many prejudices. The
conduct of certain women is open to criticism, but that is not the full
explanation. Lindsay's heroes flee from women because they are
afraid of them.[14] For many of them, this fear is, above all, a fear of
the unknown, and of sexuality, and a confirmation of the gulf that
divides the two sexes.

Men, no less than women, return to the world of their own laws,
their own characteristics, and their own values. Male and female are
often irrevocably opposed to one another. Between the two, it is
difficult to find common ground. Male and female are poles apart,
just as, with electricity, one speaks of positive and negative charges
(*Philosophical Notes*, Number 443). If Lindsay is to be believed, the
world could be reduced to this simple division of male and female.
Genius, in his view, is the union of the female and the Sublime.[15]
Laws are by nature feminine, through being constraining. The true
male is free, and hence outside the law (*A Voyage to Arcturus*, page
200). Scenery will be sometimes feminine, and sometimes masculine,
according to whether the outline of mountains or hills is smooth or
jagged (*A Voyage to Arcturus*, page 82). The straight line is masculine
in character, while the curved line is feminine. Women share with
insects this predilection for curves, and Lindsay adds that women
and insects are well known for their intuition (*Philosophical Notes*,
Number 324).

Lindsay often shows a tendency towards generalisation. His characters are not so much individuals, seen at a given moment of their
lives in a particular situation, as stereotypes of male and female.
Whatever the accuracy of his analyses, it is all too easy to accuse
Lindsay of lack of finesse. His characters frequently express these
generalisations on the rôle of the sexes: '. . . men happen to be the
best critics of feminine human nature' (*The Haunted Woman*, page
62); '. . . you are all the same, all you men! An unattached girl is fair

game to you' (*Sphinx*, page 98); 'It's a lovely thing to be a woman, isn't it? You're nine parts reputation and one part human being!' (*Sphinx*, page 175).

Whether it be through ignorance, inexperience or prejudice, man is a stranger to woman. The converse is still more true. From the very outset, there exists a fundamental lack of understanding, based upon a differing approach as much as upon biological differences. History, asserts one of Lindsay's male characters, has been written by men. The result is a presentation of women that is inevitably false. From this, there has developed man's feeling of superiority. Man knows nothing more comforting than the moment when he discovers that his consort is, after all, just a woman amongst so many others, subject to the limitations of the weaker sex. It is curious reasoning that one should find in the inferiority of his partner the means of revaluing her. 'The new conception of Celia as a weak and imperfect being, subject to the petty animosities of her sex, at once had the effect of raising her to a higher level in his esteem. He felt, with a thrill, that she was a *woman*, and, as such, was separated from him by a hundred million miles!' (*Sphinx*, page 115).

### *Types of women*

'Women may be divided into three classes; the sexual, the gay and the dull. The first seek lovers, the second women-friends and society, the third a home' (*Philosophical Notes*, Number 247).

The 'sexual woman' is unquestionably the type who appears to the best advantage throughout Lindsay's writing. *A Voyage to Arcturus* is as much a discovery of women as it is an imaginary journey. The hero is put to a severe test. Women constitute the greatest danger faced by Maskull. He resists, more or less successfully, the onslaughts of Joiwind, Oceaxe, Tydomin and Sullenbode. Oceaxe, in particular, is the prototype of this provocative woman who tries, by every possible means, to seduce the hero. The courtship has nothing chivalrous about it. Intentions are revealed at first sight. Later, they will be declared with even greater boldness. 'Still, if you have male instincts, as I suppose you have, you can't go on resisting me forever', says Oceaxe to Maskull (page 78). She sacrifices her husband for the pleasure of a new lover. Maskull is not slow to recognise that 'Oceaxe in her drapery appeared more dangerously feminine . . .' (page 78). The Hator adventure is another version of the man-hunt. He was drawn towards a mountain by 'a handsome girl who knew sorcery ...' (pages 120–121). When he arrived there, she destroyed the only foot-bridge by which he could get back, and then attempted to seduce Hator by means of lascivious looks and poses 'to see how long the famous frost man can withstand the breath, smiles and perfume of a girl' (pages 120–121).

The list of these siren-women, as they are called in *Sphinx*, is a long one. The 'two sirens' referred to are Lore Jensen and Celia Hantish. The latter, in particular, embodies the element of 'dangerous femininity'. She is 'a very charming widow, ... reputed, like all other young widows, to be dangerous' (*Sphinx*, page 25). Celia is a 'vamp'. She has her 'victims'. Elegance, charm, perfume, a teasing manner, treachery, plus an indefinable and unique quality are her weapons which prove almost irresistible.

Like *The Odyssey*, *A Voyage to Arcturus* is an epic of triumph over femininity. It is because he rejects Sullenbode that Maskull finds himself granted the revelation of the Sublime. Nicholas Cabot does not resist the song of the siren so well. He is fascinated by the grace of Celia Hantish. When she invites him to her home, the young man can scarcely contain his delight.

Lips are the symbols of this dangerous sensuality. They express the fascination of the woman, and the temptation of the flesh. Sullenbode, in *A Voyage to Arcturus*, even before she becomes the example of the amorous woman, reveals her nature. Her lips are the only expressive part of her face (page 211). Mrs Trent has 'lips so crimson and full that they seemed to be bursting with blood' (page 18). Lips are already an invitation to love. The 'siren' can be recognised by her mouth, just as others have clothes as their distinctive mark.

The second type defined by Lindsay is the 'gay, frivolous woman'. In contrast to the sensual woman, she no longer seeks the company of lovers and admirers. She likes to be surrounded by women. She cannot bear solitude. In order to develop herself, this 'gay woman' must have company. For her, life in the country means a life of solitude, so she prefers the town. Country life is tolerable only to the extent that neighbours pay endless visits. Isbel, the heroine of *The Haunted Woman*, epitomises the 'gay woman', at least up to a certain point. She lives the whole year long in the company of her aunt. Both lead a nomadic existence, going from one hotel to another. She enjoys luxury and likes the animation of towns. 'Streets, shops, crowds, any form of human activity enabled her to forget herself.'

Lore and Mrs Brion, in *Sphinx*, constitute another of these pairs of women. Like Isbel, Lore cannot bear solitude. She assures herself of the services of a companion, a kind of confidante whose very presence is enough to comfort her. Women and society belong together in Lindsay's analysis. Women cannot live outside a group of some kind, he thinks. In that way, they are limited, being too much attached to the principle of the herd instinct to have sublime aspirations. They remain 'women of the world'; mundane, attached to the physical world. In contrast, there is no such being as a man of the world, according to Lindsay. The picture of the male 'couple' scarcely appears anywhere in his work.[16] Man's nature, unlike that of woman, urges him to seek solitude.

There remains the homely woman, the third type according to Lindsay's classification. Contrary to what might be suggested by the epithet 'dull', used to describe the homely woman, the criticism here seems to be muted. There is certainly a lack of the fascination provided by the 'siren', and the vivacity displayed by the 'gay woman'. The dull woman, however, is not entirely bereft of qualities. Of all women, she is the one who best submits to her destiny of looking after her home and family. In Lindsay's eyes, this is a great virtue. In contrast to the man, adventurer, vagabond, and lone cowboy, the woman needs roots, he repeats. She is not a 'woman of the world' for nothing. Between her and the world, affinities exist that have their origins as far back as the Creation. The Demiurge, creator of the world, and of the human race, was feminine. The nature of the sexes has been determined for ever. This need of roots, and of stability, is a return to origins, and a way of declaring not passivity but grandeur. The virtues of the home are also gentleness and charity. Those of the adventurer are temerity and struggle. 'Because a man was rootless, he was first free-moving, then competitive, then hard, merciless, and military; while because a woman was rooted in the Demiurge, she was first sedentary, then attractive, then soft, pacific, and compassionate' (*Devil's Tor*, page 475).

Behind these lines emerges an apology for the woman in the home which will make members of the Women's Liberation Movement shudder. To add fuel to the fire, Lindsay goes on to say that this sedentariness is designed to allow her to bring children into the world at her leisure. At this stage, the definition of the sexes borders upon reaction. Nietzsche also wrote 'Man must be bred for war, and woman for the repose of the warrior.' Intelligence, daring and freedom are a man's business. A woman must be content with her own prerogatives; children, intuition, beauty and gentleness. Hence, feminine experience scarcely extends beyond the limits of the home and family. Women's rôle does not lie in the conquest of space, nor in scientific discoveries, but rather in 'a long subordination of one's will to the little duties of the day' (*Devil's Tor*, page 63). It is at this price that she achieves inner peace. Woman's nobility depends upon her resignation, as if, by this tendency, she forms part of suffering humanity which provides the sole hope for the renaissance of the world.

### Women and their transformations

The homely woman has the house as her kingdom. The man associates himself with the great open spaces. Woman's horizon is limited by the four walls of her home. When absorbed in adventures, like Isbel, she will then have no alternative than to move around, and change her house. She lives in a hotel, and moves from one hotel to another. Psychoanalysis has made the home one of women's main symbols[17], the epitome of the feminine locale, and the house carries the stamp of woman. Helga's bedroom, in *Devil's Tor*, is a 'private den'. Judge's drawing-room has preserved the aura of his wife, who has died some years previously. This is not so much the 'den' but the 'shrine'. The appellation may vary, but the significance remains the same: '. . . no man could have lived in that room, so full of little feminine fragilities and knick-knacks as it was, so bizarre, so frivolous, so tasteless, yet so pleasing' (*The Haunted Woman*, page 30).

The house constitutes a feminine world made up of fabrics, fashion magazines, flowers and clothes. Between the woman and the house, there is an identity of character. By the decoration, and the choice of curtains, it is the woman who expresses herself. For the man, the adventurer, the house is a prison, from which he tries to flee, in order not to be engulfed in the trivialities of daily life. The metaphysical quest is always located beyond the feminine house.

Perfume is one of the principal components of the feminine world. It is not enough for the house to be feminine. It is also perfumed. Hence, the bedrooms at 'Whitestone' smell both of the pure air of the moors and the scent of lavender, the latter being artificial, and the result of the ministrations of the mistress of the house. At the

door of Mrs Richborough's bedroom, the visitor is assailed by
perfume. Finally, perfume is one of the ingredients of the magic
world of the haunted room, 'a new kind of feminine scent'. The
value of perfume surpasses all considerations of hygiene. It is the
aura of the place, the feminine soul and the certificate of probity.
'For her, that scent of lavender was no sweet disguise, but a symbol
of feminine law and order' (*Devil's Tor*, page 39). Perfume signifies
the hegemony of women. It marks the limit of the harem. The man
who, by inadvertence or in defiance, ventures there, risks becoming
a victim. Perfume becomes a love potion.

A symbol of womanhood, perfume follows her wherever she goes,
attaching itself sometimes to a glove, sometimes to a letter, and
sometimes to a handbag. It is the weapon always available for a
woman to use to assert her hegemony, and to enforce her rule. In
the words of Judge, 'You can't kill a man by a sight or a sound, but
I wouldn't like to say you couldn't kill with some smells, and not
always disagreeable ones at that' (*The Haunted Woman*, page 41).
Aware of the danger, Judge nevertheless succumbs to the
intoxication of perfume. He will die of it. 'She imperceptibly drew a
little nearer, so that the perfume of her clothes began to insinuate
itself into his consciousness' (page 57). There is the love potion in
action. We are in the classic tradition of romantic love, of which
Tristan and Isolde constitute the prototype. They, too, had their
love potion.[18]

The importance of perfume in Lindsay's writing has not simply to
do with association of ideas, as between perfume and women.
Perfume is certainly a symbol of womanhood, but it is more than
that; it is the epitome of the feminine element. From the symbolic
level, one passes to the philosophical level. Behind the frequent use
of perfume, there emerges a philosophy, a reflection on the nature of
perfume. 'There is no more vital experience known to us than
perfume' (*Philosophical Notes*, Number 375). 'Perfume', he wrote
again, 'arouses feelings which are unique. Things therefore must
possess internal qualities which are capable of influencing people in
other ways still more vividly; for the sense of smell conveys only a
faint approximation to the real character of the object' (Number
417). The nose is an imperfect organ, but is certainly better than the
eye, which is the source of illusion. The 'unique sensations'
awakened by perfume are proof of an exceptional perception. The
true nature of anything is better revealed by its smell than it is by

any other of its aspects. The only organ that is superior to the nose is
the ear. Animals have preserved the importance of the sense of
smell. In man's case, this has become more and more atrophied.
Lindsay revalues the sense of smell in defining places and people in
the context of the criterion of smell. The visitor must know where he
is by the sheer smell of the place. The perfume of Mrs Richborough's
bedroom already projects the character. Conversely, the acrid
smell of tobacco which emanates from Lore Jensen's drawing-room
(*Sphinx*, pages 69, 195), places this character apart from the
traditional feminine world. One later learns that she does not care
for toiletries and perfume; her feminism draws her towards the male
world to which she aspires.

### Size and limitations of the feminine world

A world that was entirely feminine would be, according to Lindsay,
'one big mass of heavy sweetness, without individual shapes' (*A
Voyage to Arcturus*, page 206). To perfume, there can be added the
metaphors of sweetness and the sugary; the kind of sweetness which
evokes a feeling of revulsion. It is not the best term for describing
the feminine world. The music of women, a shade too sentimental,
suggests the sweetness of perfume. 'It's all perfectly sweet. A woman's
music, I always think, has a delicacy of sentiment one never meets
with a man's. It's like a very subtle perfume' (*Sphinx*, page 16).
Perfume, women and sweetness are all part of the same chain of
metaphors. Lindsay never tires of denouncing this sweetness of the
feminine world. He sees extensions everywhere. The sweetness that
revolts him is not softness. It is a flavour that is mawkish and
nauseating. *A Voyage to Arcturus* already contains this obsession with
the sugary. Tormance has the sweetness of an unworldly paradise
under feminine domination. At the end of the voyage,
Nightspore–Maskull can no longer bear 'a scent of disgusting
sweetness' which emanates from Crystalman's body.[19] The same
revulsion appears in his other books. Isbel, for instance, contrasts
her conception of love with that of her contemporaries. For her, love
is more than just a 'syrupy sentimentality', she says.[20] The
atmosphere of 'Mereway', in *Sphinx*, is so unbearable that Lore
compares it with sugary water.[21] Peter Copping lacks character, like
a 'sweet apple'. The apathy which accompanies aesthetic
contemplation suggests both sweetness and lack of virility. 'It's like
being unmanned by the slow penetration of our veins and organs by

some sweetly-poisonous Oriental syrup' (*Devil's Tor*, page 146).
Sugary water, Oriental syrup and emasculation are terms which
border upon the insulting.

Lindsay never ceased to denounce a certain picture of women. He
saw, in twentieth-century women, superficial creatures whose field
of interest extended little further than dresses and perfume. He did
not forgive them for their effeminate life, but, at the same time, he
deprived them of any wish to live otherwise. 'A spoilt and capricious
young woman of fortune' is the verdict which often confines them to
an inferior status. Women have no virtues. Money is put at their
disposal. They are born rich, just as they are born women. Wealth
serves them as a passport to success. They have made no effort. Like
Isbel, women are naturally attracted towards sweetness, comfort,
luxury, ease, and everything that makes life agreeable. Lindsay does
not forgive them for this tendency.

Their character is affected by this taste for easy living. Women
are vain, frivolous, affected and egotistic. Men succeed, in certain
circumstances, in making an abstraction of their masculinity. A
woman, on the other hand, can never become an impersonal
creature. She is the product of her sexuality and femininity; she
cannot detach herself from it. This servitude precludes her from
access to philosophy and reasoned argument. Abstract intelligence is
the prerogative of men: '. . . the most gifted lady of them all cannot
live by intelligence alone. She needs romance' (*Sphinx*, page 207).
Lindsay discovered in women an inborn sense of intrigue that he
never tired of describing. Sometimes, they detested one another for
no reason. Sometimes, they invented reasons for detesting one
another. 'Place two women side by side', argues Lindsay, 'and they
will unquestionably quarrel.' They cannot help being jealous. Celia
criticises Evelyn; Evelyn criticises Lore; Lore criticises Celia. The
chain of these animosities is endless. Curiosity, jealousy, a taste for
lies and dissimulation, a susceptibility for everything which affects
honour and reputation, all feed these countless feminine quarrels.

In the face of all these subtleties, man remains dumbfounded.
How can this pillar of rationality comprehend a 'natural antipathy'?
'Can't you understand that it's perfectly possible for two women
to loathe and detest each other without a reason?'[22] Nicholas
Cabot, recently named as Celia's fiancé, finds himself abruptly cast
aside for not having dared to take at its face value one of Celia's
lies. Women have their own code, which often leaves a man per-
plexed. Hence, affection can turn into hatred, without a word of
warning.

Lindsay holds women responsible for the decadence of the modern world. They are the source of corruption. It is even too late for men to remedy matters. The harm is done. Man has been transformed into a 'man-woman'. The hybrid is the symbol of general decadence. From the first page to the last, *A Voyage to Arcturus* exposes the contamination of the male by false femininity. Lindsay's Devil, the false God of the book, Crystalman, has a woman's face. He is neither woman nor androgyne, but a man-woman, or man corrupted by women. 'Why should you disguise yourself like a woman?' Krag asks Gangnet (*A Voyage to Arcturus*, page 236). Many are the characters met in Arcturus whose sex is indeterminate, such as Panawe, Haunte, Gangnet, and not forgetting the prototype androgyne, Leehallfae. All have something effeminate about them, be it voice, complexion, long hair, manners, or, especially, dress. Even the young man materialised by the medium is a precursor of the aesthetes to be encountered on Arcturus. The contrast between these beardless young men and Maskull, the male hero from elsewhere, hairy and bearded, is most marked. The androgyne is the degradation of masculine values, and does not appear here as an example of purity or Platonic plenitude, nor as a refuge from the aggression of the female vamp.[23] We have proof of all this in the use Lindsay makes of the term 'effeminate', which ends by being virtually synonymous, in his writing, with 'corrupt'. Those beings who yield to the temptations of Crystalman are 'effeminate and corrupt, that is to say absorbed in the disgusting and nauseating life' of pleasure. Behind the use of the term 'effeminate' emerges the conception of women. Lindsay comments, for example, that there is something effeminate in Arsinal's obsession with archaeology.[24] With Lindsay, the pleasure of aesthetic contemplation becomes an emasculation.[25] Love is an effeminate sport (*A Voyage to Arcturus*, page 79), a feminine occupation just like tea or croquet. In order to understand these surprising pronouncements, one must refer to a passage from the *Philosophical Notes*, in which Lindsay explains the meaning of the word 'effeminate'. 'By effeminacy, we do not mean that a man possesses the good qualities of a woman, but only the bad. It follows that it should be considered just as disgraceful for a woman to be effeminate' (*Philosophical Notes*, Number 292).

This very negative presentation would seem to indicate that in Lindsay's eyes, women were the image of Satan, and nothing good could come from a creature whose vices and failings were so obvious.

In fact, one of the most surprising paradoxes in Lindsay that a woman can suggest to him as much an angel as a monster. The important point is that nothing exists between these two extremes.

Behind the revulsion so often proclaimed, there is hidden, in reality, a profound attraction. Whatever may be his reaction, Lindsay never ceased to be fascinated by this mysterious creature, so unpredictable, and capable of the worst meanness, along with the most admirable self-denial. The following aphorism from the *Philosophical Notes* could well be applied to the author himself. 'Just as the Holy Trinity is a mystery only to Christians, so women are mysterious only to admirers' (Number 64). Vamp, destroyer and siren woman may be, but, if a man distrusts her, indeed criticises her, is this not the reflex action of fear? Is it not the fear of succumbing to her, and of becoming her object, and her toy? Lindsay's heroes are young, and too inexperienced to play with fire. They know their weaknesses too well to venture to tempt the devil. 'I don't pretend that I'm proof against natural forces', says Nicholas Cabot, referring to women, 'that's another reason for keeping away' (*Sphinx*, page 19). All recognise this eventuality, including Cabot, Saltfleet and Maskull.

Sometimes, the criticism gives way to a presentation that is more flattering. Lindsay is willing to recognise feminine virtues, such as beauty, intuition, devotion and elegance. In *Devil's Tor*, he ends by declaring that the most attractive aspects of the world in which we live bear the stamp of women. He reproaches women, above all, for their 'sexuality'; a word which, in his writing, designates both sexual impulses and, in a more general sense, sexual dispositions. Lindsay ceaselessly accuses women of being slaves to their 'sexuality'

The degeneration of man, and of the world, began with the division of the sexes, once unified in the primitive androgyne. The state of natural harmony has thus been broken. Between man and woman, a barrier has appeared, which henceforward conditions their behaviour towards one another. A dissociation is created, obliging each to be careful in the presence of the other, and to assume the rôle that his, or her, sex demands. The woman must be passive and serving, the man managing the budget, with the woman spending the money. Such circumspection and stratagems cannot be natural, reasons Lindsay.

One can see that this analysis, briefly summarised, remained close enough to certain ancient beliefs which made the difference between the sexes a necessary accident. To Aristotle, for instance, Nature spontaneously tended to perpetuate the male of the species. 'Nature tries to do what is most perfect.' The production of a female seemed to him to be a 'deviation' of Nature, although essential for the reproduction of the species. Lindsay's argument closely resembles the reasoning of Aristotle, but with one difference, which is a considerable one. Nature tends not towards the male, but towards the female, in the shape of a primitive Goddess–Mother figure, creator of the universe.

The 'deviation' of Nature is nothing but the transition from the maternal state of the Goddess–Mother to the bisexual state.[26] It was in bringing about the original maternal state that Lindsay reinvested woman with the importance that he had seemed so obstinately to refuse her. The paradox is surprising, and says much about the ambiguity of Lindsay with regard to women. Women would henceforward be goddesses, but appearing only with the characteristics of courtesans. As in the case of Baudelaire, Lindsay's thinking fluctuates between these two extremes.

It would be tempting to attribute this deprecation of women, simply because it seems so excessive, to some amatory disappointment suffered by Lindsay. There is nothing to justify this, however, in any biographical research. There seems no reason to believe that Lindsay was unduly affected by the termination of his first engagement, for example. David Lindsay's relations with his mother are still too little known to justify any kind of psychoanalytical explanation.[27] More important was the influence of the puritanical environment in which Lindsay lived, surrounded by his mother, his sister and his aunt, all three of whom were very religious. One has only to recall the disapproval of Mrs Moor with regard to the modest pleasure of a Sunday morning walk on the Brighton promenade to imagine what hostility there must have been towards sexual pleasure. It is possible to surmise that, behind Lindsay's theory of 'the fall into bisexuality', which he also represented as 'the fall into sexuality', there lies concealed an uneasiness towards sexuality in general. This work which is full of seduction scenes and troubled relationships remains basically very chaste. With Lindsay, one never recalls a love scene with voluptuousness or nostalgia. The prevailing feeling is that of shame. Hence, Maskull, questioned about his amorous relations with the Terriens, replies '... the meeting of sexes is sweet, though shameful.

So poignant is the sweetness that the accompanying shame is ignored, with open eyes. There is no hatred, or only among a few eccentric persons' (*A Voyage to Arcturus*, page 218). Elsewhere, Lindsay speaks of 'the shame-carrying passion of a male' (*A Voyage to Arcturus*, page 172).

His argument leaves one to guess the reasoning behind it. The revulsion awakened in him by the sexual act has nothing physical about it, he says in essence, but, recalling Schopenhauer, it is a humiliation. The sexual act engenders shame because the enjoyment signifies a degradation of the ideal man, and a fall into bestiality. The argument appears in *A Voyage to Arcturus*, in the words of Catice.

'Say just this, before we part company, why does pleasure appear so shameful to us?'

'Because, in feeling pleasure, we forget our home.'

'And that is –'

'Muspel.'[28]

The shame that accompanies sexuality is the feeling of the most noble part of man for the most vile. It is a hostile reaction of his superior soul. It is necessary to understand it in the way that Nietzsche interpreted it, when he declared 'This is what a superman feels for a man; a grievous shame.'

In spite of the explanation, it is difficult to understand this shame, which, in essence, attaches itself to all pleasure, and especially in the case of sexuality. Lindsay has said that he condemns pleasure, sexuality being just one of its many forms, but the association of love with shame, and the vehemence of his remarks, point to a strong revulsion towards anything concerned with sexuality. 'Dirt follows sweetness, as a lamb follows its mother. Every love-affair is in one aspect an idyll, in another aspect an orgy. By this is meant, not physical connections, but merely the effect of desire' (*Philosophical Notes*, Number 266).

### The search for identity

This picture of human relations is astonishing in many respects. Such meditation does not succeed in concealing the author's anguish. Of all the themes approached, this is the one that stands out by virtue of its vehemence and frequency; bisexuality or division of the sexes. Reflection upon this theme fills a great part of *A Voyage to Arcturus*. One can go back, for instance, to the chapters devoted to

the discovery of Tormance to notice the extent to which the author
has been obsessed with this definition of the sexes. It is interesting to
consider each character separately. The first one, Joiwind, on all the
evidence, is the very essence of femininity when she proclaims her
basic philosophy; compassion, sacrifice and kindness. Oceaxe, on the
other hand, embodies feminine perversion. Biologically feminine, she
contradicts her sex by her character and tendencies. 'The curves
were womanly, the bones were characteristically female, yet all
seemed somehow to express a daring, masculine underlying will'
(page 77). Finally, Tydomin is the symbol of oppressed
womanhood, forbidden to stay in the male sanctuary, Sant. One
should not forget, either, the hero himself, Maskull, who asserts by
his very name, in a manner that is perhaps too brutal to be above
suspicion, that he belongs to the stronger sex. This catalogue of
sexual affinities could be pursued much further.

When he does not define the sex of each character precisely,
Lindsay is careful to stress the ambiguities. He hastens to show that
the clothing offered to Maskull by Joiwind is ridiculous dress for a
true male. In the case of another character, Mrs Moor, he reveals a
similar inconsistency. She is a woman, but her tastes are essentially
masculine. She detests frivolity, knows how to appreciate music, and
knows nothing about dress. Logically, such reflection upon the
distribution of sexual characteristics was bound to lead Lindsay to
the conception of androgyne characters, such as Leehalfae and, to
some extent, Crystalman.

Such persistence in exploring the 'great differences', even if it is
not rare amongst writers, raises the question of how this theme
is chosen and used. To understand the meaning of this fascination,
it is important to connect this theme to an enquiry that is no
less insistent, and which bears upon the identity of the characters.

This investigation of the ego appears clearly in *The Haunted
Woman*. It concerns the book's heroine, Isbel Loment. Her repeated
visits to Runhill Court, and more especially her entering the
haunted room, invite many interpretations. It can be seen simply as
a fantasy story, resting upon an animistic conception of the world;
or as a quest for some Golden Age buried in the depths of the past.
One can also reveal there the discovery of sexuality, the haunted
room becoming an alcove for lovers, unreal and uncanny because,
for once, instincts can be given free rein. Discovery of passion then

becomes sanctified, according to Lindsay, but nevertheless retains its undertones that are both carnal and sensual. This is a false discovery, however, since Isbel finds nothing that is not already there, in herself. Behind the meandering visits to a haunted house, and behind the vertical axis of the magic staircase, there lies one of the central themes of the book, which is the investigation of the self. One could scarcely ask for better proof of this than the title of Chapter 5, dealing with the entry into the haunted room, which is styled 'Isbel sees herself'. The mirror which awaits her there does not, as in so many fantasy stories, mark the entry into a strange world.[29] It is certainly the threshold of strange things, but it opens only onto the depths of the human soul. The mirror, so recently the tool of the flirt, regains the significance that it had always held in the imagination, in the form of depth, ambivalence and identity.[30] 'She didn't wish to admire. She wished to understand herself.' The avowal is clear.

*Sphinx* contains a similar enquiry into the identity of Lore Jensen. Is she woman or man? Thus ponders Lindsay, like Oedipus in front of the Sphinx with the head of a woman and the body of a lion. Is she a serious musician or a failed artist? The hero of *A Voyage to Arcturus*, for his part, does not know the problems of Lore Jensen and Isbel Loment. If they are not perceptible, is this not evidence of a repression which precludes the least hint of self-analysis? If Maskull has no identity problem, is this not because he has no identity? He is the non-being, gone out in search of himself. The question is no longer one of knowing who he is, but what he will do, although, in the last analysis, the two enquiries are identical. 'Why am I here? Who *is* Surtur? ... Am I a secondary character? Is he regarded as important, and I as unimportant?' (page 137).

The importance of this search for identity will appear still more pronounced if it is seen in the context of Lindsay's writing. The author's anguish, in face of the question which haunts him, can be discerned in the recurrences of the themes of truth and reality. Arcturus, like the background of the later novels, is a world of doubt and false pretences. Nothing there is certain. Constantly deceived by appearances, man stumbles. He seeks something, or someone, that escapes him. Truth never ceases to evolve. By skilful degrees, Lindsay evades the issue, and obscures the picture that, a moment before, was as clear as if seen through binoculars. From one book to the next, the same enquiry into reality and truth repeats itself, with such contrasts as outside–inside, appearance–reality, clothing–nudity, substance–shadow and sunshine–fog. Reality ends by being put in doubt, until the appearance of a world that is 'more real than reality'. This quest for truth, and this denunciation of false pretences, would probably not be so tenacious if it were not linked to Lindsay's own anguish as regards *his* identity.

He is intent upon the subject with evident predilection. A taste for genealogy is one of its aspects. When a publisher asked him to provide a biographical note, he immediately felt obliged to point out that a certain Nordic prince, Ivar, was an ancestor of the Lindsay family.[31] Even if he disowned his father, Lindsay nevertheless preserved from the relationship anything that could serve his own interests, and provide an answer to his questions. He erased from his father's past the links with the City of London, in order to preserve only the Scottish origins of the family. His numerous stays in Scotland had a particular sentimental significance. Lindsay saw them as a return to his roots, rather than as an appeal to his interest and taste. Scotland, he was accustomed to saying, was too wet, and the sound of the bagpipes depressing. Genealogical research did not stop at Scotland. The first roots came from Scandinavia, whose virtues and merits Lindsay never ceased to praise. Men, he believed, are determined by their origins, so he took great care to define these. To be born a Jew, or in the Mediterranean region, was to be forever condemned to exile and mistrust. Only the Scandinavians, the Anglo-Saxons and the Celts deserved respect.

His characters live in England, but proclaim, with evident satisfaction, their foreign element. There will always be, in their genealogy, some ancestor, more or less distant, to come to their aid. The names of these characters are derived directly from Scandinavia, such as Ingrid, Helga, Jensen and Colborne. Lore Jensen has a Swedish mother. In spite of her English ancestry, 'The whole family regarded Ingrid as the typical Norse Colborne' (*Devil's Tor*, pages 12–13). She is even the image of her grandfather, whose connections with the Scandinavian countries were close. As for Hugh Drapier, he retains, in spite of his Latin name, traces of his origins that were Scottish and Gaelic, including splendid red hair.

Genealogical prejudice did not stop there. The world was soon divided into two clans that were irrevocably opposed, one having all the faults, and the other all the virtues. The Nordic race was proud and free, loving mystery, and living in harmony with nature. The members of it knew how to discover life and the manifestations of a supernatural world. They knew, on occasions, how to be hard. They did not flinch from sacrifices. They were polytheists, and proclaimed, by this fact, their tolerance and love of liberty. Semites, on the other hand, and, more especially, the Latin races, were distinguishable by their tribal instincts, their corruption, their rigid monotheism, their materialism and their inability to reason and to comprehend anything spiritual. With Lindsay, there is a Viking cult in blue eyes, indeed a veneration of slaughter and cruelty; aspects no less disagreeable than those in the Nordic complex that one also finds in Lovecraft.[32]

Research into his ancestry is only one aspect of the search for identity. If the assimilation with the Scandinavian race was accomplished without difficulty, the same could not be said of the next aspect of the investigation of the self, which was sexuality. Everything leads to the belief that Lindsay encountered a few difficulties in manifesting virility. If the world is badly made, reasons Lindsay, this is in large measure due to the division of the sexes; this obligation imposed upon the new-born to assume the sex accorded to it, with no personal option. The great tragedy of humanity has been the Fall into bisexuality, he asserts in *Devil's Tor* (pages 152–156). The life of every human being begins with an injustice, in the form of the murder of the child of the opposite sex, vanquished by the stronger one. Such, in all its simplicity, is Lindsay's theory of heredity. The chance distribution of the chromosomes is replaced, as early as procreation, by the concept of destruction, and of struggle for life. A similar version of this battle of the sexes in the embryo is to be found at the beginning of *A Voyage to Arcturus*. The terms are identical. Panawe recounts the disturbing adventure of Broodviol. At birth, Broodviol was found to be asexual, as neither sex had been able to dominate and prevail. How does one explain this phenomenon? 'Every man and woman among us is a walking murderer. If a male, he has struggled with and killed the female who was born in the same body with him; if a female, she has killed the male, but in this child the struggle is still continuing' (*A Voyage to Arcturus*, page 65).

The injustice of the arbitrary conferment of a sex haunted Lindsay. There is discernible in his writing a questioning of his own sexuality that is scarcely disguised. His preference, it should certainly be said, was ultimately towards the female rather than the male. If the modern woman was not above reproach, it was only the man who was to blame. Assimilation to woman was accompanied by an assessment of feminine virtues, such as gentleness, kindness and artistry. These are the manifestations of the feminine complex in a man. It is scarcely surprising, therefore, to find Lindsay, especially in *Devil's Tor*, eulogising motherhood. From Christianity, he retains one solitary aspect, which is that of the Virgin and Child. In his letters, he equates the creative genius of the artist with the pregnancy of a woman.[33] Would it be an exaggeration to consider Lindsay's decision to become a writer as being another manifestation of this envy of the vagina? Art becomes childbirth, and the artist becomes a hybrid.

The desire to be a woman rarely presents itself in so simplistic a form. Let us not forget that attempts at identification are, in general, subconscious, and that the outward demeanour of the individual can never betray the least desire. Envy of the vagina is frequently accompanied by a subconscious fear of being a woman. The first step towards femininity finds itself thwarted by a feeling of guilt which reinforces the disapproval of one's immediate circle. It then happens that the results of the femininity complex are the very opposite from those desired. 'When men criticise women, it is often because of their frustration at not being able to be women', writes one psychoanalyst.[34]

To the desire to be a woman, there is opposed the fear of being a woman. Criticism becomes, in the subconscious mind, a defence mechanism against the tendencies one has refused to admit. Hence, psychoanalysis explains the ambiguity which characterises Lindsay's relations with women. He admires them, secretly or publicly, but creates characters who do not conceal their misogyny, and who tirelessly denounce the frivolities and shortcomings of the weaker sex.

This reaction of self-defence leads to another attitude that is no less conventional, when criticism of femininity goes hand in hand with glorification of the male. If Lindsay depicts, with apparent benevolence, female characters endowed with marked masculine characteristics, such as Lore Jensen, Mrs Moor, Oceaxe, Tydomin and Gleameil, the converse is certainly not true. The least suspicion of effeminacy in a man is immediately, and vigorously, denounced, as we have shown earlier. The masculine ideal so far passes reality that Lindsay embellishes it. The complex of femininity, just because it is accepted as being part of *normal* sexuality, leads Lindsay to produce a complex of normality. From the powerful wish to be a man at any cost, he goes on to create men who are more masculine than any that ever existed. Far from agreeing with Freud that 'the majority of men fall far short of the masculine ideal, and all individual humans, by virtue of their bi-sexual constitution, and of their crossed heredity, simultaneously possess both masculine and feminine traits, to such an extent that the validity of the theory of pure masculinity and femininity remains in doubt',[35] Lindsay invents a pure masculinity that, in reality, does not exist in nature. It is this glorification of the male that is certainly personified in Lindsay's first hero, Maskull. Carved in strength, hairy and bearded, he constitutes the first theoretical creation aimed at resolving the anguish and doubts of the author about his own sexuality. With no more difficulty, one can see in the depiction of Saltfleet another variation of pure masculinity. 'He was big of build. The forehead was noticeably wide, the features were strong, masculine, severe, the grey eyes direct and uncompromising. He was clean-shaved, and the rest of his mouth fascinated Helga instantly by its expressive virility' (*Devil's Tor*, page 171). We know also that the Roman Emperor Sulla was one of Lindsay's idols, and that the portrait of Saltfleet was partly inspired by him. Sulla, sanguinary tyrant though he may have been, served Lindsay as a model of virility. If he admired the Vikings so much, this was no doubt because he saw in them 'qualities' similar to those of Sulla.

In order to try to explain Lindsay's ambiguities, the uneasiness he felt in defining himself as regards women and sexuality, there is no need to embark upon a lengthy enquiry. Lindsay's case is too much of a pattern. Inability to confront women was the result of the education he had received, and of his parental relations. The opening chapter describes the difficulties experienced by David Lindsay in his relations with women. His late marriage, almost unhoped for, is an example of this. His first engagement, which lasted some fifteen years, marked by long evasions, reminds us no less of his embarrassment. If he showed himself, in these circumstances, to be so ill at ease, this was because he lived for so long protected, and pampered, by the women in his family. Firstly, there was his mother, and then, after her death, his aunt and his sister, who became mother-substitutes. The natural attachment of the boy to his mother was reinforced, at a very early stage, by his father's attitude. One must remember, indeed, that the latter left his wife abruptly, never to return to the home. The flight of Alexander Lindsay prevented the transfer of David's affections from his mother to his father, and blocked the development of his personality in his tender years. Everything leads to the belief that Lindsay never succeeded in overcoming this complex.

Lindsay's writing contains many declarations that are worthy of consideration in the light of the teaching of Freud. The quest for the mother presents itself in a form that is scarcely disguised, since Lindsay avows, quite unambiguously, in *Devil's Tor*, his cult of the Goddess–Mother. The attributes of the Goddess are those of the mother, and, under the cloak of religion, one sees a regression towards the past, and, at the same time, towards the mother. Only the Great Goddess, or Goddess–Mother, Demiurge creator of humanity, like the mother bearing her son, is worthy of love. Other women, almost without exception, are relegated to the level of flirts and sirens. If the misogynist heroes of Lindsay are so exacting towards women, it is because they do not recognise in them the virtues of their own mothers. With Lindsay, nearly all marriage plans miscarry. Successful marriage seems to belong to the sphere of the forbidden. To be permissible, it must be on a metaphorical level, such as the 'marriage of true minds' in the case of Saltfleet and Ingrid, or the union in death of Lore Jensen and Nicholas Cabot.

The mistress is the rival of the mother, and, for this reason, cannot be tolerated. The man is in the service of his mother, and pursues the old Oedipean dream of marrying her. Nothing could be less ambiguous than the journey of Hugh Drapier in *Devil's Tor*. Setting out from Asia, he makes his way as far as a tomb, where a Queen, or Goddess, of old awaits him. The tomb, or grotto, is frequently associated with women. To enter the tomb is to commit an act of defloration, in symbolic terms. When one knows that the woman buried there is a transformation of the Goddess–Mother, the meaning is all too evident, as has been shown by Jean Markale through analyses of numerous Celtic legends where the fairy waits in her grotto for a fearless bachelor to come to 'release' her.[36] Lindsay's description of this deserves attention. Hugh Drapier enters the tomb. 'He supposed that the confinement of the place was recalling to him the forgotten fears of infancy; a psychologist doubtless could have explained it all' (page 83). Drapier does not know what is in store for him, but he already has a presentiment that this discovery has a sacred significance: '... hesitating before the invasion of the last bedchamber of a high-born wife or daughter of primitive times, defended throughout her life by her own savage purity; now defenceless ... Only, he had still been fetched here from across the seas. They could not say of him that he was here to spy and peep' (page 84).

The simulation of the sexual act could not be more explicit. With desire, however, is intermingled the fear of remaining a prisoner, and a sense of profanation, which are no doubt echoes of the son's guilt at the idea of incest. Moreover, the site of the grotto is a reminder of the presence of the father whom Drapier must confront at the exit. This figure of the father is none other than the rock of Devil's Tor, which normally bars access to the grotto, and which is an enormous rock *having human shape*, giving the impression of wishing to crash down upon whomsoever shall approach too close to the sanctuary. Presently, in hurling defiance at the father, the son is able to flout him, and to treat him as an 'emasculated crest'.[37] Once the incest has been committed, it is time to settle accounts. One knows that no pardon is possible. The crime committed by defiance, in usurping the power of the father, will be punished by death. Hugh Drapier will perish on his next visit, crushed by a piece of rock that breaks away, thus ending the revolt against the father.

There is, however, another way of rebelling against paternal pre-eminence. This one, much more subtle than the first, has its origin in the author himself. If there certainly are united families in Lindsay's novels, this is because the father, the disturbing and undesirable element, is absent. Lindsay makes it his task to crucify and bury him. The death of the father is, for Lindsay, the ransom for his worthlessness. This is indicated by the main characters of each of his novels. Ingrid's father is dead, as is Isbel's. As for Lore Jensen, she is the result of an illicit union. She does not know her father; the paternity is hidden, and hence absent. Maskull, in *A Voyage to Arcturus*, is an orphan, unencumbered with any ties, having 'neither wife, land, nor profession' (page 27). Finally, Saltfleet is no better off, being a 'bastard', since his mother refused to marry the father of her child (*Devil's Tor*, page 209). With the exception of Polecrab, a character in *A Voyage to Arcturus*, there is not a single real father throughout Lindsay's writing. Sturt, in *Sphinx*, the father of three daughters, is still alive, but Lindsay has mutilated him. In making him the victim of an accident that has ended his career as an actor, Lindsay inflicts upon him a symbolic wound which is both castration and death. Lindsay keeps him alive only to heap a second ignominy upon him, by making him the hypocritical, shameful father of Lore Jensen.

Lindsay, first as a child and then as an adult, can never have forgotten his father's desertion. This was a wrong that it was quite impossible to forgive, and the importance of which was increased tenfold by the attachment he felt to his mother. The condemnation of the father spilled over upon all men, known or unknown. The flight of Alexander Lindsay prevented belief in men, indeed in Man, who is judged henceforward as base, and a predator of women. With what anger he turned upon him is shown by his making him infirm, or, more often, making him die as soon as possible, filling his books with bastards and orphans. One travels, and lives in company with an aunt or mother, as was the case with Lindsay, but never with a father. The father is dead and buried, unknown or absent. Not content with submitting his characters to all manner of infamies, Lindsay goes on to colour his illusions with his own metaphysical theories. There remained one father to destroy, and this was God the Father, the spiritual father. Who would not see in the systematic denigration of the male God the supreme example of the revolt against the Father? Just as he hounded all the fathers of families in his books, Lindsay took it upon himself to stigmatise God as an impostor and a liar. God the Father could not have existed, he reasoned. Only a Goddess–Mother could explain the creation of the world. If he admired matriarchal societies that he regarded as being the result of the Eternal Female, it was because he could not tolerate the idea of a male God as the source of Good, since, from experience, he knew that the father brought nothing but misery. Hence, the matriarchal society must prevail, on Earth and in Heaven, as a guarantee of peace and security.

# 4

# THE WORLD OF CRYSTALMAN

Hitherto, we have made only brief references to *A Voyage to Arcturus*. This omission appears much more serious in that this book is the most famous of all David Lindsay's writing. The time has come, therefore, to do it justice. It has been called 'an irritatingly-undefinable' book, which has scarcely anything in common with other novels, English or foreign, contemporaneous or otherwise. It is, in truth, a book of many facets, being at once a work of imagination, a philosophical novel and a symbolic novel.

## *A VOYAGE TO ARCTURUS,*
## WORK OF IMAGINATION

### *The cosmic journey*

It will be necessary to wait nearly half a century for *A Voyage to Arcturus* to take its place in the first rank of fantasy literature. This view is shared by the author of quite a recent study.[1] To-day, as we know, the wonderful, the mysterious, the strange, all appeal to current tastes. It may possibly be due to the books of Tolkien, and also to an unprecedented effort on the part of literary critics, that homage has at last been paid to this old genre that has now become one of the most lively forms of literature.

It must be conceded, however, that only the most die-hard fanatics will enthuse unreservedly over the writing of Rider Haggard, A. E. Van Vogt and Clifford D. Simak. Only a few titles from the output of these authors are remembered as more than a pleasant form of diversion. This is the view expressed by an expert in this field, M. R. Hillegas. 'Occasionally this kind of fantasy achieved some sort of significance, as it did with the better stories of H. P. Lovecraft, E. R. Eddison's *The Worm Ouroboros*, David Lindsay's *A Voyage to Arcturus*, or Mervyn Peake's *Gormenghast Trilogy*.'[2]

One possible explanation for the reputation of the authors mentioned by Mark Hillegas might be the seriousness of their approach to literature. Eric Rabkin emphasises this point regarding *A Voyage to Arcturus*. 'One of the most soul-wrenching and mind-distorting Fantasies in English ... a deadly-serious book.'[3] Kingsley Amis, in declaring himself to be openly hostile to any dilution of pure science-fiction, makes an admission of the deepest significance. According to him, for all science-fiction fanatics, 'entertainment is not incidental but essential.'[4] In other words, works of science-fiction are of value only because they entertain. Whoever comes to them with the object of discovering, for example, 'new perspectives and insights', places himself short of the experience of the enthusiasts of this genre.

This attitude is poles apart from that of Lindsay. Far from approaching literature with a smile, because it offered him an escape or relief, David Lindsay took up writing because contemporary literature seemed to him, in the main, to be frivolous. Anyone who voluntarily sacrifices his material comfort to live for some twenty years in precarious circumstances, sometimes approaching complete destitution, can only have been motivated by a driving inner necessity, to which any idea of mere entertainment would have been alien. To want to place him in the ranks of public entertainers appears even insulting, and reveals, at the very least, a certain lack of understanding of his objectives and thought. Once its nature is recognised, this kind of literature becomes 'a mode valuable for presenting moral or spiritual values, which could not be presented in realistic fiction; a way of transcending the limitations of human existence to attain new perspectives and insights'.[5] It is from this standpoint that Lindsay deserves to be studied, and not as a representative of science-fiction.

One of the first to recognise the value of *A Voyage to Arcturus* was C. S. Lewis. Novelist, essayist, professor of Mediaeval and Renaissance Literature at Cambridge (1954–63), Lewis never ceased to be interested in types of fantasy literature, such as the supernatural stories of MacDonald, the early novels of H. G. Wells,[6] and the utopian writings of William Morris. He had himself entered this field of literature, since he had finished, in 1938, the first of a 'cosmic trilogy', comprising *Out of the Silent Planet* (1938), *Perelandra* (1943), and *That Hideous Strength* (1945). The first two of these books, whose action was placed on Mars and Venus respectively, described the struggle between the forces of Good and Evil; on one side the Martians remained in a state of primitive innocence, in a kind of extra-terrestrial Paradise, whilst, on the other, the Evil is embodied in one Weston, the apostle of science and earthly civilisation. The imagination here is applied to an idea that is basically religious. The lesson of Christian morality, apparent from the earliest pages, emerges in this quotation, which also summarises the way Lewis makes use of distant planets. 'If we could even effect in one per cent of our readers a change-over from the conception of Space to the conception of Heaven, we should have made a beginning.'[7]

This quotation has been chosen because it can be considered as a defence, and illustration, of Lindsay's method, in that Lewis had borrowed it from him. As proof of this, we have the author's own admission, written in 1944, 'I had grown up on Wells's stories of that kind; it was Lindsay who first gave me the idea that the "scientifiction" appeal could be combined with the "supernatural" appeal.'[8]

This presentation of Lindsay's book, however, is rather clumsy, for, as we shall see, it contains scarcely anything of the supernatural, if by that one means ghosts, unexplained happenings and visitations from the hereafter, nor, indeed, is there much science-fiction in *A Voyage to Arcturus*. Lewis had another opportunity to define his thinking in a fresh essay. 'There is no recipe for writing of this kind, but part of the secret is that the author, like Kafka, is recording a lived dialectic. His Tormance is a region of the spirit. He is the first writer to discover what "other planets" are really good for in fiction. No merely-physical strangeness or merely-spatial distance will realise that idea of otherness which is what we are always trying to grasp in a story about voyaging through space; you must go into another dimension. To construct plausible and moving "other worlds" you must draw on the only real "other world" we know, that of the spirit.'[9] In simple terms, this means that these planets are not only different from our own world as regards the topography and the inhabitants, but also by their way of life and thought.[10] To Earth, a fallen world, put in quarantine at the end of the interplanetary war, Lewis contrasts Mars and Venus, remaining sheltered from Evil. It is certain, however, that this 'dimension of spirit' is much less distinct in Lindsay's novel than Lewis imagines. The whole purpose of *A Voyage to Arcturus* is to mislead the reader by a picture of surprising exoticism, while, in reality, the morality, or 'dimension of spirit', remained close to what it would be on Earth.

C. S. Lewis, however, had the great merit of stressing that this form of literature, the story of adventures in an imaginary world, cannot limit itself simply to transplanting the reader. In itself, the exoticism is not enough, and only arouses a deep longing, without necessarily adding to the value of the book.

*A Voyage to Arcturus* belongs to the long tradition of the 'cosmic novel', a variation of Utopia and the imaginary journey, which developed particularly from the seventeenth century. With the advent of science, and especially the advance of astronomy, there appeared several works on the exploration of space, such as *Somnium* by Kepler (1634), *Man in the Moone* by Godwin (1638) and *The Other World* by Cyrano de Bergerac (1650), all of which were rather far-fetched. In the nineteenth century, on the other hand, the stories became much more realistic. The Moon itself, even, seemed to lose its fascination, as compared with the 'conquest of space' and the difficult technical problems to be overcome. Jules Verne's *From the Earth to the Moon* clearly shows this evolution towards a realism that was almost excessive. Fiction became scientific.

Compared with the Jules Verne book, *A Voyage to Arcturus* both disappoints and surprises. Preparation for the voyage is non-existent. To the journey itself, Lindsay devotes no more than seventeen lines (pages 43–44). Whilst other novelists, such as H. G. Wells and C. S. Lewis, stop to admire the sky, and depict the wonderment of the travellers,[11] David Lindsay, for his part, is impatient to reach the end of the journey. Moreover, encapsulated in the air-ship, the traveller has no opportunity of looking outside, and, in any event, he loses consciousness.

Scientific laws are shamelessly mocked. Not a single calculation is made to determine the angle of flight, nor is there the slightest hesitation as regards the risks involved in the operation. It is abundantly clear that the interplanetary journey is of no interest to the author. What counts is the scene that awaits the traveller, *on his arrival*. Maskull regains consciousness shortly after the landing. The real journey now begins. This awakening marks a beginning, and is virtually a rebirth.

To reach the star, Arcturus, David Lindsay has recourse neither to a chariot drawn by swans nor to the rocket of modern times. There is no motor. In order to move, the airship uses a law of attraction of luminous rays, whose principle is as simple as it is ingenious. Just as a pendulum returns to its starting-point, certain luminous rays from Arcturus have, according to Lindsay, the characteristic of returning to their source. All that is needed, therefore, is to put these rays into a bottle which is firmly fixed to the front of the 'rocket', and the latter will immediately be propelled as far as Arcturus with the speed of light.[12]

In spite of certain liberties taken with regard to plausibility and scientific truth, Lindsay defined, with great precision, the star that he chose to explore. Although little known, Arcturus is a star that does really exist. It is situated in the Northern Hemisphere, in the extension of the Great Bear. Its brightness makes it easily identifiable. Lindsay respects this data, since, as early as page 26, he presents Arcturus to us as being 'the brightest star in the south-eastern sky'.

Although important, this orientation does not strike us as being sufficient to explain a choice which, at first sight, seems surprising, since it would have been so easy to choose one of the better-known stars, the Moon, Mars or Venus. In addition to its brightness, Arcturus is distinguishable from the other stars by two important characteristics which are emphasised by all astronomical tracts, these being that it is a *double* star, and *blue in colour*. Far from being insignificant, these two elements served to assist the author, and to such an extent that it is certainly no exaggeration to assert that they explain his choice.

That it is a double star is indicated by Lindsay in the first description, when, before their departure, the travellers look at Arcturus from Earth, with the help of a telescope. 'The star, which to the naked eye appeared as a single yellow point of light, now became clearly split into two bright but minute suns, the larger of which was still yellow, while its smaller companion was a beautiful blue, but this was not all. Apparently circulating around the yellow sun was a comparatively-small and hardly-distinguishable satellite, which seemed to shine, not by its own, but by reflected, light' (page 28). Behind this division into two stars, there emerges, not only the ambiguity of values on Arcturus, but also the fundamental contrast between the blue sun and the yellow sun, so often met in the book, between Crystalman and Krag. What might have appeared to be a gratuitous device becomes the basis of an idea, and evidence of a course which will confirm itself throughout the entire book.[13]

### The extra-terrestrials

Arcturus is not a dead star. Scarcely has he set foot there than Maskull finds himself face to face with one of its inhabitants. It must be admitted that one awaits with no little interest this meeting of the two worlds. Previously, writers had had as much difficulty in imagining these extra-terrestrials as in explaining cogently the means of the journey itself. Certainly, during the Middle Ages, the Kingdom of God was conceived as being somewhere beyond the stars, but how could one accept the idea of a habitable world? Throughout the nineteenth century, life in outer space is inconceivable. Space becomes cold. Beyond the stars, there reigns a Void, the black night, the Mare Tenebrarum.[14] To conceive the inhabitants of space was difficult, and to describe them became a guessing game. For a long time, the extra-terrestrials would be presented as monsters. The Martian, as seen by Paul, one of the great illustrators of American science-fiction, resembles a huge grasshopper, ten feet high, raised on its paws, with bulging eyes, and an enormous thorax.[15] The description has scarcely evolved since H. G. Wells, whose Selenites had the appearance of monsters wearing cylindrical metal shells. Their arms were more like tentacles. Writing more than forty years later, C. S. Lewis admits that it is difficult for him to conceive anything other than creatures with bulging eyes and terrifying jaws.[16]

What does Lindsay's extra-terrestrial resemble? The meeting with Joiwind is reassuring. Arcturus is not inhabited by monsters out of H. G. Wells and his contemporaries. Certainly, the inhabitant of Arcturus is not the son of Adam. A tentacle extends from the chest at the level of the heart. A kind of huge ear grows in the middle of the forehead. As for the skin, it changes colour according to the emotions being felt, but, in spite of these new organs and characteristics, the form is human, beyond any possible doubt. These inhabitants of Arcturus are clothed in ancient fashion, like prehistoric man. They are not encased in iron, or covered with a shell. They have no feelers at the top of the skull. After the initial surprise, they lose their strangeness, so close do they seem to Earth people. On meeting Joiwind, Maskull makes no attempt to flee, as does C. S. Lewis's Dr Ransom in a similar situation. For his part, Maskull is fascinated by the 'angelic purity of the features' of the young girl who comes to welcome him to this new star. No terror affects these two beings, but rather an immediate liking, indeed a tenderness similar to that felt by a Stephen Dedalus, in discovering, on this Earth, the model of beauty from which the young man, shortly to be an artist, would learn to draw his inspiration.

Liberties taken by the author reappear when we come to examine the problems of communications posed by the meeting of extra-terrestrials. From one book to another, a number of writers have resolved these problems with more or less success. In his novel, *Star-Maker*, Olaf Stapledon resorts to a form of transmission of thought, which allows the narrator to put himself, to some extent, in the place of the extra-terrestrials, and so to discover their mode of life. C. S. Lewis, for his part, attributes to the inhabitants of Venus a language which, although different from our own, can be under-stood. To facilitate this, Lewis makes his hero, Dr Ransom, an eminent Cambridge linguist.

Lindsay and Maskull lack Ransom's fondness for foreign lan-guages. What is the language of the inhabitants of Arcturus? One never finds them talking any language other than English. In this book, the traveller has made no effort to attune himself to the extra-terrestrials. It is the very opposite that occurs. The inhabitants of Arcturus understand, and speak, English without any difficulty. Joiwind can read Maskull's thoughts,[17] and then answer him in English. To communicate, she uses an organ called a 'breve' situated in the middle of the forehead. How does she accomplish the transition from reading thoughts to speaking? Lindsay does not say. 'I can now understand your language', says Joiwind to Maskull. 'It was strange at first. In the future, I'll speak to you with my mouth.' The second character met by Maskull seems still more gifted. When Maskull marvels to hear him speak English so well, Panawe answers him 'Thought is a rich, complex thing. I can't say if I am really speaking your tongue by instinct, or if you yourself are transmitting my thoughts into your tongue as I utter them' (page 58). This says much for the ability of Lindsay to avoid embarrassing questions. Basically, he offers no real solution, preferring, sometimes, by means of a side-step, to invoke superior wisdom, and sometimes to leave everything vague. Before long, Lindsay ceases to make any allusion to this problem of communication, retreating behind a convention that one can summarise in these terms; everyone speaks English without difficulty, and, apparently, without having had any in-struction. The author's explanations are obscure.

Arcturus is a star which nobody, before David Lindsay, had sought to explore. The reader waits with interest to discover this new star. The names of places and characters immediately introduce a note of strangeness: Maskull, Krag, Tormance and Night-spore. The names of the inhabitants of Arcturus, Joiwind, Corpang, Crimtyphon, Dreamsinter, and so on, are no less surprising, and serve to mark the distance that separates Arcturus from the Earth, from this society of the 1920's which appears at the beginning of the book, and whose representatives have names that are traditional enough, such as Jameson, Trent and Backhouse.

Apart from the effect of remoteness, indeed of uneasiness, that these names evoke, one wonders whether there should not be seen in them the symbolic intentions of the author. Lindsay seems to suggest this hypothesis to us when he makes one of his extra-terrestrials say 'Naturally we don't take our names from you, Maskull. I don't think our names are very poetic, but they follow nature' (page 49).

However inviting this explanation may be, it is nevertheless dangerous. Would it, perhaps, not be better to see, behind this vindication by Nature, one of the many traps set for the innocent Maskull? All these names are composed of several elements that are easily recognisable, such as Joi-wind, Crim-typhon, Pan-awe and Brood-viol. Quite often, one of these elements suggests something precise. Spadevil can be broken down to 'Spa' and 'Devil'. Dream-sinter would become 'Dreams', with the addition of the suffix 'inter'. There scarcely exists a single one of these names which the patient reader cannot decipher. Unfortunately, this game is purely acad-emic, and serves little useful purpose. It does not seem that, behind all these subtleties, there is any overall principle. The name 'Maskull' can certainly be broken down into several parts, but how should one interpret it?[18] Should one see, in this character, the representative of the ideal mascul-ine, fearless bachelor setting out to conquer the women of space, at once Prometheus, Everyman and Adam? Or should one divide his name differently, as Mask-ull, whose true face is concealed, masked by his double, Nightspore? To dissect each name in order to draw some kind of significance from it is to run the risk of losing one's way in the inexplicable. It is better just to accept the strangeness, without too much questioning. Joi-wind is no more worthy of admiration than any other inhabitant of Arcturus, notwithstanding the pretty name she bears.

*The metamorphoses*

*A Voyage to Arcturus* begins with the description of a psychic phenomenon. In the course of a spiritualistic séance, a medium succeeds in
creating a human form; a cloud that is slightly luminous turns into a
young man. This episode sets the tone of the book, and serves as an
introduction to Tormance. We enter a universe of metamorphoses.

From the time of his arrival on Arcturus, Maskull notices that he
is no longer the same man. Arcturus has contaminated him. His
blood has become almost white. In the middle of his forehead, a
kind of ear has grown. From each side of his neck, there is a
protuberance.

At the outset, Arcturus seems idyllic. Very soon, however, it
becomes evident that this world is not as uniform as it might seem.
Physically, the beings differ from one region of Arcturus to another.
The metamorphoses continue. On the second day, the 'breve' has
become a 'sorb', a third eye. The tentacle is extended to form an
arm. While he follows his route, Maskull sees his own physique
constantly being transformed. Soon, it is a membrane which grows
in the middle of his forehead, and then it is a new pair of eyes. One
day, after having walked in a stream, through water that emits an
unknown energy, he puts his hand to his forehead, and discovers
four pairs of eyes.[19]

The marvels of *A Voyage to Arcturus* do not end there. The animals,
the landscape and the events all contribute to confuse the protagonist. Fabulous animals have always been linked with man's
history. From the Bible to Maupassant, the panorama is vast. Swift
has his Yahoos, the Bible its Behemoth, and Flaubert his Sadhuzac.
*A Voyage to Arcturus* also contains its fabulous array of beasts; a horse
and a dog, each with five legs (pages 141 and 165), enormous
'insects' with an iron shell and 'jaws like scimitars' (pages 101–102).
The most remarkable of all these animals are the 'shrowks'. Let us
leave to Lindsay the pleasure of presenting them to us. 'They were
not birds, but creatures with long, snake-like bodies, and ten rep-
tilian legs apiece, terminating in fins which acted as wings. The
bodies were of bright blue, the legs and fins were yellow' (page 84).
It should be added that these beasts, many feet in height, are
covered with scales, and suck the blood of their victims; only then
do we have some idea of these monsters.

Strange Arcturus! One would never finish describing all the
unusual events. Here, the trees live, and become animated. Lewis

Carroll's Alice asked whether bats eat cats. In Arcturus, cats no longer imprison mice; they are themselves prisoners of the trees (page 116). Plants whirl around (page 51). As with Swift, islands float and drift in the sky (page 87). Everywhere, strange beings appear and disappear before our eyes, for no apparent reason. Lindsay defies logic and plausibility, spontaneously introducing avalanches, streams, vegetation, gravitation and procreation. What metamorphoses! Lindsay sets about multiplying them. From one stage of the journey to the next, the reader travels through lands beyond human imagination. Between men, animals and plants, boundaries no longer exist, and the novelist becomes, like Crystalman, the father of strange hybrids, and the creator of shapes.

Invention is not enough. There are numerous readers who cannot help seeing, in the best works of fantasy literature, a gratuitous game. Invention can only be the alibi for the art. David Lindsay does not always avoid this danger. *A Voyage to Arcturus* contains numerous episodes that seem justified only by the desire to astonish. It would have been wrong, however, to stop at this primary standard of invention.

One of the most striking features of the novel is the transformation of Maskull's bodily organs. This mutation is not only surprising, but also charged with meaning. The first two episodes of the quest on the new star must be compared. Considered separately, they have no other value than their strangeness. Taken side by side, however, they function as counter-weights, with Joiwind's kindness balancing the harshness, and indeed cruelty, of Oceaxe. The change from one scene to the other is accompanied by an overthrow of philosophies. The transformation of the organs justifies, and accentuates, the evolution of philosophies, introducing into the book the conception of relativity. When Maskull arrives at Sant, one of the regions of Arcturus, his body is transformed to the point at which it resembles the physique of the people of the country. On his forehead, he has two membranes called 'probes', which serve him as a kind of pass through 'the gates opening into a new world' (page 118). The old organs are destroyed, while an ideological upheaval occurs to parallel the physical mutation. The preceding organ served to register harmony between man and the outside world, reacting to pleasure and sorrow. Once this organ is destroyed, the function disappears. Pleasure and sorrow matter little. A new code of values is presented to us, this one being based upon duty (pages 119–120).

Another character arriving on the scene, Catice, loses no time at all in referring to the point. 'With this stone I strike out one of your probes. When you have but one, you will see with me, and you will recollect with Spadevil' (page 127). In fact, Maskull rejects the values preached by Spadevil, and becomes a disciple of Catice. The new creed may be summarised by the words 'Do not fear change and destruction, but laughter and joy' (page 130). In *A Voyage to Arcturus*, there is an alchemy of the senses.

The novelist's imagination applies itself to philosophy in order to attack accepted ideas. Many are the episodes in the novel which, by virtue of their incongruity, disturb complacence, conservatism and accepted ideas. Few amongst us pity the mouse for being the plaything of the cat before being devoured, but who would not be shocked, like Maskull, that worthy representative of the human race wandering in strange lands, when the cat, by a reversal of fate, becomes the prisoner of the branches of a 'living' tree, and is shaken about, without respite, until death ensues? (page 116). Finally, what can one say of this man transformed into a plant at the will of a more powerful enemy, and who slowly takes root amid general indifference? (page 92). That could only be a practical joke, thinks Maskull, but, alas, no. One of the characters even offers a justification, in the face of which the reader feels nonplussed. 'It's you, Maskull, who have peculiar ideas. You rave about the beauty of flowers and trees; you think them divine, but when it's a question of taking on this divine, fresh, pure, enchanting loveliness yourself, in your own person, it immediately becomes a cruel and wicked degradation. Here we have a strange riddle, in my opinion' (page 94).

What is astonishing is not so much the invention in itself as the feat of skill of a writer who succeeds in putting his imagination in the service of his beliefs. Even incidents that are seemingly incoherent fit into the overall conceptual framework. The appearance of new organs is confusing. It should not be seen as a game in which the author indulges, but rather as the affirmation of a new mode of life by his characters. Each organic transformation bears witness to a change in the significance of life. This artificial Paradise that is Arcturus knows neither order nor sensual pleasure, as it is the domain of permanent mutation. To change the organ is, to a large extent, to change life. At each modification of his body, Maskull abandons a part of himself; that little spark of fire which makes him a Promethean hero (pages 58, 123, 155), engaged in a quest whose outcome he foresees far from clearly, but of which he senses the nobility. The metamorphosis is degradation, and loss of humanity. It is, as Pierre Brunel wrote, 'felt like an impoverishment of the human being'.[20]

The discovery of each region of Tormance, with all the upheavals that accompany it, is a new contamination of the Promethean hero. As soon as he arrives on this new star, Maskull must submit himself to an initiation rite, which makes him a member of the brotherhood of the friends of Crystalman. With a knife, Joiwind makes a cut, in one of her arms and one of Maskull's. Then, placing the two wounds one upon the other, she exchanges the blood (page 47). It certainly operates as a contamination, as we are shown in a later episode. When Maskull is 'constrained' to kill Digrung, a brother of Joiwind, the family blood that he now has in him serves to torment him, and to remind him of his crime (pages 106–107). According to the law of relativity between the visible and the invisible, each organic transformation is a spiritual degradation, and marks the progressive penetration of the stranger into the world of Crystalman. The creation of new forms is nothing but the subconscious desire to resemble Crystalman, so the author tells us.[21]

## THE CHARACTERS

There are unquestionably very few novels whose principal character, at the end of the book, is so unidentifiable. Where does Maskull come from? What does he do? Who is he? All these questions remain, to a large extent, unanswered. He lands in the middle of a spiritualistic séance, invited at the last minute by a lady who admits knowing nothing more than his name (page 18). Of all the characters that Lindsay introduces at the beginning of the book, only three will reappear, and these are the very three that nobody had expected, Maskull, Nightspore and Krag. The others are quickly forgotten.

Of Maskull, the reader has, at first, a physical portrait. Is he human, this individual whom the author presents to us as a 'kind of giant, but of broader and more robust physique than most giants'? (page 20). Bearded, strongly-built, with coarse features, he recalls the primitive beings so often encountered in Scandinavian tales, giants or Gods, in the imaginary exploits that David Lindsay knew so well. To a small child encountered on the road, Maskull would represent the very ideal of virility.[22]

We know nothing of his past. He scarcely mentions it, except to assert that he has no professional, or family, commitment to keep him on Earth. He seems to live aside from a world which gives him little satisfaction, and which he ends by leaving at the first opportunity, without even trying to explain his departure. In the society of the time, he is an 'invisible man', whose absence is not noticed.

The psychological picture seems no less superficial than the physical one. Only a few characteristics stand out. Maskull presents himself as 'a simple man', with no great ambitions (page 71). He does not set out with the object of returning with great revelations. He is drawn to this adventure because there is nothing to hold him on earth. From the beginning to the end of the novel, he never stops asking himself what is happening to him. He submits to events rather than provoking them. He has an inherent innocence that ill prepares him for the discovery of Tormance, and which certain of his prejudices do not succeed in destroying (page 173). He has sound common sense, which does not prevent him from being duped on many occasions. As a general rule, Maskull does not allow himself to be swayed by sentiment. He listens, questions and observes, but reveals little of himself. No doubt, there can be seen, behind this wall of silence, the defence mechanism of a man well aware of his own weaknesses. 'Now you understand the sort of man I am', he says to Sullenbode. 'Much brutality, more weakness, scant pity for anyone' (page 219).

Maskull is first presented as being accompanied by Nightspore. These two characters are linked, although the relationship is not apparent at the time of departure. Nightspore disappears immediately upon arrival in Tormance. He will be heard of no more until the last pages of the book. Nevertheless, Nightspore is not a secondary character. It is worth remembering the title that Lindsay originally chose for his novel, 'Nightspore in Tormance'.

As a companion for Maskull, Nightspore could scarcely be more different. While Maskull shows interest in the medium's metaphysical experiments, Nightspore, for his part, turns his back, hides his head in his hands, and bites his nails impatiently, as if ashamed to witness such a spectacle (page 22). If Maskull passes easily for the man in the street, Nightspore is an 'aristocrat of the universe' (page 40).

Indeed, Nightspore is Maskull's second self, his *spiritual* double.

One exists only because he has a body. The other exists only because he has a soul. Nightspore, Lindsay tells us, is 'consumed by an intense spiritual hunger' (page 21), so devouring that he always seems to be living elsewhere, deep in thought of which he alone is aware. He, too, though for different reasons from Maskull, is an 'invisible man', since, *materially*, he should not exist, and so he disappears. One of the objects of the quest on Arcturus is the rediscovery of Nightspore. The physical man, Maskull, sets out to discover his soul.

This is certainly a laborious quest, but how easy compared with what must be the meeting of the body and the soul. Between the two, no union is possible. One or the other must disintegrate. Nightspore, craving for the ideal, is 'like a hungry caged animal' (page 42), the prisoner of man, and his triviality. When Maskull, with one sacrifice after another, has fashioned his own soul, and is prepared to die for it, it is his body which becomes a prison.[23] The body is only the prelude to the soul. When Nightspore reappears, it is Maskull who disappears. 'Where's Nightspore?' asks Maskull, to which Krag replies 'You are Nightspore' (page 240).

There remains a third character, Krag, in many respects the mediator between Nightspore and Maskull. Krag is the instigator of the journey. It is he who persuades Maskull to accompany him. Nightspore is content to follow, although well aware of the object, unlike Maskull. Krag and Nightspore know more about it than they say. There is a complicity between them that Maskull guesses. 'I'm beginning to regard you as a second Krag', says Maskull to Nightspore (page 34).

Of all the characters in the book, Krag is the most vividly portrayed. Physically, he does not pass unnoticed, with his yellowed teeth, hairy chest and bronzed skin resembling an animal. He snores noisily. His voice is shrill and disagreeable. He introduces himself to people with heavy slaps on the back. Krag is irritating. He is the intruder of whom one would like to be rid discreetly. However, we must not trust appearances too much. Krag is not one of those louts in whom the lack of good manners means stupidity. This man, small in stature, has a head well above average size (page 23). He has a ready repartee, and is a past master in the art of using irony. He teases deliberately, and aggravates. His temperament is 'a mixture of sagacity, brutality, and humour' (page 23).

So much for the picture of this astonishing man. For the reader, the real Krag remains unknown for a long time. Like Crystalman, Krag has a gift for ubiquity.[24] He is everywhere at once. Who is he, then, in the last analysis? The book offers several kinds of answers, many of which, far from being of any real assistance, merely add to the confusion. Krag is first presented to us as enemy number one, and then as the kill-joy.[25] One must wait until the last page of the book to discover his real identity. Having striven to present himself as a devil, he turns out to be none other than Surtur, the representative of the ideal Sublime, and the advocate of suffering. Krag can only be the Devil, whom one discovers through making a cult of pleasure (page 228). Krag remains a kill-joy from first to last, but he does so in order to show that life is not one long round of pleasure. He reminds Maskull that, without suffering, without effort, without ugliness, even without death, grandeur cannot exist. From that time, everything becomes clear. Each episode appears in a new light. One can better understand the physical repugnance of the character, his bantering, and even the feeling of pain which overcomes Maskull each time Krag touches his arm.[26]

## THE QUEST

### The journey

Before becoming a quest, Maskull's adventures are a journey. We have described the journey in space. When the star, Arcturus, is reached, the journey does not end there. It merely begins. In fact, the entire book is made up of false starts. Scarcely has Maskull reached one point of Arcturus than some incident or disappointment impels him to set off once more. If the book really has an ending, that does not mean that the quest itself is over. The end is the signal of the start of a new crusade. Just like those wheels in perpetual motion, the book seems to return to its point of departure.

Before being a quest *for* something, *A Voyage to Arcturus* is a long, blind journey. It becomes a crusade only in the later pages of the book, when the enemy, hitherto unknown and invisible, appears. It is no doubt because they have no precise object that Maskull's wanderings closely match the configurations of the terrain. There scarcely exists any region of Arcturus which, to make clearer the details of its ideology and morality, is not distinguishable by its topography.

Alone in an unknown world, Maskull is confronted by an infinite landscape. Meeting each new feature assumes the importance of a discovery for him. Often, too, he is guided more by the terrain than by people he meets. He makes a rule always to walk in a northerly direction.[27] The existence of a mountain that is strangely tall, at the edge of a scarlet desert, is, in itself, almost an invitation to the traveller. Often, Maskull cannot resist the strange fascination that these mountains exercise upon him, as if such obstacles exist only to be overcome.

Between the man and the landscape, an affinity exists. The map of Arcturus is not neutral, not just intended to accentuate the 'exotic fantasy', as Todorov expressed it. Poolingdred, for instance, is characterised by the extent of its plain, its meagre vegetation, and the contours made by its 'cup-shaped mountains'. The softness of its features is matched by a philosophy of life based upon kindness and generosity. Quite different is Ifdawn. The mountain is high and jagged, like a barricade. The inhabitants of Ifdawn have inherited something of the hardness of their landscape; they are aggressive and ruthless. For them, only force counts. The beauty and generosity of the inhabitants of Poolingdred strikes them as being ridiculous. As Oceaxe says, 'That's typical of Ifdawn. Nature is all hammer blows with us; nothing soft and gradual' (page 82).

Once a place of residence is assigned to a people, the latter are already well-defined. Threal is 'a land of mystics' (page 143). Sant is a man's country. Polecrab knows, from one look at Maskull, that he has passed through Ifdawn, as he recognises in him the tragic expression of the inhabitants of that region (page 143). In the structured world of Arcturus, to leave one's country is tantamount to destroying a part of oneself, and often risking death. To pass through Ifdawn without a 'sorb' is simply to commit suicide (page 76). Tydomin cannot go to Sant as women are forbidden there. When Gleameil decides to leave for the island of Swaylone, she stresses that she will never return.

This journey in Arcturus is manifestly not an excursion for blasé tourists. It would be, for a critic, a never-ending task to count all the mountains and precipices encountered. On at least two occasions, Maskull's life is threatened by earthquakes. He crosses swamps, skirts precipices, and goes underground.

In all these wanderings, the most persistent image is that of the precipice. It is encountered even before leaving Earth, when Maskull and Nightspore set out to discover the 'Gap of Sorgie', in

Scotland (pages 35 and 36). From all the evidence, Arcturus is the
extension of the Gap of Sorgie.[28] Death lies in wait for the traveller
at every step. The whole of Arcturus resembles 'Shaping's Causeway', a crest of some twenty miles in length, but only about four
inches in width, and so narrow that two people cannot pass through
together, one having to throw himself into the void to allow the
other to pass. It is difficult not to see, behind this ruthless law, an
allusion to Maskull's adventures. He, too, skirts precipices, and
meets characters on the way who try to seduce him, and stop him,
in order to fling him into the void afterwards. On several occasions,
Maskull must avoid involvement with sirens, such as the kindly
Joiwind, the passionate Sullenbode, and the enchanting Gangnet.

### Reasons for the voyage

*A Voyage to Arcturus* ends with the announcement of a struggle, in
cosmic dimensions, between Good and Evil. Maskull has become
the hero of this struggle, whereas, at the time of departure, he was
little prepared for it. He allowed himself to be taken off on this
adventure, not against his will, but without knowing exactly why.
He admits this to Joiwind, when she tries to find out the reason for
his presence on the star, Arcturus. 'Will you think it foolish if I say I
hardly know? I came with those two men. Perhaps I was attracted
by curiosity, or perhaps it was the love of adventure' (page 48).

Curiosity and love of adventure fail to conceal a further reason,
which was the deep dissatisfaction that Maskull felt with contemporary reality. From one allusion to another, a picture emerges
of a man ill at ease in the society of the period, and who seeks, in
adventure, a way of escape. It seems scarcely necessary to stress that
this picture also fits, to a very large extent, the author himself. 'Why
did you come here?' Maskull is asked once again, at the end of the
journey, to which question he replies 'To meet with new experiences, perhaps. The old ones no longer interested me' (page
218). Elsewhere, he denounces the vulgarity of the modern world[29]
the gregarious instinct of men, and their conformity.[30] Maskull fits
very well into Lindsay's gallery of heroes, which includes Nicholas
Cabot, Saltfleet and Hugh Drapier. The Earth, seen from a distance
of millions of miles, appears no more attractive for that. Whether
the words are those of Maskull or Nicholas Cabot, the condemnation is identical. The Earth is 'small, and overcrowded with
men and women. With all those people, confusion would result but

for orderly laws, and therefore the laws are of iron. As adventure
would be impossible without encroaching on these laws, there is no
longer any spirit of adventure among the Earthmen. Everything is
safe, vulgar and completed' (page 218). Dissatisfaction impels the
journey. If adventure is impossible, or forbidden, on Earth, it must
be sought outside Earth. Such seems to be the moral of *A Voyage to
Arcturus*. The space-craft constantly pushes back the frontiers of
possibility.

Maskull is certainly a rebel, but with certain qualifications. He is
no theorist of permanent revolution, nor even of the philosophy of
the absurd. He proclaims neither his struggle nor his disgust. A giant
in stature, he remains, to some extent, a child in spirit.[31] He is a false
pessimist or, put another way, naive. Throughout his adventures,
Maskull never ceases to repeat that he understands nothing that is
happening to him. He is often the plaything of men and events.

Maskull knows scarcely anything of the real object of the journey.
At the time of departure, Krag gives him enough information to
arouse his curiosity, though refraining from revealing everything to
him. When Maskull questions him, he resorts to evasions, or to
answers that are incomprehensible at this stage of the adventure.
Poor Maskull no longer knows if he is the victim of a practical joker
or the protagonist of a suspense novel. The disappearance of his
travelling companions increases his perplexity. He constantly repeats that he would like to know who are these characters around
him.

Maskull is not the only victim of Krag's machinations. The reader
is exposed to them just as often as the hero. Behind this presentation,
there must be seen the author's intentions of deliberate ambiguity.
The whole interest of the quest lies in the ignorance of the hero. It
would have been easy to warn the traveller, at the time of departure, by revealing to him the manoeuvres of Crystalman; in short, to
arm him for his adventures. The result, however, would have been
completely different. Lindsay's method is much more subtle, since it
consists of abruptly plunging an ingenuous individual into an
unknown, and dangerous, world, whilst striving to obscure the
divisions between Good and Evil. When Maskull wonders why
nobody helps him to discover the meaning of his adventures, he fails
to realise that his questioning already constitutes a kind of answer,
inasmuch as the answer can only come from himself. That is what
explains the disappearance of Krag. That is why, in the episode

entitled 'Barey', Krag remains aside, refusing to intervene between Maskull and Crystalman.

## The significance of the quest

*A Voyage to Arcturus* is a novel about initiation and submission to ordeal. To be in any sense valid, the values of this ordered philosophy must emerge from individual experience. It is in contact with the world that the individual becomes enriched. Even if he does not see the object of his adventures very clearly, Maskull understands that this journey is not useless, and that it undoubtedly has a hidden meaning. He remembers the lessons passed on to him by those he meets, such as the story of the man called Broodviol, who 'became wise by making up his mind never to ask questions, but to find things out for himself' (page 150). Is this not the basis of all philosophy? For Plato, amongst others, reality was not a given fact, and only a long and arduous path could lead to its attainment. In this lies the superiority of Maskull over so many others in search of truth. A few days in Arcturus would have sufficed for Maskull to become the holder of a measure of wisdom, albeit minute, but enough already to have enabled him to set about philosophising upon life and the transcendent world. Communication with the beyond, he discovered, could never be the object of a profession. To those who questioned him on his wisdom, he replied 'It has sprung together somehow; from inspiration, from experience, from conversation with the wise men of your planet. Every hour it grows truer for me and takes a definite shape' (page 193).

It is at the end of the initial day passed on the new star that Maskull, for the first time, has the intuition that his presence has significance. A man suddenly appears in his path, declaring himself to be Surtur, the instigator of the adventure and calls upon Maskull to put himself at his service. 'His brain was all dark and confused, but one idea was already beginning to stand out from the rest; huge, shapeless and grand, like the growing image in the soul of a creative artist; the staggering thought that he was a man of destiny. The more he reflected upon all that had occurred since his arrival in this new world, and even before leaving Earth, the clearer and more indisputable it became, that he could not be here for his own purposes, but must be here for an end, but what that end was, he could not imagine' (page 73).

Maskull's intuition becomes reinforced by the encounters he has.

The first characters are of little significance. On the contrary, they try to keep him amongst them, to seduce him, and to 'absorb' him. The following characters, on the other hand, are, in a sense, closer to him, to the extent that they, too, are searching for something. Between them and Maskull, there is achieved a unity of purpose, which explains why, quite often, these characters are not just people he meets, but also travelling companions. Even if their quests differ, they have something in common. This is sufficient to bring them together. Gleameil is not going, like Maskull, to a meeting with the Sublime, but this does not hinder her decision to leave her husband and children, in order to set out on the adventure that draws her to Maskull.[32]

Generally speaking, the influence exercised upon Maskull by the inhabitants of Arcturus is more disastrous than positive. The majority of them try to mislead rather than guide him. It is important to note that the realisation of having been entrusted with a mission comes to Maskull, not so much through contact with people he meets, but rather through the revelations of transcendental nature, apparitions and intuitions.

There are two incidents in *A Voyage to Arcturus* which, in themselves, define Maskull's quest. The first is the sudden appearance of Surtur–Krag already mentioned. The second, contained in Chapter 13, is still more important. Once again, a sudden appearance upsets all the given data, with the vision of three characters, Krag, Nightspore and Maskull himself, marching in determined step, straight ahead, to the sound of an invisible drum. To appreciate the importance of this episode, it is enough to remember that it occurs exactly in the middle of Maskull's adventures in Tormance. This marks the end of the first part of the wandering. Never has the quest seemed more vain to him. Never has he been so discouraged. 'What was this nightmare journey for, and would it continue in the same way?' (page 132). It is, however, at the very depth of his despair that the truth manifests itself.

It is no mere chance that, at this moment, Maskull finds himself in a forest; a closed place of darkness, where the trees and the roots are such barriers and obstacles to the path of the wanderer. Above all, it is a place without horizons, where the traveller loses himself, and despairs of again seeing light.[33] Crossing the forest marks one of the most dramatic moments in Maskull's quest. After having spent several days on Arcturus, Maskull still does not know the reason for his presence on the star. At the end of his tether, having scarcely eaten since his arrival, disturbed in his moral convictions by the murders he has committed, Maskull has reached the limits of his endurance. He has just considered committing suicide, in order to put an end to his anguish (page 129).

In David Lindsay's writing, however, there is no death which is not, to some extent, a prelude to birth and renaissance. The nightmare ends in illumination. The forest, a place of death, is also a place of life and birth (page 129). Dark and closed upon itself, the forest easily becomes a symbol of the maternal uterus, like the cave or the house. One can see in the very name of this forest, *Wombflash*, a direct allusion to birth, and to the re-birth of Maskull. The crossing of the Wombflash forest constitutes a rejuvenation for him, of which he will be very conscious. 'Since I've come out of that forest ... a change has come over me', he says (page 144). The narration itself suggests the pain of the birth. 'Incapable of enduring such shocks', Maskull loses consciousness.

What does this mean? Before leaving this forest, Maskull is literally in the dark. He has only the vaguest ideas about the significance of Tormance, and the rôle that he has been given to play. Then comes the revelation; the meeting with the three marchers. Immediately, some of his illusions are dispelled. When he leaves the forest, he recognises, for the first time, that his adventures are linked to one Surtur, still scarcely known, but whose name has already been mentioned several times. Finally, to mark more clearly his rejuvenation, Maskull makes this assertion for the rest of his adventures. 'This world of yours, and perhaps of mine too, for that matter, doesn't give me the slightest impression of a dream, or an illusion, or anything of that sort. I know it's really here at this moment, and it's exactly as we're seeing it, you and I. Yet it's false. It's false in this sense, Polecrab. Side by side with it another world exists, and that other world is the true one, and this one is false and deceitful, to the very core' (page 145).

In the course of his journey, Maskull is guided by a mysterious beating of drums. He hears it for the first time on the occasion of the visit he pays to the Gap of Sorgie, before the departure for Arcturus. The author even suggests that the difficult, and perilous, walk to this cliff has been solely designed for the purpose of hearing this mysterious sound, which seemed 'to belong to a different world' (page 36). Before leaving the edge of the Gap, Nightspore tells his companion that it is possible that he will hear this sound elsewhere, and then advises him that he should 'try always to hear it more and more distinctly'. Nightspore's prediction proves correct, since, on the star Arcturus, the same noise is heard,[34] consisting of four beats, with the third one slightly more stressed than the others.

Just as previously, this sound seems to emanate from somewhere other than the everyday world,[35] often originating from the depths of a lake.[36] Only at the end of the novel will the reader know that the drumbeat represents the call of the Ideal Sublime. It guides Maskull towards the goal of his quest, and, at the same time, gives a cadence to his progress with ever-increasing frequency and force, until becoming, in the end, an uninterrupted roll of drums. From chapter to chapter, this roll of drums becomes more and more distinct. Maskull eventually recognises two different rhythms, one being that of a march, and the other of a waltz (page 243). The sound, Lindsay tells us, comes from Muspel, but the drumbeat is a distortion caused by the transit of Crystalman through the universe. The roll of drums is the call of the Sublime world, but is degraded by conflict with the vulgar world (page 241).

As David Lindsay indicates, the noise of the drum exists outside man, but is also an emanation from him. In the Wombflash forest episode, there is a synchronisation of Maskull's heartbeats with the roll of the drum (page 132). This identification is taken up again at the end of the book, when Krag appears, an enormous hammer in his hand, in the act of striking a red spot. 'Presently Maskull made out that these sounds were the familiar drum beats. "What are you doing, Krag?" he asked. "Beating on your heart, Maskull", was his grinning response' (page 239). In other words, the Ideal Sublime exists *in us*, and is carried by us. In the last analysis, the Ideal is the creation of the individual, and the sound of the drum is an echo of man's heart.

### A mythical quest

The interest of the journey in Arcturus goes far beyond the bizarre walk into another country. As Maskull emphasises,[37] it is not a trip organised for tourists. Maskull loses no time in divesting himself of the image of Mr Everyman. He becomes Prometheus, the artful ancestor of the human race who, for the benefit of everyone, does not hesitate to defy the Gods. Panawe recalls the myth of Prometheus, when he tries to discover the meaning of the name

'Maskull'. '"Has there been a man in your world who stole something from the Maker of the universe, in order to ennoble his fellow-creatures?" "There is such a myth. The hero's name was Prometheus." "Well, you seem to be identified in my mind with that action, but what it all means I can't say, Maskull."' (page 58).

The sacred fire that Maskull has come to seek in Arcturus is Muspel, the first sign of what will become the Sublime in Lindsay's personal philosophy. The choice came quite naturally to his mind since, in the Nordic sagas, Muspel denotes the kingdom of fire whose heat, according to legend, is the source of the Creation of the world.[38] Before the Creation, there were only two regions, Muspel and Niflheim, the latter being the province of darkness, ice and fog.

In *A Voyage to Arcturus*, the two myths of Muspel and Prometheus are closely linked. Allusions to the Promethean quest are numerous, but Maskull's adventures are clearly distinguishable from the traditional myth. The 'theft' of the sacred fire does not really exist in Lindsay's book. Surtur, the holder of the fire, is closely connected with Maskull's quest, since he is the instigator of it. One can talk of theft only in the sense that Crystalman opposes Maskull's efforts. There remains, however, the mission which has been assigned to Maskull of returning to Earth for the purpose of bringing the truth to mankind, and to combat Crystalman.

Upon the myths of Prometheus and Muspel, there are superimposed allusions to Christianity. The religious implications in *A Voyage to Arcturus* are self-evident.[39] One finds there the dichotomy so dear to Christian-inspired literature. Between Good and Evil, Surtur and Crystalman, there are intermediaries, but that does nothing to alter the fundamental struggle. Minor ambiguities must not conceal membership of one or other camp. Good makes no concession, so strong can be the temptation to assimilate love or beauty.

Maskull's quest is essentially a religious one, even if it is very clearly distinguishable from all the traditional religions. Maskull scarcely notices this in the course of the journey, much less at the beginning, when he meets Joiwind. Evidence of this is provided by his astonishment when Joiwind, in order to describe Tormance to him, refers to her God. 'What does all this mean, Joiwind? Why speak of God?' One does not leave Earth in order to escape to God, since, in Tormance, nothings exists detached from its creator. Even

before setting foot on the new star, Maskull knows its name, which is
the world of Crystalman.

Several of the inhabitants of Arcturus have anxieties of a religious
order. Amongst these, mention should be made of Spadevil, an
austere preacher, who, at the end of a long period of meditation and
reflection in the desert, travels through the country. His language,
his aphorisms, the parables with which he embellishes his speeches,
reveal him to be an apostle of duty. He finds, in Maskull and
Tydomin, his first 'witnesses and followers' (page 118). Also worthy
of mention is Leehallfae, last representative of a dying race, whose
only worry is never to have found her creator (page 175). Finally,
there is Corpang, whose entire life has been devoted to 'never-
ending prayers and mortifications', in the hope of reaching God
(page 194).

Maskull's quest is different. It is just as mystical, but less feverish
and anxious. For him, 'to hear voices perhaps can't be made a
profession'. One must deserve grace, and, for that matter, submit to
rites of initiation, purification and penance. Maskull goes through
each of these stages. First of all, he sets off unarmed and stark naked.
In the new world, man arrives naked, clothes having been left on
Earth (page 42). A knife-cut in the back serves as a passport to
Muspel, being the introduction to pain, without which the quest
cannot succeed. The wound that Krag inflicts upon Maskull functions as an initiation to the Ministry of Pain. Next, the new stage of
the introduction of the hero to the Sublime is the oath of allegiance.
This is the meaning that must be attached to the surprising meeting
with Surtur (page 73). 'It is necessary for you to serve me', Surtur
tells him. 'You are my servant and helper.' To this, Maskull replies
'I shall not fail.' The oath given, Surtur disappears into the sky.

The penance is encountered at every stage. Lindsay is very
familiar with John Bunyan's *The Pilgrim's Progress*. Perhaps he was
inspired by it. Parallels are not lacking between Bunyan's hero,
Christian, and Maskull. The straight and narrow path of the Gospel
certainly exists in Lindsay, too.[40] In order to attain it, Lindsay
invents a route strewn with pitfalls, and as difficult as Christian's,
consisting of marshes, pain, danger, peril, nakedness, dragons, darkness and death. Only the sword and the lions are missing from the
dangers that confronted Bunyan's pilgrim.[41] Dreamsinter is the
Narrator from Bunyan's book, looming up at the right moment to
guide the wandering pilgrim. Like Christian before him, Maskull

discovers the skeletons of other travellers who had died before achieving the object of their quest.

To say that Maskull resists temptation would be an exaggeration. Quite often, he falls headlong into the traps set for him. By the time he realises this, it is too late. In spite of all these pitfalls, however, he never ceases to advance, which is a victory in itself. Maskull is no better, and no worse, than anyone else, but is simply confronted by an enemy who is stronger, and more cunning. Lindsay shows this clearly. Maskull, like so many others before him, is the victim of Crystalman. His idealism does not withstand the traps set for him. With or without extenuating circumstances, Maskull has committed several murders. Each of them has marked a regression, and a disgrace. Krag will reproach him for having delayed on the way, and for not having followed Surtur with sufficient determination. When the hour of judgment arrives, Maskull is not spared. His body is delivered to Lucifer–Crystalman, but his soul is saved. 'Maskull was his, Crystalman's, but Nightspore is mine', Krag will say (page 240).

Muspel transcends life, whilst Crystalman *is* life. That is why Maskull cannot attain this ideal in his lifetime. This death is a deliverance. Maskull is reunited with his travelling companion, Nightspore, and then becomes obliterated in front of him. *A Voyage to Arcturus* is a metaphysical journey. Starting out with the body, it ends with the discovery of the soul. The body itself is no more than an instrument that is destined to be utilised, and then broken. Each step brings Maskull nearer to his own death. The reader guesses this. It is necessary, and has been foretold several times.

### The world of Crystalman

The lord and master of Arcturus is Crystalman. This star belongs to him. He has made it in his image of a man of crystal. Crystal is perhaps also Christ; a new-style Christ who would have exchanged humility for arrogance, and the suffering freely accepted for an unrestrained search for happiness. Whether he be God the Father or God the Son, Crystalman has his kingdom, which is an almost exact copy of the world of Genesis. It is erroneous to say that no churches nor real religious symbols are to be seen.[42] On the contrary, an attentive reader is able to detect a dense thread of symbols which unite to form a parody of Christianity.

Crystalman is an usurping God. He knows better than anyone the basic elements of propaganda. The veneration with which his subjects surround him is itself proof of the efficacy of his performance. Tormance has its religious rites, like all regions where fidelity dominates. If there is no church, this is because everything there is 'natural'. Prehistoric man had no need of a temple in which to worship. A cave was enough for him. There are few trees in Tormance, but then the most pitiful shrub is a miracle, and its site a sacred place. The Arcturus tree with 'translucent and crystal leaves' is a shrine dedicated to Crystalman, and the totem of primitive people. For a spring to originate at the foot of this tree is to add one marvel to another. The imagination races, and builds cathedrals. 'Shaping's Well' is one of these sanctuaries of Arcturus, where Crystalman's devotees assemble to invoke their God (page 53). Maskull's adventures begin with a prayer addressed to Crystalman, at which he steals away most adroitly, on the pretext of his impurity.

There is no church without sacred water. The source is there at the foot of the tree, also crystalline, in the image of the God that it represents. This water gushes forth to the four corners of Arcturus. It flows, spreads and stagnates. It is called 'gnawl water', and must be drunk before prayer. From Lusion Plain to Barey, Maskull's walk follows the course of a stream, sometimes invisible, but which soon reappears in the form of a fountain, a lake, the sea or a river. Still more curious is the effect produced by the gnawl water upon Maskull. Sometimes, the water acts upon his senses to intoxicate him, as if Tormance did not signify a land of torments but delights. Sometimes, in contact with the water, he receives an electric charge which stimulates him.

This sacred water with astonishing properties, therefore, is a weapon used by Crystalman. It intoxicates in order the better to deceive. It appears to be a source of life, but the life that it offers is that of Arcturus, which means, in Lindsay's eyes, a certain form of death. The stream, one learns, comes directly from Crystalman's body (page 174). The water transmits to the drinker the characteristics of Crystalman. It transforms, sometimes insidiously, and sometimes brutally, the entire personality, like a powerful drug.[43] Those who live only upon this water have already reached the point of no return, and are prisoners of Crystalman.

What, then, is the significance of Crystalman? At the root of the book, there are a few values which Lindsay means to condemn, such

as beauty, art, love, morality and the will to live. The inhabitants of
Arcturus are, in varying degree, defenders of these values. Crystalman, for his part, gives them his guarantee. He is both their author
and their sponsor.

The interest of the author's vision lies particularly in its masterly
presentation. By brusquely thrusting an ingenuous individual into a
sordid world, the author strived to mix Good and Evil, refusing to
intervene in aid either of his hero or the reader. Before the final
outcome, when all is revealed, there is a deliberate ambiguity.

At the outset, the proposition is one of absolute clarity. 'Good and
evil in the world don't originate from nothing. God and Devil must
exist, and we should pray to the one, and fight the other.' Lindsay's
ability consists of reversing the rôles. Whilst Crystalman is ultimately despicable, according to Lindsay, he is presented to us as a
gracious being. His opposite, Krag, then becomes 'the author of evil
and misery, whom you call Devil'. The confusion of values has been
carefully maintained by the author.[44] Moreover, Krag is as ugly as
Crystalman is attractive. Just as the one is surly, vulgar and brutal,
so the other is refined. The ambiguity is still more accentuated by
the many names behind which Crystalman hides himself. Sometimes
he calls himself Shaping, sometimes Faceny, and sometimes, yet
again, Gangnet. The author's 'explanations' are scarcely more
satisfactory. The economy of detail is sometimes too remarkable not
to be intentional. Elsewhere, the information is false, and, far from
assisting the reader, helps to confuse him even more.[45] Finally, when
the reader expects the truth to be revealed, the character who
withholds it escapes at the last moment, feigning forgetfulness, youth
or some other excuse.[46]

Irony is the favourite weapon of David Lindsay, or saying the
very opposite of what one wishes to convey. Crystalman is the
double of Satan, and so he is presented as a God. One of Maskull's
main preoccupations, during his stay on Arcturus, is to discover the
real identity of Crystalman. Each character that he meets gives him
an answer, often fallacious. At first, he believes that Crystalman is
the God and creator of Tormance, since the inhabitants invoke him
in prayer, and venerate his name. Tight, amicable links unite him
with his subjects. This presentation, however, is far from satisfactory. Crystalman's identity escapes Maskull, just as it eludes the
reader. Are Crystalman and Thire two different names for the same
man? Is Surtur another name for Crystalman? At the beginning of

the novel, hero and reader are plunged into the same uncertainty as to the nature of the world they are entering.

To avoid the truth becoming revealed too soon, David Lindsay has cast his hero in the mould of an ingenuous individual, thus adopting a technique that satirists, ever since Voltaire, have known very well. Maskull never ceases to be enraptured by what he discovers. The world of Joiwind strikes him as being so idyllic that the existence of Evil seems unimaginable in such a setting. It takes all Krag's perseverance for Maskull to recognise in Crystalman the true face of Satan. His initiation is so laborious that, even in the very last pages of the book, he still does not understand Krag's philosophy (page 233). In defence of Maskull, however, it should be added that nothing is done to help him. The disappearance of his travelling companions leaves him to face the mystery alone. For his part, he has little idea what to do on the star Arcturus.

The author himself certainly takes care not to intervene, contenting himself with presenting the many facets of Arcturus with detachment, leaving the reader with the responsibility of forming his own opinion. Each episode, however, brings its own complements and modifications to the initial proposition, according to which Krag is the root of all Evil. The discovery of Ifdawn is a clear warning, coming after the meeting with Joiwind. Goodness is succeeded by cruelty. To-day's truths are to-morrow's heresies. This would seem to be the moral of the tale. Nothing could better indicate the sense of irony than this alternation of extremes.

The structure of the book also increases the ambiguity. The reader is confronted by a 'spatial structure' that is astonishingly modern, and very difficult to puzzle out[47]. Any question remains unresolved until some thirty pages later. The author gives his information only very gradually. Isolated from the overall context, this often means nothing. One has to wait nearly two hundred pages for the egg, at first presented as a symbol of beauty, to become a disgusting, slimy stain. The identity of Krag, the instigator of the journey, is revealed little by little. The sense of irony is so effective that one has to wait until the final pages for the meaning of the adventure to be eventually explained. Krag is none other than Surtur. Both are representatives of redeeming pain.

The star Arcturus, one notices, is not so different from our own planet as might be thought from its position in the sky. Lindsay wanted to show, in an indirect form, life such as it is on Earth. The ultimate judgment that he reaches is categorical. Life is mediocre, vulgar, made up of false pretences and trickery. It is not worthwhile to be alive, unless there exists another world, supernatural and superior, to which it serves as a necessary introduction.

To make the contrast between these two models more obvious, Lindsay has chosen to represent them by two worlds; namely, Tormance, or the world of Crystalman, on the one hand, and Muspel, or the world of Surtur, on the other. The former is the copy of the world in which we live, whilst the latter symbolises a certain ideal. The first reference to the parallel world of Muspel is found in the story of Panawe. One day, in his youth, a certain Slofork made this revelation to him. 'This is Shaping's world. He that is a good child here, knows pleasure, pain and love, and gets his rewards, but there is another world, not Shaping's, and there all this is unknown, and another order of things reigns. That world we call Nothing, but it is not Nothing, but Something.'[48] From that time, this dichotomy is revealed with increasing frequency. It is clear, however, that this parallel world is not perceived in the same way by all the characters on Arcturus. For some, it is a world of grandeur, built on suffering, but, for others, it is a badly-cut object, the very antithesis of the concrete world.

As soon as the existence of this supernatural world has been perceived, albeit confusedly, life becomes an illusion, a dream and a fraud. Lindsay employs many times the concepts of reality and unreality in order to depict this crisis of conscience. The surrounding world exists; it is real, and can be touched. It can even destroy, but, at the same time, it does not exist, inasmuch as the real world is elsewhere. 'Reality and falseness are two words for the same thing', writes Lindsay (page 145).

Pursuing his analysis, he shows that our everyday world is a false copy of the ideal world. The master down here, Crystalman, is but an usurper, he repeats. Aware of this shortcoming, Crystalman does everything in his power to conceal from men's eyes the existence of the other world, and to portray himself as the real creator of the universe.

This is the kind of language which was employed, over the centuries, by the Gnostics, those men classed as heretics by the Christian Church because of their claim to secret, wonderful knowledge.[49] What part does Gnosticism play in Lindsay's thinking? It is difficult to determine, as its ramifications extend into numerous systems of associated thought. The convergence, however, is clear enough. How can one fail to see, in Crystalman, the Prince of Darkness, or evil God, who, nearer to our time, has also inspired Lawrence Durrell?[50] With David Lindsay, one meets the same obsession with the problem of evil, the same feeling of being a stranger in the world, the same search for spirituality, and, converse ly, the same denigration of the body, and everything connected with it, such as pleasure, sexuality and illness. The spark of spiritual fire, imprisoned in the bodily exterior, that Lindsay attributes to every being, seems equally to come in a direct line from Gnosticism.

The ambiguity of Arcturus is not only due to a perverse desire on Lindsay's part to mislead his readers. There is also Crystalman's effort to cloud the issues, and to deceive. Everything is two-sided on the soil of Arcturus. The star is composed of two parts, one yellow and the other blue. Tormance is the inhabited part of Arcturus. It is lit by two suns, Alppain and Branchspell. Two men compete there for pre-eminence, Crystalman and Krag. The creation of Arcturus is consistent with this dichotomy. 'They say that, when the world was born, Krag was born with it, a spirit compounded of those vestiges of Muspel which Shaping did not know how to transform. There-after, nothing has gone right with the world, for he dogs Shaping's footsteps everywhere, and whatever the latter does he undoes. To love, he joins death; to sex, shame; to intellect, madness; to virtue, cruelty; and to fair exteriors, bloody entrails' (page 155).

Tormance is a world of two faces. Appearance ceaselessly clashes with reality, and the interior with the exterior. Between the voice of Oceaxe and her nature, there is a gap. The most beautiful of the beings on Arcturus has a most horribly deformed face at death. Joiwind's kindness is immediately contradicted by the cruelty of Oceaxe and Crimtyphon. Beauty sometimes hides ugliness. Conversely, what seems repugnant at first sight is not so in reality. Krag, for instance, in spite of his complexion, and his yellow teeth, is better than Crystalman. The horse which, from the outside, is so ugly, is not thereby any less a living creature, and is, in fact, an organism of such complexity that it arouses our admiration (page 167). It will take four days of adventure and danger for Maskull to realise the trap set by appearance. 'To-night is like life (...); so lovely above and around us, so foul underfoot' (page 223). After four days of initiation, the fruit of experience is bitter, and there is no longer anything attractive in Arcturus.

The deceit of Crystalman, as we have said, is that of life in general, and not that of any particular country born in David Lindsay's imagination. In *A Voyage to Arcturus*, Lindsay has merely given a dramatic form to philosophical ideas that he has exposed with probably greater clarity in his *Philosophical Notes*. The quotation deserves to be given in its entirety, as it succinctly summarises the thinking of the author. 'One must not regard the world merely as a home of illusions; but as being *rotten* with illusion from top to bottom; not a sound piece anywhere, but all springs, glasses and traps throughout. The most sacred and holy things ought not to be taken for granted; for, if examined attentively, they will be found as hollow and empty as the rest. What is this vast sham? Will, Unity and Individuality, leading to the conceptions God, Art, Science, Eternal Rhythm, Virtue, Nobility, Beauty, Music and Love. Behind this sham world lies the real, tremendous, and awful Muspel-World, which knows neither Will nor Unity nor Individuals; that is to say an inconceivable world' (Number 534).

The first deceit that Lindsay denounces in *A Voyage to Arcturus* is goodness. The character who symbolises it is Joiwind. Her name itself suggests sweetness and grace. She shows Maskull the foundations of the society in which she lives. All men are brothers, and mutual aid is a pleasure. Life is the most precious thing in the world. Plants and animals are, like humans, living beings created by God, by which she means Crystalman. It is accordingly forbidden to eat animals and vegetables. To tear a single leaf from a tree is to inflict a wound. In spite of a few references to the extreme simplicity of Joiwind's doctrine, and to the boredom that such a belief must engender, Maskull is seduced by the goodness of his hostess, and promises to follow her precepts. 'The brotherhood of man is not a fable invented by idealists, but a solid fact', he tells himself (page 61). Lindsay does not denounce Joiwind's ideas directly. He waits for Maskull to leave Joiwind before demonstrating that this cult of goodness is totally impracticable. Subsequent events indicate, in fact, that Joiwind's clan is very isolated. Arcturus is more a world of discord and cruelty than one of fraternity. In Ifdawn, for example, will-power is the natural law. Murder is legitimate there.

Between goodness and will-power, Lindsay has made an attack upon art and beauty. Their representative is none other than

Joiwind's husband, Panawe. Lindsay presents us with a satirical picture of this artist, depicting him as effeminate, with an extremely pale complexion caused by the cloistered life that he leads. 'His hair was white; but again, from vigour, not decay.' Quite by chance, Maskull is present at the production of a 'work of art'; an egg coming out of the artist's ear, like 'an overflowing of beauty', adds Lindsay. Elsewhere, in his *Philosophical Notes*, Lindsay says 'the more gracefulness, the less honesty' (Number 26) and 'a beautiful person is only a living corpse'.[51]

With Spadevil, we reach the heart of the problem. For the first time, pleasure is presented as the basis of existence. Beauty, art and fraternity are accordingly only derivatives of pleasure; the pleasures of contemplating, pleasing, creating, helping. Spadevil's doctrine constitutes an important step towards truth. Crystalman, who has hitherto been presented to us as the creator of the world, is partially unmasked. He is only the creator of pleasure (page 121). The sense of the book is certainly the struggle between pleasure and pain, between Crystalman and Krag. From this first novel, *A Voyage to Arcturus*, there appears what will be the constant theme of Lindsay's books. One has only to glance through the *Philosophical Notes* to realise the importance that Lindsay attached to this question. Of the first five reflections to be found recorded there, three already have pleasure as their theme. This indicates an obsession which says much about the austerity of the author, the result of a puritan background, a personal neurosis and perhaps too much reading of Schopenhauer.

Pleasure has long been the subject of numerous philosophical treatises. Aristotle was one of the first thinkers to link human activities to this notion of pleasure. After him, Epicurus asserted that 'pleasure is the supreme good'. If, like Aristotle and Epicurus, David Lindsay declares that 'Man's nature is pleasure', this is in order immediately to separate himself from them in deploring this supremacy of pleasure, placing himself in a metaphysical and cosmological perspective. The sole justification for the existence of the world is pleasure, according to him.[52]

To prove this, Lindsay has little difficulty in finding examples. His rigour is such that nothing is spared, neither joy, nor beauty, nor aesthetic contemplation, nor love, nor even stoical endurance, solitude[53] and boredom.[54] All are derivatives of pleasure. To conclude, from that point, that pleasure is the basis of the physical world, there is but one step for Lindsay to surmount. Only the parallel world, the Sublime, is free from the tyranny of pleasure. The order of things there is different.

In varying degree, all the characters met in Tormance are worshippers of pleasure, and creatures of Crystalman. To help her neighbour is Joiwind's greatest pleasure (page 47). Panawe certainly recognises the existence of degrees of pleasure, going from the Sublime, and passing through pain and love (page 67), but his situation as an artist, and the cult of beauty that he preaches, prevent him from rejecting pleasure. Spadevil clearly declares that to hate pleasure can itself become a new form of pleasure, but his proposed solution of a morality of duty is only, according to Lindsay, yet another fraud. Finally, Gangnet is the very incarnation of pleasure. He proudly repeats that 'the world could not go on being without pleasure', and pities Maskull for having crossed the most perilous countries of Arcturus. Gangnet is the 'Prince of Poets', dressed in strange fashion, like a man disguised as a woman, and exhibiting a treacherous sentimentality.

After the pleasure of helping, the pleasure of killing, and the pleasure of creating, there remains one form of pleasure that is perhaps the most remarkable, and this is the pleasure of loving. Women are not absent from Arcturus; very far from it, indeed. Their presence will make itself felt even more strongly than that of the men. The first extra-terrestrial met by Maskull is a woman, Joiwind. She avoids actually falling into the arms of the male hero who arrives from elsewhere, but that means but little, as the situation is clear. Henceforward, Maskull will have to take account of women, and their seduction techniques.

In the courteous world of Joiwind, fraternity is synonymous with chastity, and brotherhood excludes sexual love, but disturbing thoughts persist, and bring blushes. The sweetest kiss is given with a tentacle interposed. 'Before he realised what she was about to do, she threw her tentacle round his neck, like another arm. He offered no resistance to its cool pressure. The contact of her soft flesh with his own was so moist and sensitive that it resembled another kind of kiss' (page 52). Oceaxe, for her part, does not have Joiwind's reserve. With her, Maskull knows what is wanted of him. 'If you have male instincts, as I suppose you have, you can't go on resisting me for ever' (page 78). The extra-terrestrial appears more often in the shape of a woman than of a man. The lord of Arcturus, Crystalman, is 'naturally effeminate'. The interplanetary rocket also invites us on a journey to a wonderland of love and pleasure, in the shape of the dull fraternity of Joiwind, the ardent desire of Oceaxe, the resignation of the feminist, Tydomin, the sensual egoism of Leehallfae, and the passion of Sullenbode.

Basically, love, like beauty, art and duty before it, is rejected. It hinders the discovery of the Sublime. One must cast oneself off entirely from all that is human, repeats Lindsay indefatigably. The episode with Sullenbode is evidence of this. There, love is presented as a violent, and *painful*, passion, whose apogee is the sacrifice of one of the lovers for the other. Seen from this standpoint, love is an experience that is infinitely rich, but not sufficiently so, however, for it to be reconciled with the sense of the Sublime. Sullenbode dies instantly when her reason for living, love, disappears. Love has lasted only for the space of a dream. Maskull continues his walk 'like a suddenly-awakened sleeper'.

In order to reject totally all the doctrines of Arcturus, David Lindsay makes use of a very complex system of symbols which unite all the characters into one large family, quite regardless of detailed difference. The most remarkable aspect of this family atmosphere is the famous 'Crystalman grin', which is a sort of grimace that appears at the death of each character, as if he is scoffing at both readers and hero for having been caught in the trammels of beauty, love and pleasure. This 'vulgar, sordid, bestial grin', which darkens and freezes the heart by revealing moral corruption, is Crystalman fully exposed. The most beautiful Apollo has a face that is most horribly deformed in death. Characters on Arcturus who appear to be most noble and deserving are not spared. Even Sullenbode does not escape her situation as a daughter of Crystalman, but Maskull will never learn this, thanks to a subtle irony on the part of the author. 'Beneath its coating of mud, her face bore the vulgar, ghastly Crystalman grin, but Maskull saw nothing of it. She had never appeared so beautiful to him as at that moment' (page 226).

Physically, the inhabitants of Arcturus resemble one another. 'You are naturally effeminate', Krag accuses Crystalman. It is no mere chance that the purest product of Crystalman's diabolical creation, Leehallfae, is a hybrid being. Nearly all the inhabitants of Arcturus have inherited something from their creator, such as the sweet voice, the long hair falling upon the neck, the pink, beardless face, and the scent. When we meet Crystalman in person, his physique is so familiar to us that we are not surprised. 'His dark hair curled down to his neck, his brow was wide, lofty and noble, and there was an air of serious sweetness about the whole man that was strangely appealing to the feelings.'[55]

It is not just the characters that resemble one another. The landscapes, too, carry the mark of their creator, notwithstanding a misleading diversity. Crystalman, man of crystal disguised as God, has his world of crystal. Since his arrival on the new star, Maskull notices that the mountains seem to be made of 'transparent glass', which does not shine in the sunlight (page 62). The careful reader will have little difficulty in finding this vein of crystal which appears in many places on Arcturus. The forest resembles 'a roof of glass' (page 70). The bushes and the leaves are of crystal (page 61). The water is of crystalline transparency. The crystal egg is presented to us as the most beautiful model of artistic creation (page 59).

The coincidence is far from being fortuitous. All these references constitute a symbolising of crystal that Lindsay is at pains to explain in the episode concerning Polecrab. As so often in the book, we are confronted with a digression that seems insignificant, and which, in its context, remains obscure. Polecrab recounts what has previously been revealed to him by Broodviol. 'He said that Crystalman tries to turn all things into *one*, and that, whichever way his shapes march, in order to escape from him, they find themselves again face to face with Crystalman, and are changed into new crystals' (page 146). Hence, the crystal is the material of the world of Crystalman. Whoever is won over to his ideas is a crystal, this 'ruin'd piece of nature' (*King Lear*, Act 4, Scene 6), whose beauty hides a cold material, situated at the opposite pole from the Sublime fire. 'The test of real life is originality', writes Lindsay in his *Philosophical Notes*, 'and all that part of us that does not create and branch out into unique forms is already crystallised' (Number 386). Elsewhere, he adds 'To be a "thoroughbred", to be a perfect specimen of a race, is to be a perfect crystal' (Number 483), as they have reached the limits of evolution, and can progress no further. The crystal symbolises the renunciation by human beings in the search for Sublime origins. The character who best expresses this, to the point of leading, single-handed, a quest in the reverse direction, towards Crystalman, is Leehallfae. A willing prisoner of Crystalman, Leehallfae has lost all humanity, to be no longer anything but a crystal. 'The bones were so flat and angular that the flesh presented something of the character of a crystal, having plane surfaces in place of curves' (*A Voyage to Arcturus*, page 173).

Far from being a delightful excursion in wonderland, *A Voyage to Arcturus* is a descent into hell. Tormance, the zone of torment, is the theatre of a combat of giants, the outcome of which will determine the future of the human race. Unlike so many religions, Lindsay's God is not above the conflict, but stands in the arena. The time has passed when Muspel could wisely contemplate the world that he had created. The enemy has invaded this world, and Muspel himself struggles for his existence, 'against all that is most shameful and frightful; against sin masquerading as eternal beauty, against baseness masquerading as Nature, against the Devil masquerading as God'. When the last step of the tower has been climbed, Maskull discovers his solitude. In the world of Crystalman, he is the sole emissary of Muspel.

# 5

## THE SUBLIME WORLD

David Lindsay is an ideologist rather than a philosopher, as the reader will be quick to notice. If it is the invention, the exoticism and the strange that make the first impression, one soon discovers, behind these flights of fancy, a kind of thought that lacks neither richness nor interest. While his novels gravitate towards imaginary worlds, the writer's thinking, in itself, leaves the beaten track, and takes the form of intuition of a vivid intensity. All Lindsay's determination is needed to ensure that his plots adhere to the reality of this world. As a general rule, the realistic picture gives way to intimations of the hereafter.

To analyse this thinking is no easy task. The novel, as a literary form, does not always lend itself very well to the exposition of ideas. It is necessary to tell stories, to bring characters to life, to achieve verisimilitude. At worst, one will have a didactic dissertation that is incompatible with the liveliness of the story. At best, there is a fragmented narrative, with the rhythm of the adventure jarring uneasily with the rhythm of the thought. To the limits of the genre, there are added further difficulties which are linked to the quality of the experience described. If Lindsay's convictions cannot be called into question, it remains no less true that the message he tried to convey is not of the kind to which we are accustomed. Truth does not take the form of a single mass, imposing itself by force alone, but manifests itself by passing intuitions.

### THE SUBLIME

The whole of Lindsay's writing is based upon the experience of duality, or the feeling that life as we know it, whilst being scarcely enriching, contains elements which testify to a possible grandeur. Being lonely, and the prisoner from birth until death of a few years' existence, as well as a composite mass of atoms exposed to the dangers of an impersonal world, man is nothing. Nevertheless, he is

174

not destitute of grandeur, as is evident in his tenacity in surmount-
ing unhappiness, his intelligence and his aspirations. From this point
of view, man asserts his place in some superior order of things. This
model, as some kind of ideal, Lindsay calls the Sublime.

The theory of the Sublime constitutes the ultimate point of the
whole of Lindsay's ideology. Its importance is considerable, since it
claims to be nothing more nor less than an explanation of the
universe. It is accordingly essential to understand it properly.
Lindsay himself repeatedly insists upon the importance he attaches
to this theory, which he also considers to be one of the most original
aspects of his thinking. He adds that his entire ideology, in his view,
must be an exposition of the Sublime.[1]

Before examining the content of this doctrine, it is necessary to
resolve an ambiguity as to the word itself, which differs, when used
by Lindsay, from current usage. According to Lindsay, the term was
chosen, for want of anything better,[2] to denote a certain transcendent world. The interpretation is accordingly his own.

The word is one of long standing, since it is found, for the first
time, in the third century A.D., in the writings of a Greek orator
called Longinus, author of *On the Sublime*. It is principally in the
eighteenth and nineteenth centuries, however, that the term
achieved its period of glory, thanks notably to thinkers such as
Boileau and Edmund Burke.[3] Burke's definition, that the Sublime
was founded upon profusion, irregularity, pain and darkness, as
opposed to the Beautiful, sets the tone for a whole stream of
literature, typified particularly by the 'Gothic novel'.

Kant takes up the term, and then comes Schopenhauer. His
theory of the Sublime is taken directly from Kant, but it embodies
the conception of free will, unique to the author. As with Burke, the
Beautiful and the Sublime conflict with one another. Certainly, both
tug at man's will, in order to plunge him into a state of contemplation, but contemplation of the Beautiful is serene rapture,
whilst, at the heart of the Sublime, there is a feeling of anguish, and
a reminder of our will.[4] Whereas, with Kant, the contrast is between
reason and imagination, with Schopenhauer, the discord bears in a
general sense upon the resemblance of the functions of representation to those of will. The power of detachment resists the power
of will.

Lindsay's admiration for Schopenhauer is known. One of his
characters in *Devil's Tor*, Uncle Magnus, bears a likeness, both

physically and morally, to the German philosopher (page 108).
Lindsay parts company from his mentor, however, when it comes to
the Sublime. He does not hesitate to criticise Schopenhauer's conception of the Sublime as being 'the contemplation of Beauty under
threatening circumstances'. Is it enough for a beautiful woman to be
surprised by a storm to make the scene a Sublime one? Lindsay
poses this question by reducing Schopenhauer's theory to its essentials. He then adds that, in his view, 'The Sublime is not beauty but
something else, which is related to beauty, yet transcends it'
(*Philosophical Notes*, Number 79).

If he parts company so clearly from current precedents, Lindsay
does not break away from them completely. Otherwise, why should
he have adhered to a term in which he recognised such ambiguity?
With Lindsay, there is no systematic research of Sublime landscapes,
as we find in Burke, but there is easily recognisable a tendency to
choose, ideally, grandiose scenery. Although absent from both *Sphinx*
and *The Haunted Woman*, this traditional form of the Sublime does
appear in *Devil's Tor*. The background chosen by Lindsay as the
framework for his novel accords with the definition of the Sublime.
Dartmoor is one of those lonely places with limitless horizons. There
are neither men nor animals, and a deep silence reigns everywhere.
Such a location seems to invite meditation, because there is nothing
to engage the will, as Schopenhauer would say. When a storm breaks
upon this background the landscape only becomes more Sublime.
Faced by a storm, man knows that he is at the mercy of the
elements. At the same time, however, he is, according to
Schopenhauer's description, 'the pure-minded subject who casts his
eyes upon the fury of nature, and upon the picture of vanquished
will'. The rock of Devil's Tor, the thunder with which the book
opens, the barren and denuded background of Dartmoor, the mist
and the wind, are so many elements favourable to the Sublime.

Sometimes, it certainly seems that Lindsay employs the term
'Sublime' in accordance with accepted common parlance, as, for
example, when he defines the Sublime of Nature. 'The real Sublime',
he writes, 'consists only in action. Therefore the ocean is sublime,
mountains are not, except insofar as they cause atmospheric distur-
bances. Mountains are masses of decaying rocks; thus huge grave-
yards' (*Philosophical Notes*, Number 440). He returns to this same idea
when he asserts 'the true Sublime consists only in energy and
activity. Therefore the sea and music are Sublime, but mountains

and architecture are pseudo-Sublime' (Number 444). Mere grandeur of dimension is not, then, enough in itself. To the effect
produced upon a spectator, there must be added an essential that
belongs to the very nature of the Sublime object; namely movement,
which is a sign of life and energy.

The conception of the Sublime did not come to David Lindsay
through reading such philosophers as Kant and Schopenhauer. It is
more accurate to say that it established itself through contact with
the world, and that it was born out of the very experience of the
author. Lindsay indefatigably repeats that the Sublime world, in his
view, is more real than the tangible world. 'The Sublime world is
not a metaphysical theory but a terrible fact, which stands above
and behind the world, and governs all its manifestations'.[5] Far from
being immaterial, and populated by ghosts and illusions, the Sublime has a body whose substance is more real, and more solid, than
'this coloured, cubic and heavy world of ours'.

Born out of experience, the Sublime appeared very early, and, in
fact, well before Lindsay started to write. In the beginning, there
was a feeling of the unreality of our physical world. Lindsay begins
by exposing the mediocrity and vulgarity of life. Apart from a few
exceptions, such as martyrs, mystics, musicians and philosophers,
man seems to him to be a creature deprived of imagination, a
prisoner of his comfort and security, and exclusively preoccupied
with money, food and distractions.

All these inclinations have, as their common denominator, pleasure or well-being. Pleasure appears, therefore, as the world's motive
power. This law, however, clashes with one piece of evidence;
namely, the universality of suffering. There scarcely exists any living
being who does not suffer in one way or another. History recalls the
Greek tragedies, the lamentations of Job, and the suffering of
Phaedra. As between suffering and pleasure, it is certainly the
former which constitutes the primordial state. It is futile, therefore,
to regard life as being a negation of pain, as we are taught by the
majority of moral philosophies. Between the pre-eminence of pain
and the search for pleasure, there is a contradiction, asserts Lindsay.
The dissociation of pleasure from pain is simply the characteristic of
our physical life. Far from trying to abolish the one by the other, we
must try to reconcile them, as the sole means of regaining henceforward a vanished state in the form of a kind of Golden Age, in which
pain and pleasure are but one.

This vanished world is unknown to us. Nevertheless, we pass through moments of exultation which sometimes enlighten our existence with a rare intensity. We find ourselves alone with Nature, and see a countryside become suddenly transformed, as if peace, solitude and the atmosphere had combined to recreate the scenery. The hearing of a beautiful piece of music can also produce this state of euphoria, when a man can, in certain circumstances, lose his individuality, and forget the background surrounding him, in order to bring to life that other world of the music. In Lindsay's eyes, the Sublime is that other world, attainable in certain conditions, whose manifestation he compares with water coming to the boil upon reaching a certain temperature.[6]

The first approach of the Sublime is met in *A Voyage to Arcturus*. This is the picture of Muspel, which is hardly precise, because the book tries, above all, to denounce the pitfalls of the conscious world. The choice of the Scandinavian myth of Muspel, as a symbol of the Sublime, was determined by other reasons. Besides the symbolic use to which Muspellsheim,[7] the world of fire of Nordic mythology, lends itself, it did not escape Lindsay that Muspel was, according to legend, the original world. The giant, Ymir, father of the human race, united fire and ice. Lindsay returns to the idea of a world that existed before the Earth and Heaven, and imbues the legend with a certain Platonism and Gnosticism, in order to arrive at an original conception of a pre-existing world, whose actual universe would only be a much inferior derivative. By the device of the myth of Muspel, Lindsay similarly explains the end of the world, and the reconquest of the Sublime world. According to legend, at the end of a combat between the armies of the Gods and the Giants, the sole survivors will be the sons of the Gods who, under Surtur's command, will have, as their mission, the destruction of the world by fire. The massacre is a beneficial one, however, since it is a purification and a renewal. Just as before the creation of the world, Muspel will reign.

In order to justify the pre-eminence of the Sublime world, Lindsay affirms that the explanations of the universe by earlier religions and philosophies are scarcely satisfactory. The message of *A Voyage to Arcturus* is the negation of traditional codes, and the discovery of a new principle of explanation in the Sublime. According to Lindsay, theories of evolution, the virtues of education, human fraternity, and the idea of God, are all deceits which have had the sole effect of concealing from men's eyes the existence of the Sublime world. The only true explanation that remains is that of Schopenhauer, making the will, or powers striving towards something, the basis of existence. All our unhappiness arises out of that. The will to live is tyrannical and sad. The misery of man on earth comes from the overriding necessity to satisfy the demands of the will. All privation is painful to it. Starting from there, Lindsay adds that a world whose insufficiencies are so evident can present no interest whatsoever. Its limitations are explicable by its nature. The tangible world is secondary, created from an ideal model which is itself set free from the servitude of will.

The history of the world, and of humanity in particular, is the story of a disgrace. This degradation, it must be stressed, however, has nothing to do with the Christian conception of the Fall. The three standards of this evolution are the Sublime, the self and morality. The Sublime state is the example of an entirety that is free from all imperfection. The transition from the Sublime to the self is due to the interference of the principle of individuality that Lindsay likens to Nature. Morality, for its part, particularly appears as a repressive force of the self (*Philosophical Notes*, Numbers 196 and 17). Such, in broad terms, are the principal lines of Lindsay's ideology.

The conclusion that man must draw is clear; namely, to live fully is to penetrate the outward appearance of the tangible world, in order to become aware of the reality of the ideal world. Life, in spite of its monotony and insufficiencies, is not bereft of privileged moments when man can break away from his surroundings, in order to glimpse this superior reality. 'Heavenly Sublimity was like a violent rent in the noisome fogs of life, affording an unforgettable narrow blinding of heaven' (*Devil's Tor*, page 418). The attraction of existence is henceforward limited to this secret moment of bewilderment when the soul again finds its creator, and when the restraints of the common herd are forgotten, so that it is possible to rise to a superior plane.

## THE CONQUEST OF THE SUBLIME

The Sublime is not of this world, repeats Lindsay. The conquest of the Sublime, therefore, begins by detachment from the world. In *A Voyage to Arcturus*, after long preparation, it is necessary to await the death of Maskull in order to begin to reach for the Sublime. 'His body was like a prison. He longed to throw it off, to spring up and become incorporated with the Sublime universe which was beginning to unveil itself' (page 225). In *Devil's Tor*, it is the storm which acts as the catalyst of the Sublime. The walk taken by Hugh and Ingrid is an ascent, far removed from the everyday world. Already separated by distance and height, they are still more isolated by the tempest which rages around them. The rain encloses them like a prison. It forms a wall between them and the rest of the world (page 21). Nevertheless, it is a false prison, as the isolation is the first of the conditions necessary to be free. The storm reveals a new mode of existence of which Hugh and Ingrid have previously had only a vague intuition. Within a few minutes, the significance of life is overthrown. Values commonly accepted, such as life, love and fraternity, lose their importance. All that is human becomes obliterated in the face of the terrible grandeur of the Sublime world.

One solitary experience of the Sublime is enough to transform the course of existence, as if something at the very foundation of oneself has been broken. The pessimism of Lindsay and his heroes has no other source than this impossibility of seeing the tangible world as our reason for existence. Out of this is born the psychology of 'the outsider', immortalised by Colin Wilson in his best-selling book,[8] concerning the permanent dissatisfaction of the man who has become aware of the unreality of his existence, and whose most ardent wish is to distance himself from his fellow-beings, in order to devote himself to an inner quest for a reality that only he perceives.

The experience of the Sublime engenders more anguish than satisfaction, because it disturbs one's life. Anguish is a component of the Sublime. In contrast to the Christian Paradise, which one need only await in tranquillity and virtue, the Sublime has the effect of making man depressive. It is accompanied by 'disturbance, sullenness, infinite longing, sadness, despair' (*Devil's Tor*, page 68). Sublimity is nothing but the subconscious desire of the soul to regain its origin, and a nostalgia to return to the intangible world, or the Paradise Lost from which our real world emanated. The dissatisfaction is that of 'the outsider', who knows that he belongs to the hereafter. 'Men, you see, are not only men, they are also and essentially *spirits*. The world is not their right place ... Accordingly, in their unconscious depths, men are unhappy in the world, which is not their place, and which confines them.'[9] What some call 'redemption' is no more, in Lindsay's eyes, than the soul's return to its first condition.

The instrument of learning is the soul or the spirit. Truth does not lie within the gift of the senses. It is only discovered inwardly, by an effort to free oneself from surrounding influences, in order to respond to a transcendent need. Between the human soul and the driving force of the world, there is an identity of nature which explains that knowledge of the world concerns only a part of man, his eternal soul. Men are 'also and essentially spirits', writes Lindsay, meaning that human nature combines a mental life with an organic one. Of these two, only the former is of interest in enabling one to discover a fundamental knowledge of life. David Lindsay begins, therefore, by dividing his characters into two categories. On the one hand, there are the initiates of the body, and, on the other, those of the soul. The doctor, as a servant of the body, is placed in the ranks of latter-day charlatans.[10] Women, unceasingly preoccupied with dress, ornamentation, beauty and bodily cares, do not escape criticism. Lindsay denounces barbarity, and the return to animalism. Man has lost his soul, he cries, and is no longer anything more than a 'human biped, whose stomach is paramount in the existence of a mystic universe' (*Devil's Tor*, page 68). At the polar opposite are found nearly all Lindsay's heroes and heroines, such as Hugh Drapier, Lore Jensen, Ingrid Colborne and others, each of them being almost without substance, for whom the body scarcely exists. Hence, Ingrid's eyes provide the evidence of an intense internal life, and her body seems to give way before the force of her gaze (pages 13, 190). The irony of life is that man discovers only a few moments before death that this body that he has cared for and nourished is going to disappear in a fraction of a second (*Devil's Tor*, page 79).

Without examining it very deeply, David Lindsay takes up again the philosophy of Plato, with its contrast of two worlds; the creation of the world by a Demiurge, the human soul considered as part of the Universal Soul, the traps of the tangible world, the possibility of man recovering his divine, eternal origin, and the unhappiness of man on earth, subjected to this nostalgia for his first existence. In spite of this borrowed philosophy, Lindsay loses no time in parting company from his illustrious predecessor. To the Platonic theory, there are now added other currents of thought, particularly Stoicism, Eastern philosophy and Gnosticism.

Man is aware of existing independently of the world which

surrounds him. Experience proves to him his individuality. This division constitutes, in Lindsay's eyes, the first stage of the Sublime. Individuality is the opposite of the Sublime, and Sublimity represents, to a large extent, the effort of man to regain the whole. Human experience, in the sense that it is narrowly linked to individuality, is, in the nature of things, anti-Sublime. The *Sublime man* cannot exist, these two ideas being contradictory. Several important conclusions proceed from this. The Sublime feeds upon solitude in the human order. One cannot accede to the Sublime in society, since the group is the image of an assembly of individuals. On the contrary, the Sublime needs to be emancipated from individuality. Every assembly of people can serve only to remind man of his attachment to individuality, or what Schopenhauer calls 'the painful reminder of the subjection to the will'.[11] The universe is divided, therefore, into tendencies that are either Sublime or vulgar, according to whether one escapes, or becomes reconciled to, individuality. Emotions, for example, belong to individuality, insofar as one can isolate and analyse them. The Sublime sentiment itself is indivisible; an example being the rapture induced by a beautiful piece of music, when one does not register the notes or the sounds, as the music has become a sensation that it is not possible to analyse into separate parts. Between these emotions and the Sublime, there is all the difference that exists between colours and light.

To overcome individuality constitutes one of the first necessities in the conquest of the Sublime. Schopenhauer's solution does not attract Lindsay. Not once does he make any reference to the celebrated morality of pity by which man, according to the German philosopher, suppresses the pain of individuality in comparing his experience with that of his fellow-beings, in sharing the suffering of the world. Perhaps Lindsay remembered the criticisms Nietzsche levelled at Schopenhauer, asking how a philosophy calling itself pessimistic could be beguiled by a theory so 'false and sentimental'.

The method to which Lindsay adheres does not consist of drowning individuality in a mass of other individualities, but in *abandoning* individuality altogether. The conquest of the Sublime is achieved by a renunciation of the self, which has long been seen as one of the foundations of any mystical quest. The necessary condition for all progression towards Divinity, and any kind of illumination, is moral detachment. This abandonment of the principle of individuality is presented to us in several forms, including sacrifice, acceptance of Fate, magnanimity and altruism.

The most spectacular of these gifts of oneself is sacrifice. This is one of the most baffling aspects of *A Voyage to Arcturus*. Several times in this book, characters disappear by jumping into a void, from the top of a cliff. One of the most striking examples is provided for us by Panawe, in the story he tells of the adventures of Slofork. One day, on Shaping's Causeway, Panawe met a character called Slofork. The path was so narrow that it was not possible to pass on this mountainous crest, surrounded by empty space. After a brief discussion on the meaning of life, Panawe saw his companion suddenly leap up, crying 'You will never rise above mysticism ... but be happy in your own way.' Having said this, Slofork jumped into the void (page 67). No explanation is provided, since it is clear that Panawe did not understand the motive for this 'suicide'. Even with Joiwind, sacrifice is a necessity for the achievement of Divinity (*A Voyage to Arcturus*, page 49). Maskull is so convinced of this that he comes within a hair's breadth of losing his masculinity when Tydomin, tired of being the slave of men, offers him a curious exchange of sexes. Here again, the argument put forward by Tydomin is that of a sacrifice freely made.[12] Previously, Lindsay had described another version of this exchange of sexes. Panawe recounts that, as a child, he was taken for a freak. He was asexual. Neither sex had been given to him at birth, leading to embarrassment for him and his parents. This thorny problem was resolved by a sacrifice, the feminine half abdicating in favour of her brother.[13] When Spadevil finds himself accused of charlatanism, he immediately agrees to sacrifice himself, so as to die for his ideas. Truth, he declares, 'will not perish by my death, but by my efforts to escape from death' (*A Voyage to Arcturus*, page 129). Finally, there is the example of Hator who, for his part, died not through throwing himself from the top of a cliff, like Slofork, but by ceasing to breathe (page 122).

So many examples could not be adduced by mere chance. They emphasise a philosophy of sacrifice dear to David Lindsay. Sacrifice, says one of the characters in *A Voyage to Arcturus*, is not utilitarian, but a ransom that one pays (page 102). It constitutes, therefore, the first step towards the discovery of the Sublime, in the sense that this sacrifice is both a gift and a renunciation. If one accepts that the Sublime is not of this world, man must agree to die, the will to live being the manifest proof of attachment to this world. Whosoever wishes to rise above life, indeed 'above mysticism', must be ready to sacrifice his own material existence. That which constitutes the nobility of life, and which gives a meaning to life, is this faculty to give, of one's own free will, that which man will see forcibly removed in death.[14] The gift of oneself is not the answer of someone who is tired of life, and disgusted with existence, but an act of heroism. Suicide is desperate, cynical or bitter, but sacrifice is joyous and grandiose.

Sacrifice is not concerned solely with life. The proposition which Tydomin makes to Maskull is not to sacrifice his life for her, but only his personality as a man. One can meet many forms of sacrifice. To sacrifice is to give a part of oneself, and to go towards the other person, instead of being drawn towards oneself. One understands from that why Lindsay is so interested in relations between men and women. Friendship and, especially, love are the sentiments which constitute the acid test. If Lindsay is so prone to depict love, it is certainly because he sees in it the beginning of the Sublime, combining sacrifice and a mixture of pleasure and pain. Love, in this conception, has nothing frivolous about it, being a total abnegation by lovers, one for the other, as shown in the episode involving Sullenbode in A Voyage to Arcturus. Sullenbode, at first 'a mass of pure sex', becomes a woman, thanks to the passion that Maskull feels for her. This love gives her a soul, whereas, previously, she had possessed only a body. For the first time since his adventures began, Maskull is in love. If this love does not endure, it is for two reasons. In the first place, Maskull's love for Sullenbode cannot withstand the call of the Sublime Ideal, since love and the Sublime are ultimately in opposition to each other. In the second place, Lindsay cannot conceive the idea of love without sacrifice. A Voyage to Arcturus ends with the definition 'Love is that which is perfectly willing to disappear and become nothing, for the sake of the beloved' (page 214). The same idea is found in The Haunted Woman. To the passing love-affair, Judge opposes real love, with its tears and pain. It is easy to flatter one's partner, but rare indeed are those who, for love, agree to sacrifice everything.[15] From the moment that it is born, love can only grow. If it diminishes in its intensity, then it is already no longer love. There is certainly no happy love with Lindsay, not only because this passion is, above all, painful and demanding,[16] but also because it can end only in sacrifice. When the intensity has reached its peak, beyond which love can no longer increase, one of the two beings must sacrifice himself, or herself, for the love of the other, so that love may survive (*A Voyage to Arcturus*, page 222).

If women appear to David Lindsay to be more noble than men, this is largely because they instinctively possess this sense of abnegation. In the case of Panawe, already mentioned, it is the *feminine* half which sacrifices itself for the other living half. When, at the end of *A Voyage to Arcturus*, Maskull reviews his adventures, he comes to the conclusion that the women he has met have shown themselves to be more noble than the men, for a reason he explains. 'We men often sacrifice ourselves, but only for a substantial cause. For you women, any cause will serve. You love the sacrifice for its own sake, and that is because you are naturally noble' (page 219).

A number of mystical doctrines are known to have, as their object, the loss of oneself in ecstasy, and the fusion of self and Divinity. Before reaching this final stage of contemplation, methods exist for the abolition of the self, whilst retaining awareness of the tangible world. The first way of detaching oneself presupposes a total abnegation as regards the exterior world. This is presented by Lindsay in two main forms; namely, contempt for oneself and acceptance of destiny. Both these constitute the principal themes of *Devil's Tor*. Saltfleet, the adventurer, is first seduced by the audacity, originality and tenacity of the archaeologist, Arsinal. The passion for archaeology, which at first appears so admirable in Arsinal, is, in reality, only a form of vice. It hides a fundamental egoism. Certainly, Arsinal scorns honours, money and power. However, his quest remains no less lacking in grandeur, stresses Lindsay, since he shows himself to be incapable of despising his own ambitions. The affinity which the two men believed to have found for each other now wears away. To the possessive instinct of the one, Lindsay contrasts the 'philosophical' temperament of the other. 'Without *self-contempt*, nobody, man or woman, can rise past a certain determinate level of willing' (page 310).[17] The self is contemptible. One must learn to despise its demands.

The second form taken by abnegation of the self is the acceptance of the decrees of Fate. The theme scarcely appears in *A Voyage to Arcturus*. It will be remembered, however, that it is present in *The Haunted Woman*. The love of Judge and Isbel totally overwhelms them. When they meet in the haunted room, they act in defiance of good sense and convention. They are drawn towards one another, as if by a magnet. Finally, in *Devil's Tor*, there reigns a fatalistic atmosphere. Men are the playthings of forces which overtake them. The different intrigues are improbable. There are too many coincidences, and too many unexplained events. The book would have scarcely any value if there were not, behind the improbability, the principle of an inexorable Fate. The actions of the characters are explicable by intuitions, and by impulses that are but little understood. Hence, Hugh hastens to return from Asia to England, because he feels that he is soon going to die. Ingrid feels irresistibly drawn to a hill close to her home. Uncle Magnus Colborne has decided to build his home in a place where he formerly had a dream. It is 'chance' that throws Hugh into the path of Saltfleet and Arsinal, the archaeologist having had a dream in the night and so having changed his itinerary the next morning. Without this decision, he would never have met Hugh Drapier, who alone knows of the existence of Devil's Tor. The birth of Ingrid seems to have been wrought by Destiny. Providence saved Ingrid's father from a terrible accident, but, as soon as the young girl was conceived, Destiny had no more use for the father, who died soon afterwards.

Coincidences, chance, luck and intuitions are just so many modern forms of that Fate which the ancients knew so well. The improbability of *Devil's Tor*, therefore, conceals the very ambitious plan of restoring some nobility to the idea of Fate, which has not ceased to be degraded over the course of centuries. The ancients had a sharp sense of the existence of this superior world which both surrounded men and governed their actions. This world in which the ancients believed would be one form of the Sublime world. The Sublime world has disappeared, and with it the idea of Fate, replaced by the conception of an all-powerful God, this modern 'insipid' form of determinism, created by a people incapable of accepting the idea of an inexorable Fate (page 293).

## THE VIRTUES OF SUFFERING

The beliefs and values of David Lindsay involve pain and suffering, which take the form of endurance or sacrifice. In itself, suffering has nothing Sublime about it, but it is the instrument of the Sublime. 'If one were set the problem of causing men to acquire their original Sublime nature, no other means could be found than by making them *suffer*. Thus pain is justified', writes Lindsay, in his *Philosophical Notes*. Lindsay's ideas approximate to certain trends in asceticism and stoicism, whilst always retaining their own originality.

In order fully to understand Lindsay's use of the term 'Sublime', one must refer to the nature of the Sublime. Nearly all definitions of the Sublime, whether by Kant, Burke or Schopenhauer, stress the violence involved therein. In all cases, there is a contrast between opposites. A Sublime spectacle is at once attractive and agonising. It evokes as much fear as pleasure. If it is not yet pain, this fear is a projection of pain. It can be said that the Sublime is the amalgamation of pleasure and pain. When he conceives his Sublime world, Lindsay starts from this same idea. He imagines an order of things in which pain and pleasure would be united. The degradation that has characterised the transition from the Sublime world to the actual world would only be the dissociation of pleasure and pain, which were formerly united. 'Just as complementary colours joined together form white light, so, by the prism of individuality, the Sublime is split into pleasure and pain ...' (*Philosophical Notes*, Number 177.) Man feels either pleasure or pain, but rarely both at the same time. When these two feelings are joined, we are in the presence of the Sublime, and of a return to the first condition of man. The most violent emotions are at once both painful and agreeable. Man cries with joy in Sublime moments.

What happened to this primitive state? As between pleasure and pain, it is clear that man has made a choice. Man flees from work, and seeks rest, comfort and sweetness. Scarcely has a child been born than he is offered a lollipop or a sweet. Later, he will learn to associate Evil with suffering. The most celebrated philosophers, from Aristotle to Leibniz, have made pleasure the supreme blessing. In contrast, doctrines that are based upon pain are depicted as perversions. The idea of physical suffering being an end in itself has hardly any advocates, recalls Jeanne Russier.[18] As for moral suffering, contemporary Western thought no longer pays it much attention since Schopenhauer. In order to find its adherents, one has to return to the Stoics of ancient times, or look towards the Buddhism of the Orient.

What is quite apparent is the universality of pleasure, in that it appears in the form of physical love, aesthetic contemplation, art, fraternity or beauty. To regain his Sublime origin, man has no better means than to submit himself to the beneficial effect of pain.

Pain becomes the 'solvent of pleasure'. It must be clearly understood that it is not a matter of replacing pleasure with pain, but to attain, through the effect of pain, a union with the interior pleasure of the Sublime. The Sublime state does not separate them.

The arguments used by Lindsay to justify the positive value of pain are certainly not lacking. Without pain, pleasure is insipid. Boredom is nothing less than a search for pleasure that is bereft of any definite purpose. Suffering is a proof of life. The man who suffers should congratulate himself each time he feels pain, since it is better to have a pain in the leg than to have no leg at all. Moreover, adds Lindsay, pain brings satisfaction, since pain brings the benefit of inducing man to surmount it. It impels change. While certain people benefit from pleasure, others seem to flourish much more under the influence of pain. Their nobility in no sense diminishes. 'There is one thing worse than pain, and that is pleasure. So long as men suffer, there is still room for Sublimity, but, in the happy society of the sociologists, men will think and feel in battalions, and no one will any more feel himself an individual rooted in Eternity' (Number 133).

This revaluation of pain is as noticeable in the *Philosophical Notes* as it is in the novels. Krag, Maskull's guide on Arcturus, is known to be the very personification of redeeming pain. A cut made in his arm serves as Maskull's initiation in the pain that remains with him throughout his adventures, 'just strong enough to make life one long discomfort'. The cut is already the first step to the Sublime, as the rest of the story proves. The pain that he feels allows Maskull to resist the 'Tormance gravitation', which means, in essence, the disastrous influence of Crystalman. This search for the Sublime is symbolised in the novel by the climbing of the tower, which is made possible only by the cut in the arm (pages 39–40). In a world such as that of Arcturus, where pleasure reigns, only pain is positive. The hero is spared no suffering. The ordeal is as difficult as the stakes are high. In opposition, there is a 'fierce, mocking enemy, crouching and waiting at every corner of the road of life, in order to kill with its sweet sting the naked grandeur of the soul' (page 120). More as an endurance test, Maskull comes to wish for pain. He remembers the example of Hator, who knew how to protect himself, through pain, from the corruptive effect of pleasure (*A Voyage to Arcturus*, pages 120 and 129). In eventually separating from Sullenbode, he does not forget her words, 'Can't we suffer? Can't we go on suffering, for ever and ever, Maskull, until love crushes our spirit, finally and without remedy, and we don't begin to feel ourselves?' (page 223).

No doubt, David Lindsay takes as his own the axiom of Baudelaire, expressed as 'You are a happy man. I pity you, sir, for being so easily happy.' Like Baudelaire before him, Lindsay sees pain as being 'the divine miracle for our impurities'. He also denounces those people who laugh too easily, to the neglect of self-discipline. Happy people are the slaves of modern times, satisfied with monotony and meagre rewards. For the true 'aristocrat of the universe', something more than half-measures is needed. Either one must abandon oneself to an orgy of pleasure or else one must eschew all forms of pleasure.

Between these two extremes, Lindsay has made his choice. The supreme blessing is pain, and he goes on to explain his reasoning. Failure represents the best springboard to success. Man is like a boxer. He must train himself to receive blows. He must accept insult and injustice without faltering (*Philosophical Notes*, Number 167). In order to remain above the conflict, one must never show oneself to be troubled, if one is a wise man. In moments of acute emotional upheaval, feelings must be hidden. 'The only wise course is to endure and wait.' To try to free oneself by expressing what one feels is to court disaster. Lindsay admires the Viking spirit, and the ease with which these Scandinavian warriors treated death, pain, work and anxiety. He recognises in them a detachment which he immediately adopts as being the best means of confronting the world.[19] Without this ruggedness and determination, he adds elsewhere, man remains a dilettante who can scarcely be taken seriously.[20]

It is towards the philosophy of endurance, therefore, that Lindsay's preference is directed. Schopenhauer, for his part, has taught that 'pain is the basis of life', and he advocates a means of overcoming suffering. Nietzsche, in turn, has shown yet another way in the barren paths and deserts where Zarathoustra took refuge, fleeing from easy solutions. 'Philosophy consists of voluntarily seeking even those aspects of life that are hated and scorned', he declares.[21] Nietzsche denounces sensual pleasure, morality and the gregarious instinct of man. There are no solutions outside a certain cruelty. In order to protect man, and to resist omnipresent vulgarity, it is necessary, first and foremost, to be strong. One must

eschew preconceived notions. Pain, adds Nietzsche, is what separates us from our humanity, and prepares us to be Supermen.
Perhaps it does not improve us, but it assuredly enriches us. Lindsay
says nothing different, and we know that Saltfleet, one of the
characters in *Devil's Tor*, has something of the aura of Nietzsche's
grandeur about him.

Hinduism offers still another means of overcoming suffering,
simply by denying its existence. According to this philosophy, pain
is part of life, but, in suppressing attachment to existence, it is
possible to exterminate the cause of pain, which is desire. The wise
man achieves deliverance by meditation, in discovering that his ego
is part of the universal ego, and that, in consequence, pain is a
stranger to him.

Finally, of Christianity, which he repeatedly condemns, Lindsay
especially remembers those aspects which integrate with his own
philosophy of pain and renunciation. The great men whom he
admires, therefore, are the Christian saints and martyrs, along with
the Puritans. In the general decadence, the only people for whom he
reserves any credit at all are 'the Aryan Brahmins, the Stoics, the
Christian saints and martyrs, the Puritans, the makers of noble music,
and the Sublime philosophers' (*Devil's Tor*, page 69).

## THE NATURE AND CREATION OF THE WORLD

The three novels by David Lindsay with the richest philosophical
content are unquestionably *A Voyage to Arcturus*, *Devil's Tor* and *The
Witch*. Many years separated the writing of these books, and so it is
scarcely surprising to find that the thinking of the author, during
the interval, grew to substantial proportions. Certainly, he never
abandoned his conception of the Sublime, but its forms are different,
even if the basis remains unchanged.

The theory of the Sublime is not expounded in any great detail in
*A Voyage to Arcturus*. This book is particularly devoted to a criticism
of the anti-Sublime, or the vulgar, in all the characters on the star,
Arcturus. The most interesting analysis, and that which explains the
different episodes of the book, is to be found in the very last pages.
From the top of the tower where he has taken refuge, Maskull sees
the world at his feet, like a planet that one perceives in the distance,
from a rocket. The universe then seems to him to be composed of
three parts, consisting of the tower on which he finds himself, a ball
of fire located in the distance, and, finally, an intermediate zone of

darkness. These three parts correspond, respectively, to the world of Muspel, the world of individuality and the world of Crystalman. The world of individuality, it transpires, is created from a disintegration that occurs when the Sublime fire of Muspel encounters the atmosphere of Crystalman. Individuality is accordingly a corruption of the principle of the Sublime. Lindsay presents this in the form of a division between, on the one hand, 'whirling rays', and, on the other, 'green sparks'. The 'whirling rays' are beams of Sublime fire, which are first stopped, and then deformed, by the effect of the atmosphere of Crystalman. The 'green sparks', in contrast, are minute fragments of Sublime fire which, degraded by thus becoming prisoners of Crystalman, try to return to their source. All living organisms are composed of these two opposites, which indulge in an unending struggle.

Although it is tempting to equate Crystalman with pleasure, it is more probable that he symbolises life in general, pleasure being no more than the prop of life. Lindsay writes 'The Sublime stream entered Crystalman's body, and the passage caused him the most exquisite pleasure' (A Voyage to Arcturus, page 246). This certainly seems to indicate that pleasure is no more than a consequence of the division of the Sublime. In contact with life, the Sublime becomes separated into two components, which are pleasure and pain, with the former being stressed as the dominant factor. 'The individual whirls were jostling and fighting with, and even devouring, each other. This created pain, but, whatever pain they felt, it was always pleasure they sought' (A Voyage to Arcturus, page 246).

Although the symbolic intention, even the allegory, is clearly revealed, it must be admitted that this cosmogony is far from being clear. For example, Lindsay says nothing to explain the creation of Crystalman's world. If Crystalman is to be seen as a symbol of life, how did this life appear? We know that it is a corruption of the Sublime, but we are never told the origin of this disgrace, or how life could have started. The only certain factor is the conflict of the two worlds. 'Surtur's world, or Muspel, is the original of which this world is a distorted copy. Crystalman is life, but Surtur is other than life' (A Voyage to Arcturus, page 193). From this, it is clear that the conquest of Muspel, if it begins in this world, can be achieved and completed only in the hereafter of this life. Death is a necessity, and it is also a beginning, 'the first stage of the voyage, although many virtuous men imagine that it constitutes the entire voyage'. Death marks only the end of individual life, the end of individuality, and certainly not the end of life itself, if one believes in any kind of survival of the soul. It is this more general life that Crystalman denotes, and one then understands how the Sublime, in contact with life, becomes degraded, and fragmented into many millions of individuals, divided between their attachment to life and a desire to improve their condition by striving towards something different, thus constituting the struggle between the 'whirling rays' and the 'green sparks'. We shall never know the meaning of this reunion of the individual and the world of Crystalman, which constitutes, according to Lindsay,[22] the prime necessity for the attainment of the Sublime. Does it signify death, or perhaps a state approaching the nirvana of the Buddhist religion? Should one understand, by 'identification with the world of Crystalman', an impulse of pity whereby man assumes the misery of the world, in order, afterwards, to overcome it by virtue of his act of devotion? This is scarcely probable if one remembers the author's satire when he depicts human fraternity in Chapter 6 of *A Voyage to Arcturus*. It is certainly difficult to arrive at an answer, since, by one of those ironic silences that occur so often in the book, Lindsay evades the issue. 'But what did he mean by our reuniting ourselves to Crystalman's world? If it is false, are we to make ourselves false as well?' 'I didn't ask him that question', replies the speaker, 'and you are as well qualified to answer it as I am' (*A Voyage to Arcturus*, page 146).

It is clear that, if Lindsay's thinking reveals some common ground with doctrines that might be classed as 'mystic', it parts company from them quite sharply when one considers that, between the Sublime world and the everyday world, there exists scarcely any link at all. Death itself constitutes the first stage, says Lindsay.

Several studies have depicted Lindsay as 'a mystic'. Colin Wilson, for instance, entitles an essay 'Lindsay as Novelist and Mystic'.[23] Harold Visiak, in his turn, presents Lindsay as 'a mystic of the most extreme kind'.[24] Certainly, by some standards, Lindsay's thinking is 'mystical'. He was very familiar with Plato, and had also read the great treatises on Buddhism, and books by Jacob Boehme. In Lindsay's writing, there are traces of traditional aspects of mystical doctrines, such as the importance of spirituality, and, particularly perhaps, the abnegation of the self, which Lindsay made one of the pivots of his philosophy.

Notwithstanding these affinities, Lindsay vigorously insisted upon distinguishing himself from so many of the mystical authors before him. Robert Barnes claims to have heard Lindsay declare, at least four times, 'I am not a mystic'. It is also worth remembering that important passage in *A Voyage to Arcturus* in which Slofork, a 'sorcerer' of superior knowledge, after having explained the two-worlds theory, exclaims scornfully to his companion 'Perhaps you are right, young man, but you have never learned that, and never will. For you, the world will continue to wear a noble, awful face. *You will never rise above mysticism*, but be happy in your own way.' (page 67. The italics are ours.) Having said this, the 'sorcerer' throws himself into the void.

This key passage is quoted because it summarises, forcefully and clearly, the difference between the sublime man, Slofork, and the man of mysticism. The mystic is an individual who, whilst recognising the existence of another world, remains attached to this world as it is. Most mystical doctrines are lessons of life. Jacob Boehme teaches that one must, above all, distinguish, *in this world*, between appearances and realities. In most cases, mysticism sees itself as being a direct participation between the enlightened man and his God. Only Buddhism regards detachment from life as being a necessity, all other mystic dogmas being content to manipulate the world that Buddhism rejects. Pantheism constitutes just one form of mysticism that reassesses the world. The perception of divine immanence shows the world in a new context. There is nothing of this about Lindsay. The pantheistic approach of Shelley and Jefferies is precisely what he condemns. 'For them, the world will continue to wear a noble, awful face.' The ultimate reality that Lindsay tries to encompass is to be found far beyond Nature, which he equates with the anti-Sublime world of individuality. It must be added that, whilst mysticism, in the strict sense of the word, denies all possibility of explaining Divinity, Lindsay goes further, offering solutions. He does not confine himself to depicting a relationship between man and transcendent reality, but goes on to try to analyse this reality.

Between *A Voyage to Arcturus* and *Devil's Tor*, more than ten years intervene. In the latter work, the thinking is more refined, and the intuition of the former is confirmed. The theory of the Sublime has been considerably developed. In *Devil's Tor*, the Scandinavian myth of Muspel has been relegated to the background with only a few references to recall what was, in *A Voyage to Arcturus*, representative of the ideal transcendent world. At the same time, this suprasensible reality is brought considerably nearer, assuming the solidity and consistency of real life. The plan is much more ambitious than in the earlier book. Lindsay attempts nothing less than the reconstruction of the world in his own style, from its very beginnings until the end of time. The Muspel of *A Voyage to Arcturus* has become 'The Ancient'. As for Surtur, the defender of Muspel, he has been replaced by a Demiurge who is female.

David Lindsay's interpretation has its origin in the simple statement that it is impossible to imagine a male God. Such a male Creator of the Universe could not have prevented himself from giving the product of his creation certain characteristics of his own. Now, reasons Lindsay, one need only open one's eyes, and look about one, to notice that the world is essentially female. 'All the great elements of the world, the universal and all-powerful incentive of love, the enormous fact and cult of beauty, the endless production of children to supply the wastage by death, the seasonal mating of free animals, and annual rebirth of vegetation, the orbits of planets and comets, the doubtless curved paths of the stars, the tides, not only of the sea, the purely-instinctive existences of all creatures, save the moral among humans, and even of them, everything of this was so peculiarly of the female stamp, emotional, blind, repetitive, that it was as if he had found himself in a house whose every room contained women's clothes, needlework, flowers, stuffs, silken draperies, fragile furniture, infants' toys and garments; and were asked and required to consent that the residence had been equipped for his own use by a man' (*Devil's Tor*, page 474).[25]

The argument is clear. All that which is beautiful and good finds itself associated, in our mind, with women, including politeness, good manners, magnanimity, love, finesse and art. Nature, by common consent a divine creation, is, according to all the evidence, essentially female, especially as only curved lines are to be found there. To-day, psycho-analysis has come to support this interpretation, by giving to nature a maternal image. The most important human function, that of reproduction, is female. Without it, the world would long since have ceased to exist.

In conclusion, according to Lindsay, nearly all the components of the universe bear witness to belonging to this femininity. After love, women, children, beauty, nature, civilisation and art, what is left? Work and war are two activities that one readily associates with men, but also with unhappiness, pain, and even hatred. Work and war are such glaring examples of imperfection that it would be senseless to regard them as derivatives of a perfect being, the creator of the universe. We are led, both by evidence and absurdity, to the only possible interpretation; that the universe has not been created by a male God, but by a female Demiurge.

To support his proposition, David Lindsay resorts to arguments provided for him by the history of religions, and, in particular, the cult of the Great Mother. From India to the Mediterranean, there existed the same cult, as evidenced by the statuettes representing a Great Mother.[26] Christianity, too, had a Great Mother, for whom it substituted a male God. This Goddess was none other than the Virgin Mary, whose importance has been minimised by the paternalistic societies of the West.

Lindsay's Demiurge can be cruel and bloodthirsty, when necessary. In this respect, the depiction still conforms to the studies of this cult, which have shown the Great Mother to be a bellicose Goddess, presiding equally well at the production of living beings as at their destruction. Suffering is a reality that nobody can escape, not even the Creator. Between the world and its Creator, there is an identity of nature, both being based upon suffering (*Devil's Tor*, pages 473–474).

More debatable, it would seem is the Scandinavian origin that Lindsay chooses to attribute to the cult of the Great Mother. Certainly, one cannot fail to see here one of the numerous manifestations of this 'Scandinavian complex' in much of Lindsay's writing. The cult of the Great Mother could only have been born in Scandinavia, he asserts, because with no other people does one meet such reverence and admiration for women. The cult must then have spread throughout Europe, where it became degraded in contact with the societies of the South and the Orient. Crete marks one of the stages between Scandinavia, on the one hand, and Asia Minor and India, on the other. 'The cult had passed slowly eastwards, from the deep-natured, deep-sighted men of the North, to brown-skinned priests and moralists, and so on to heavily-bejewelled, painted, perfumed women, with their appropriate male companions, dancing mad orgies' (*Devil's Tor*, page 271).

Human misery then, according to Lindsay, is largely a consequence of the degradation of the feminine values embodied in the Ancient and the Great Mother. This evolution occurred partly because patriarchal societies replaced primitive matriarchal societies, and partly because the female ideal was corrupted. It is this latter aspect that should now be considered.

The problem presenting itself to Lindsay is a simple one. How is it possible to reconcile the conception of women as the source of all perfection with his own evidence of the frivolities and limitations of the 'weaker sex'?

This paradox shows that there has been continuity between the Ancient and twentieth-century woman, albeit a gradual debasement. From that, the question arises as to whether this corruption was inevitable, whether time is the cause of erosion and especially whether some happening intervened, at one stage or another, to influence the course of events. It is towards this last solution that Lindsay inclines. The Ancient, he writes belonged to 'femaleness', without being 'womanly', making the distinction that Lindsay establishes between 'female' and 'woman' (*Devil's Tor*, pages 452– 453). The female finds itself dissociated here from female sexual characteristics. At the beginning of humanity, there was femininity. The appearance of man occurred simultaneously with that of woman, in circumstances that remain quite obscure, but which permit the assertion that the human tragedy is bound up with the emergence of the bisexual condition. All evil stems from this 'unnatural' division. There can be no clearer proof of life's imperfection than the need to 'choose' a sex, which confronts us at birth. Man, just as much as woman, is condemned to be an actor on the world stage, playing a rôle imposed upon him by his own sex, compelled to lie, and to dissemble in the presence of the other sex.

Just as with Christianity, Lindsay conceives a Fall from the divine state to the human state, but here the divine state is a maternal one. The Fall is nothing else than the passing from the maternal state to the bisexual state. 'Existing alone, needing no completing half, marvellously wise, solitary, ancient, awful, the *female* had in some unthinkable hour of cosmic tragedy fallen into sex, thereafter to become the slave and sport of its derivative. Thus the unnatural effeminacies of women, their animal voluptuousness and cowardly sheltering from the knocks of the world, their infantile love of dress, their intense interest in the inter-relations of men and women, their passion to outvie other women in wealth, rank, influence, society and beauty; all come from that fall to sex' (*Devil's Tor*, page 453).

## THE HEREAFTER

On 9 November 1921, a few months after his literary début, Lindsay wrote 'We are surrounded by a terribly-queer, unseen universe.' He was referring to a personal experience. One night, Lindsay and his aunt, who lived together, heard a deafening noise, as if the roof of the house was falling in. Investigation revealed no damage. The incident was inexplicable, except by recourse to the supernatural. As far as is known, this is the sole manifestation of the supernatural that Lindsay has publicly acknowledged, although it was doubtless not the only such experience. Robert Barnes has recalled that Lindsay took a close interest in the occult sciences, but that the author of *A Voyage to Arcturus* never took part in any experiment of this kind.[27]

Lindsay's interest need surprise nobody. The period in which he lived was notable for an unusual infatuation with the supernatural. In his youth, Lindsay wallowed in this background of occultism, materialisations, ghosts and legends. His Scottish origins alone were sufficient to orientate him in this direction. As an adult, Lindsay proudly insisted upon the 'mystic sense' that he recognised in his Scottish ancestors, which he contrasted to the vulgar materialism of the majority of his English contemporaries. From the turn of the century, English society was undeniably materialistic. This did not prevent it, however, from a passionate devotion to spiritualistic research. Madam Blavatski's Theosophical Society, The Order of the Golden Dawn, and the Society for Psychical Research of F. W. Myers, are just a few of the fashionable organisations of the time.

Lindsay is the heir to this tradition. Like so many of his contemporaries, Lindsay repeats 'We are surrounded by a terribly-queer, unseen universe'. His characters, too, never cease to assert this.[28] Lindsay's mother and aunt themselves occasionally organised spiritualistic séances. It is here, however, that the common ground between Lindsay and his contemporaries comes to an end. Unlike them, Lindsay scarcely took these experiments seriously. Throughout the whole of one of these séances, Barnes and Lindsay continually exchanged winks with one another. Lindsay admits the strangeness of many of these unexplained phenomena, but he is able to recognise charlatans and amateurs. He writes in his notebooks 'It is a serious thing to invoke in cold blood the world of spirits, believing it to be really existing. Table-turning, etc., is utterly antagonistic to the solemn and deadly earnestness of such a belief' (*Philosophical Notes*, Number 157).

It was no mere chance, perhaps, that Lindsay began his writing career by describing a spiritualistic séance. One must be careful to

note, however, that this first chapter of *A Voyage to Arcturus* does not
set the tone of the rest of the book, any more than it implies any
kind of approval of the aura of mystery which so delighted the
English of that period. On the contrary, it is a denunciation of
infatuation with the occult. Lindsay clearly depicts the artificiality
of such a gathering, which consists of curious people eager for
distraction, who no more believe in the supernatural than they
respect the medium. Of what value was this medium? He may well
declare that 'spirits should be treated with more deference' (*A
Voyage to Arcturus*, page 17). He seems to forget that he himself is
acting out his rôle for money. Once the demonstration is over, the
medium is given a cheque, which he pockets without hesitation. As
for the participants, they abandon themselves to a simple game
which does not deserve to be taken seriously. The real supernatural
is elsewhere, and it begins with the departure for Arcturus.

In spite of its limitations, the séance is not a negation of the
supernatural. It is simply a condemnation of certain kinds of
approach to the supernatural and to the occult. Its principle of the
séance remains no less valid, being the communication between two
worlds, and between two ways of life. It is certainly in this way that
David Lindsay describes the medium's activities. 'Through the gaps
in his mind, the inhabitants of the invisible, when he summoned
them, passed for a moment, timidly and awfully, into the solid
coloured universe' (*A Voyage to Arcturus*, page 21).

Far from rejecting fantasy as being improbable, David Lindsay
uses it in his plots with evident predilection. He himself defined his
own style as being 'a blend of common and supernatural life'.[29] *A
Voyage to Arcturus* adds to the benefits of the imaginary journey those
of exotic marvels. The unknown serves as a kind of alibi for the
strange and the supernatural. In *Sphinx*, the unknown is the dark
area of the human mind, man's sleeping unconscious for which
Nicholas Cabot's machine searches. The analysis of dreams leads to
revelations about the conduct of the characters, which would otherwise remain incomprehensible. Finally, in *Devil's Tor*, the plot comes
no nearer to being rooted in reality. Rather does it border upon the
impossible, such as intuitions, magic stones, visions of the future,
and returns to the earliest ages of man, making the book a kind of
fresco of ghosts and distant horizons.

Of all Lindsay's writing, *The Haunted Woman* is the novel which
most closely belongs to the tradition of fantasy stories. The plot
revolves around a theme which is common ground in this field; the

discovery of a haunted house. The stereotypes of fantasy literature are easily recognisable. The background is an isolated house, several centuries old, perhaps even dating back a thousand years or more. Without being Gothic, the manor's architecture is remarkable, introducing, from the very outset, that note of strangeness which the author knows how to use in order to make the reader feel the thrill of fantasy. The austere interior seems to consist entirely of a series of corridors, more or less dark, which serve as a reminder of the vaults and caves of 'Gothic novels'. The dwelling has been unoccupied for years, and left in the charge of a couple of devoted old servants.

The care with which Lindsay depicts the atmosphere of the place is evident, as he prepares the reader for the discovery of the haunted part, which is a magic staircase that suddenly appears before certain characters, leading them to places that only they will know. The staircase serves as a transition between the everyday world and the fantasy world, very much in the manner of the rabbit-hole which led Lewis Carroll's Alice into Wonderland. As a place of transit, and a symbol of climbing from one level to another, the staircase has long been one of the principal features of the fantasy world. It is on the staircase that the ghost of Peter Quint appears, in the famous story by Henry James, *The Turn of the Screw*. It is again on the staircase that the narrator of George MacDonald's *Lilith* loses sight of the person he is pursuing.

The best fantasy stories are often stamped with ambiguity. The equivocation of *The Turn of the Screw* is legendary, and one could also cite, for instance, August W. Derleth's *The Lonesome Place*, as well as a number of tales by Edgar Allan Poe. *The Haunted Woman* is no exception to this rule. It is far from being an easy book to interpret, particularly as regards the end of the story, and the part played by the musician. Can this be Crystalman, from *A Voyage to Arcturus*, presented to us in a new disguise? Alternatively, is it the ghost of Ulf, the first owner of the house, formerly carried off by goblins?[30] What meaning should be attached to the check suffered by Isbel and Judge in their relationship? Should one attribute responsibility for this deceit to Crystalman? Is this the love-trap? Again, was Lindsay trying, as he did later in *Devil's Tor*, to stress the difference between love, even of the more sincere kind, and 'passion', whose very nature is pain and sacrifice? Were Isbel's sensuality and the chivalrous nature of Judge the major obstacles?

Whatever may be the significance, the book brings well into the forefront the contrast, common to all the Lindsay novels, between the everyday world and the magical world, or, put another way, between the 'vulgar' and the 'Sublime'. The staircase ideally fulfils its function of transition from one place to another.

With the possible exception of *A Voyage to Arcturus*, there is nothing in Lindsay's writing of pure fantasy. One does not enter a world of sheer fantasy that one finally leaves at the end of the novel, as in the case of Mervyn Peake's *Gormenghast*, for example. What happens in *The Haunted Woman*, *Sphinx* and *Devil's Tor* is that the two worlds, supernatural and everyday, are tightly interwoven. There is interaction between the two worlds, of which, it is true, only certain privileged beings are aware. Of all the visitors to Runhill Court, only Isbel discovers the narrow door which leads to the magic world. Of all the members of the Sturt family, only Evelyn is initiated into the secrets of the sleeper. Finally, in *Devil's Tor*, the 'outsider' is Peter Copping, whose mystic sense has long been atrophied by town life. 'Ghosts have never done the human race one atom of good', he boldly declares (page 134).

If Lindsay's writing is examined in its entirety, it has to be admitted that scarcely any unity of style is maintained. It is indeed difficult to define each novel in terms of the categories of fantasy and supernatural. While *A Voyage to Arcturus* belongs to the tradition of the imaginary fantasy journey, the next book, *The Haunted Woman*, is clearly supernatural. *Sphinx*, on the other hand, is solidly anchored in the reality of the everyday world, which is disturbed only by the machine for recording dreams. *Sphinx* is situated in the category of 'scientific fantasy', as defined by Todorov.[31] 'The supernatural is explained in a rational manner, but by laws not recognised by contemporary science.' As for *Devil's Tor*, it seems to defy classification.

In spite of its diversity, David Lindsay's writing is very clearly distinguishable from current fantasy trends, which are 'first and foremost a game with fear'.[32] Lovecraft insists upon this element of fear when he entitles his essay, 'Supernatural Horror in Literature'. Louis Vax speaks of 'shame of reason',[33] and Caillois of 'fissure' and of 'unusual irruption', of which Machen's novels, *The Great God Pan*, *The White People* and *The Black Seal*, constitute striking examples, being tales in which malevolent forces invade the domestic world which excludes them.

One finds this irruption of a parallel world in Lindsay, but the supernatural has nothing disturbing about it. Here, one can read, in the *Philosophical Notes*, 'So-called morbid ideas, death, ghosts, the spirit-world, etc., correspond to nothing real. It is the Sublime life calling to us, which our individualistic nature mistranslates in this fashion' (Number 399). Mrs Richborough, one of the characters in *The Haunted Woman*, who possesses psychic powers, also goes out of her way to offer a reassurance. 'For me, there's nothing whatever terrifying in the supernatural', she says (*The Haunted Woman*, page 124).

The horror shown by certain people in the face of the sudden irruption from the hereafter is the reflex defensive action of the body in the presence of the unknown (*Devil's Tor*, page 29). Fear does not exist amongst the adepts, but amongst the uninitiated and the 'vulgar'. Far from regarding the rock of Dartmoor as the tomb of an ancient princess, as it should, popular imagination has distorted history to make the place a haunt of Satan, Devil's Tor. In *The Haunted Woman*, it is not the initiated owner who fears the 'dangers' of the haunted room, but the caretaker, whose judgment is clouded by legend.

The irruption of the supernatural has the effect of depreciating the everyday domestic world, the validity of which is henceforward challenged by 'the other world'. Is the tangible world the creation of Satan, as in *A Voyage to Arcturus*? 'Light, sanity, health, purity, we value these because they are invaluable to world life. When they are opposed to gloom, witchcraft, dreams, the morbid, the supernatural, etc., we naturally regard the first as the work of God, the second as that of the Devil, but how if this "Devil" should be the voice of the real world calling us out of our dreams of sweetness and sunshine? Then history would have to be re-written and in most cases "good" and "bad" substituted for each other' (*Philosophical Notes*, Number 282).

For the man, as for the novelist, the main problem is to make these two worlds relate to one another. It is particularly as a method of communication that the occult appears in Lindsay. The occult intervenes from the earliest pages of *A Voyage to Arcturus*. The medium is the intermediary between the tangible world and the world of the spirits. In *The Haunted Woman*, thanks to her gifts as a medium, Mrs Richborough succeeds in discovering the access to the magic room, and not by any kind of *revelation*, as in the case of Isbel. Without being mediums, in the strict sense of the term, numerous characters are gifted with a sixth sense, enabling them to communicate with the universe. Artists have this particular sensibility, their spirit troubling them many times a day, as if through turbulent external events. Isbel, the heroine of *The Haunted Woman*, is an artist without knowing this. Because of this, she is sensitive to occult influences. The headache that she experiences in the hall of the haunted manor is a sign of her vulnerability. Ingrid, in *Devil's Tor*, describes herself as 'a bundle of intuitions', adding that she believes herself to be gifted with the power of a medium (pages 9–10). Hugh Drapier, too, possesses this 'mystic sense',[34] which gives him a presentiment of his coming death. Finally, Evelyn, in *Sphinx*, predicts the imminence of a tragedy, the victim of which will be either Celia or Lore (page 62).

Lindsay's characters, to a large extent, are exceptional people, but not abnormal. The occult is not presented as being an abnormality. Rather is it the contemporary world that is abnormal. If, nowadays, the occult is not very widespread, it is because civilisation, science, mass culture and the modern ideal of communal life have gradually stifled it. There once existed a Golden Age when man was clairvoyant by nature, declares Lindsay. Just as dinosaurs and mammoths have disappeared from the Earth, so has the pattern of original man failed to survive the outrages of modern civilisation. Only a few exceptional beings still possess this mystic sixth sense, and these are scarcely recognisable amongst the vast majority of people.[35] The people of Norway, and those of the Scottish Highlands, knew how to preserve their sense of the occult, asserts Lindsay. It is scarcely surprising to discover the genealogy of the characters who express, to put it candidly, the prejudices of the author. All worthy individuals, all good people, are drawn from a clan that is either Scottish or Scandinavian, as in the case of Hugh Drapier, Lore Jensen, Ingrid Colborne and many others. From one novel to the next, it is just a matter of an extension of the great family of the men of the North, eager for mystery and the supernatural, with whom are contrasted the Saxons and the Southerners, materialist and down-to-earth.

Communications with the hereafter could not become a profession, we learn from *A Voyage to Arcturus*. This is certainly because the quest is situated outside the will and intellect that, in *Sphinx*, and also in *The Haunted Woman*, direct it towards mysterious zones of the unconscious mind, of dreams and of death. The discovery of a haunted manor is the pretext for an internal quest, as evidenced by the very title of Chapter 5 of *The Haunted Woman*, 'Isbel sees herself'. The magic staircase does not just lead to the haunted room, but also marks the transition from the conscious to the subconscious. The passion that Isbel suddenly feels for Judge was not born out of nothing, she recognises, but had always existed in a deeper part of her, without her knowledge. The division produced between her deportment inside and outside the haunted room duplicates the division of herself, as between conscious and subconscious. Her bewilderment, and the shame that she then feels in denying her recent conduct, are the reflex defence mechanisms of the super-ego in face of actions which, in the light of conscience, appear irrational, and even unimaginable. From that point, the demands of the subconscious conflict with social conventions. While the conscious allies itself to normality, quite properly, the subconscious, on the other hand, appears as a disturbing force. If the breaking of her engagement, in Isbel's eyes, is an act of liberation, her relatives, for their part, view it as a catastrophe (page 120).

The investigation of the subconscious, started in *The Haunted Woman*, is pursued and amplified in *Sphinx*. While, in the former case, the dichotomy of the two worlds contrasted the haunted room and the hotel, in the latter it concerns the dream, and the state of insomnia. The rôle of the subconscious, and its links with the Sublime, could not be more clearly presented. The value of the dream does not differ from that of the subconscious in general, of which it is, according to Freud, 'the royal road'. Like the occult, dream and subconscious are doors leading to a world that is more real than the world of full consciousness. Dream and subconscious are, it seems, comparable to the Sublime, or more or less parallel to a suprasensible world.

## MUSIC

To a large extent, David Lindsay discovered the Sublime through his own personal experience, and especially through music. This last point is one that needs to be emphasised, especially as earlier studies have not dealt with this fundamental aspect.

Mention has already been made of Lindsay's musical tastes (see Chapter 1 herein). Although he played no instrument, and could not even read a musical score, he had reached a stage where music held few secrets for him. He was never a theorist, however. He lived music, and, according to his friend, Rober Barnes, whose musical education was certainly more comprehensive, Lindsay's musical judgments showed insight. While music, for most people, is a pleasant diversion, Lindsay made it a veritable art, superior to all other artistic forms. Scorning the eye, as being the organ of illusions, he regarded the ear as a divine organ, and truly the narrow door leading to ultimate reality (*Philosophical Notes*, Number 164.) At its best, music for this Beethoven-lover was not just a simple combination of sounds, but a form of grandiose expression. Everything depended upon the composer, his intentions, and his appreciation of music. No doubt, Lindsay entertained a good number of his contemporaries to a little of that scorn shown by the musician in *Sphinx*, Lore Jensen, towards non-connoisseurs.[36]

In order to understand the importance that Lindsay attached to music, there is no need to look very far, and just one sentence sums up his thinking. 'Music is the experience of a supernatural world.' The author goes on to say 'The attempt to identify it with world-experience is a proof of the practical, utilitarian nature of Man, which always tries to change the wild into the domestic' (*Philosophical Notes*, Number 490). As 'the experience of a supernatural world', music is definitively a revelation of the Sublime. The attraction of music, therefore, stems from its power of emancipation from the Earth. Music constitutes a world apart, far removed from the imperfections and falsities of our present lives. To put it more precisely, music is the proof, and the product, of a parallel world. Lindsay scarcely develops this idea, contenting himself, it seems, with drawing the conclusions to which his personal experience has led him. It is not known whether Lindsay was content to adopt the interpretation of Schopenhauer, who saw, in music, the revelation of another world, whose existence would have preceded the emergence of the present world. According to Schopenhauer, music speaks of a 'world' that is completely independent of the world of free will. It is a message coming directly from the hereafter, free of interference from the world of phenomena, unlike the other arts. As will be noticed, this interpretation is quite close to that of Lindsay.

It is possibly because it suggests the world of our origins that music is associated more with nostalgia than with Nietzschean jubilation. Anything else would be surprising. It is primarily as a release that music appears, this 'power as a releasing factor' of which Ingrid speaks, at the very beginning of *Devil's Tor*. 'You seemed under an enchantment. I fancy you were not merely held, but seriously disturbed. Where were you?' Hugh asks Ingrid, to which the young girl replies 'In a strange sphere, unsuggested by the music, I expect. Music is never more than a releasing factor for me; and that's why I am cold to nine-tenths of music, for it doesn't release. I can secure the same emancipation from things without music at all, much more slowly, but retentively on that account, as up here, alone and at peace with everything actual. I've told you something about that. *It must be the beginning of the Sublime*.' (Page 22. The italics are ours.)

Of all the arts, music alone is truly Sublime. Hence, this writing, which is presented, above all, as a conquest of the Sublime, is permeated with this philosophy of music, which is both the catalyst of the journey to the source of life and the proof of Paradise Lost. Since it operates to suggest the other world, Lindsay knew how to use music. Thunder, another manifestation of the parallel world, is 'the greatest music' (*Devil's Tor*, pages 3, 21). The magic stone that has fallen from the sky seems to emit music. Death, gateway to the hereafter, is accompanied by 'solemn music' (page 71). The mystic union of Ingrid and Saltfleet takes place against a background of 'mystical music'.

Far from being a mere prop, music is the very pillar upon which rests Lindsay's writing. In view of this, it is scarcely surprising to find, amongst all the characters in search of another world, an exceptional number of musicians. Lore Jensen is a professional musician. Ingrid is overwhelmed by Beethoven's 'Waldstein' Sonata. Isbel and Mrs Moor are admirers of Brahms and Beethoven. Nicholas Cabot is the son of a violinist. The presence of so many music-lovers is enough to explain the importance of the theme, but one can go further. There is no book by Lindsay which does not contain a piece of music that, in some way, sets the style. Each one begins with the performance of a piece, as if the author wanted to fix the tone of the novel. *A Voyage to Arcturus* begins with an extract from Mozart's *Magic Flute*, but it is rather the music of Swaylone that symbolises most of the book. 'Now, men when they make music are accustomed to build beautiful tones, because of the delight they cause. Therefore their music world is based on pleasure;

its symmetry is regular and charming, its emotion is sweet and lovely, but my music is founded on painful tones; and thus its symmetry is wild, and difficult to discover; its emotion is bitter and terrible' (page 158). In *The Haunted Woman*, the solemn entry into the haunted manor is against the background of Beethoven's Seventh Symphony, which Lindsay calls 'the Supernatural Symphony', in his *Philosophical Notes*.[37] In *Sphinx*, the tone is different, with variations, and a crescendo that is skilfully orchestrated. Once again, however, it is the music which defines the novel, whose title, 'Sphinx', is borrowed from a musical composition by Lore Jensen (*Sphinx*, page 32). Finally, in *Devil's Tor*, Lindsay returns to his great love, Beethoven, and his most grandiose work, the Ninth Symphony. The book itself has all the massiveness and complexity of Beethoven's work. The same anguish and hesitation are found there, but, while Beethoven's symphony is a discovery of human joy, as affirmed in the final movement by the choir, *Devil's Tor* ascends, clumsily but surely, to the inhuman spheres of the Sublime. If the book ends less well than it starts, it should nevertheless be recognised that its opening has the truly impressive quality of a Beethoven overture.[38]

There is no better aid than music to suggest visitations from the hereafter. Mozart's music overwhelms the spectators, as if, according to Lindsay, there were no common dimension between the world of music and the clubs of idle, vulgar Londoners. The entry into the manor house evokes an identical impression of penetrating a world apart, 'the land of giants' of the Seventh Symphony. In *The Haunted Woman*, the spectators, Judge, Marshall and Isbel, arrive from different places, meet in the hall, and settle down for the 'concert'. The musicians are heard tuning their instruments (pages 40 and 41), in preparation for a symphony (page 34), 'as if a curtain were about to be drawn up, revealing a new and marvellous world' (page 27). Scarcely have Judge and Isbel entered this marvellous world of the supernatural, the haunted room, than the soloist appears, in the form of a flute player, whose tune, of a surprising strangeness, is both delicate and impassioned (page 132).

So great is Lindsay's love of music that it ends in dominating the ideological background, to become a technique of expression, and a style in itself. This writer may span the world, without really seeing it, and emphasis has already been given to the impoverishment of his power of realistic narration, but music is the one thing that does not pass unnoticed. In *The Haunted Woman*, nearly all the descriptions of Brighton life are confined to a limited framework, such as a hurdy-gurdy grinding out its tune in the town's alleys (page 13), or an orchestra playing on the promenade (pages 19, 36). That is what Lindsay remembers of the life of England's premier seaside resort, then at the height of its popularity.

Is it on principle, by inclination or by omission, that the writer draws most of his pictures against a background of music? The sunrise makes him think of the opening bars of a Beethoven symphony (*A Voyage to Arcturus*, page 237). An elegant pose suggests 'a lovely fall of music' (*Devil's Tor*, page 87). Mountains seen from a distance impress Maskull 'like a simple musical theme, the notes of which are widely separated in the scale' (*A Voyage to Arcturus*, page 69). Then, when he takes Oceaxe in his arms, it seems to him that the young girl's body responds to him as if it were a harp (page 86).

The inhabitants of Arcturus speak English. This does not prevent their voices being so melodious as to suggest that they are more familiar with music than with the language of Shakespeare. Panawe's voice is 'like a bewitching adagio from a low-toned string instrument' (page 71). Joiwind's voice, in contrast, resembles music from a violin (page 78), while that of Oceaxe has the sweetness of a flute (page 86).[39] It would be easy, no doubt, to set *A Voyage to Arcturus* to music, so obvious is it that the score has already been written, from the *Magic Flute* tune at the beginning to the waltz with which the book ends.

Music does not appear merely as a metaphor. There is a real orchestra to play the *Magic Flute*. There is also Earthrid, whose music, in irresistible tones, comes from beyond the sea to the ears of travellers whom he condemns to death as victims of the sirens of the island of Lotus Eaters. Finally, there is Tydomin's song, the 'grotesque melody' of the slave who sings in spite of the corpse that she carries on her shoulders. Of all the musical themes in *A Voyage to Arcturus*, there is one which predominates, by virtue of its force and repetition, and this is the beat of the drum, guiding Maskull in his quest.[40] At first only faintly heard, this beating grows in intensity, becoming more and more distinct, until the final scene, when it is like the deafening noise of a gong which reverberates throughout the world. One sees what advantage Lindsay can draw from such an idea. It is clearly as a musician that he handles it. To re-read the chapter entitled 'The Wombflash Forest' is proof enough of this. In the silence and darkness of the forest, from which he can see no escape, Maskull suddenly hears the distant noise of the drum. Immediately, he starts to walk in that direction. Though weak and intermittent at first, the beat gradually grows in intensity as Maskull approaches it. Soon, there is added music which rapidly swells in volume, to break into a deafening concert, so grandiose that Maskull feels himself carried away by the music, and ends by losing consciousness.[41] This is the first revelation of the Sublime.

Upon a closer examination of the book, it is noticeable that *A Voyage to Arcturus* rests upon the alternation of two rhythms, one being the march in two-four cadence, and the other the waltz in three-four time. The military march, timed by the beat of the drum, is a symbolic representation of the hero's quest. This is why, in a dream, Maskull's destiny appears to him in the form of a march, when three men, Krag, Nightspore and Maskull himself, move straight ahead, one after the other (page 135). It is later learned that the march corresponds to the movement of the 'green corpuscles', which, in Lindsay's cosmogony, symbolise the beings trying to regain their divine origins.

At the opposite end of the spectrum are the 'turbulent corpuscles', symbolising those beings who have renounced the quest, in order to abandon themselves to the pleasures of dancing, loving and, indeed, crime. These 'turbulents' are the human equivalent of the music in three-four waltz time. Circular movement, therefore, lacking progression, is the symbol of the corrupted life of Arcturus. Here lies the explanation of just a few of the fruits of Lindsay's imagination, and, in particular, those strange animals and vegetables of Arcturus which move in circular fashion.[42] This circular motion, or waltz, is for them the equivalent of the grin displayed by the humans on Arcturus; it is in a sense, their trade-mark, and immediately identifies them as creatures of Crystalman.

A composer would have little trouble in making use of these two rhythms of the march and waltz in order to illustrate the contrast between, on the one hand, the quest for the ideal, and, on the other, the satisfaction of immediate interests in the quest for pleasure.

'Only a very few people will ever read *A Voyage to Arcturus*, but, as long as even two or three people will listen to Beethoven, two or three people will read it', declared Lindsay, with that mixture of humility and arrogance that is so characteristic of his personality. In order to write, he had to use words, but the artist in him was closer to the musician. He contemplated the world in philosophical terms, and tried to convey his intuitions and reflections in the way a musician would have been able to do. His undeniable guide was Beethoven, whose symphonies, too, encroach upon the present in order to confront man with his metaphysical destiny. The rhythm of Lindsay's books draws its inspiration from the unfolding of a musical work, consisting of a slow introduction, followed by characteristic themes, a staccato passage, and a finale which is sometimes clear, and sometimes vague, as if the book ended with a question. The music is not only descriptive, but interrogates, suggesting bridges between the world down here and the hereafter. It is a form of expression, but also a form of life, to the point that, when he comes to describe the metamorphoses of the soul, in search of its origins, Lindsay will have recourse to the 'three musics', these being, respectively, liberation from the everyday world, discovery of the soul, and incorporation of the human soul with the Absolute (*The Witch*, pages 353–354).

## *THE VIOLET APPLE* AND *THE WITCH*

When he died, David Lindsay left two unpublished novels, entitled respectively *The Violet Apple* and *The Witch*. The former was written while Lindsay was still at the beginning of his literary career. Started in February 1924, it was apparently finished in July that same year. Hence, the writing was fairly rapid. The novel did not achieve its expected success, and, after several rejections by publishers, Lindsay returned to the typescript to make revisions. The new version gained no more success than the earlier one, however, and the author decided to put it away in a drawer.

More than half a century would have to pass before this book became available through the welcome enterprise of Chicago Review Press in the United States, and of Sidgwick and Jackson in England.[1] In the chronology of Lindsay's works, *The Violet Apple* lies after *Sphinx*, but before *Devil's Tor*. Moreover, the three books are similar in many respects, and these new publications will certainly allow many readers to discover an aspect of David Lindsay that is little known, to the extent that both *Sphinx* and *Devil's Tor* have long been unobtainable in England, and out of print. These publications, inspired by the renewed interest shown in Lindsay's books, also confirm an evolution in the writer towards a style which is his own, with a conception of plot and characters that is rather stiff.

From *Sphinx*, Lindsay took up again the essential elements of the novel form, consisting of backgrounds, characters and situations. The background is provided by another of those country houses encountered previously. Kent has replaced the Hampshire of *Sphinx*, but the house itself remains virtually unchanged. Aside from the original village, half a dozen prestige houses have been established in this rural setting. Their apparent charm, with their flower-beds and their curtains of trees, cannot hide their nature, which could scarcely be better symbolised than by the very name given to the street in question, which is Malfait Street, French for 'Badly-Made Street'. The arrival of the townspeople seems like an intrusion. The discerning reader knows that the journey of Anthony Kerr, a fashionable London playwright, cannot be anything but the confirmation of false values, or the upheaval of the community and the discovery of a reason for being different.

The reader already familiar with Lindsay's work will not be surprised to learn that the arrival of Anthony Kerr, and his friend, Jim Lytham, sets in motion a chain of marriage plans. Jim announces his engagement to a neighbour in the village, Haidee Croyland. In order not to be outdone, Anthony discovers his attachment to Jim's sister, Grace, and loses no time in announcing his own engagement, somewhat hastily. The plot of the novel concerns the setback to the marriage plans, which are thwarted by the irresistible attraction that Haidee and Anthony feel for one another, thus breaking up the couples.

Such themes as the young girl ready for marriage, the eligible bachelor, the engagements which miscarry on the ground of a higher morality that places emphasis on a quasi-mystical union to the detriment of an 'ordinary' marriage of reason or convenience, are none of them new with Lindsay. Indeed, they might even be termed recurring ones. If, to these stereotype situations, there is added an ironical depiction of the shabbiness of human relations, compromises, jealousies and selfish motives, the reader will have quite an exact picture of *The Violet Apple*.

This is not to say that *The Violet Apple* is a mere pastiche of *Sphinx*. The second part of the book is already the forerunner of *Devil's Tor*, in the sense that, for the first time, Lindsay goes beyond simple criticism, proposing a solution to the ills he has been at pains to expose so fully. *Sphinx* was a book that was full of bitterness, and even cynicism. It ended tragically with the death of the hero. The only glimmer of hope in this sombre book was the reunion in death of the lovers who had been separated in life.

*The Violet Apple* is undoubtedly more convincing, in that it reunites Haidee and Anthony in their lifetime. Ultimately, this union does not have the mustiness of mysticism evident in *Devil's Tor*, and, later, in *The Witch*. The man and woman who, at the end of the book, turn towards Nature, resolved to lead a simple existence together for the rest of their days, are beings of flesh and blood, even if their union is essentially spiritual, or 'a marriage of true minds'.

Even though Lindsay commenced his career in the manner already seen, with the experiments of *A Voyage to Arcturus*, and then, on a smaller scale, with the metaphysical upheavals of *The Haunted Woman*, one can see his conception of the novel, at the same time, assuming both form and discipline, to the point that the reader comes to regret the outpourings of imagination that both surprised and seduced the reader of his first two novels.

The novels evolve from a 'romanticism', where the imagination holds sway, to a 'classicism', where precision prevails. The fanciful element has certainly not disappeared, but its importance has diminished, while human relationships have been developed at the expense of communication with the hereafter. There remains, in *The Violet Apple*, what can only be called a gimmick, which serves once again, as a catalyst for the uncanny, somewhere between the natural and the supernatural. In this case, it is a seed, the origins of which go back to the beginning of the world, and which, once transplanted, yields this violet apple which inspires the novel's title. The apple that has come from the Dark Ages, like the magic stone in *Devil's Tor*, operates both as an introduction to the metaphysical world and also to a superior level of communication.

What could be more classical than this almost excessive respect for the unities of time and place? Never again did Lindsay compress his plot into such a limited period of time; the duration of the plot is from Friday morning to the following Sunday week, a total of ten days. The hours of the day are specified precisely. Dates are lacking, but it is known that the events take place in the month of April, and, in particular, around Easter.

Such a concentration could be damaging to the plot, but Lindsay has been careful to construct his novel around a crisis. The method is not new. It consists of introducing the characters in the few preceding days, and showing the upheaval of a routine existence, following an unexpected incident, consisting, in this case, of the breaking of a glass, which contains the seed. The pip then becomes an apple, and a veritable apple of discord, similar to the one in mythology which Paris gives to Venus. The apple introduces this discord, breaks up the couples, disrupts the families, and ruins most promising careers. At the end of the book, the Kerr family has disintegrated when the brother renounces his sisters. Hence, *The Violet Apple* contains the metaphor of explosion, which has already been emphasised.

The unity of place is observed with no less care than the unity of time. The greater part of the novel is set against the background of a

Kent village called Brasted, and, more particularly, the house of the Kerr family. The book opens with the same transition, from London to the provinces, and the same entry to the house, that has already been seen in *Sphinx* and *The Haunted Woman*. The confrontation of ideas can have no other background but a house in the country. The town is incapable of permitting such interrogation and quest. In order to discover oneself, one must be confronted by Nature.

Besides being a country-house, 'Croom' is also a holiday home. Anthony Kerr goes there to spend the week-end, even though he brings work with him. The neighbours are idle people, either, as in the case of Haidee's parents, retired, or else of independent means, like Jim Lytham. The pressures of work are not great. Even Anthony Kerr writes his plays by dictating them.

The novel technique used by Lindsay from *The Haunted Woman*, therefore, appears quite rigid. The framework, the plot and the main themes have scarcely changed. The number of characters introduced is noticeably the same from one novel to the next, that is around ten. Only the rather complex family links make *The Violet Apple* perhaps more difficult to read than the earlier books. There is unquestionably in this novel a theatrical side that is still more pronounced by virtue of the almost exclusive use of dialogue and direct style in the first part of the book, up to the point at which Haidee decides to eat the apple. At this stage, the book see-saws. Not only does one see the upheaval in the life of the protagonists, but the writing itself matches this change in the plot. Instead of dialogues, there are descriptions, such as the passage of great beauty on the rebirth of nature in the spring (page 173), a description of great delicacy worthy of a truly great writer. It is not only the style that is reminiscent of the theatre. The characters follow the pattern of drawing-room comedy. The secondary characters, in particular, are types that are easily recognisable, such as the unworthy and authoritarian father, Mr Croyland, the submissive wife, Mrs Croyland, the pseudo-intellectual, Silvester, the young madcap, and the two old-maid sisters, Marian and Josephine. Of the secondary characters, only Virginia is convincing, since she is not drawn as a caricature. Hence, what might have seemed an extravagant form becomes justified if one recognises the author's intention to give his book a theatrical sense, comprising conception of the characters, and the use of dialogue. *The Violet Apple*, therefore, must be seen as the supreme prolongation of the theatrical metaphor, of which numerous ramifications have already been introduced,[2] proceeding much more coherently this time, because the principal character, Anthony Kerr, is a playwright.

Behind this story of broken engagements, there is assuredly a criticism of contemporary society. Even though verbose, the criticism remains quite virulent. This residential complex is a collection of monstrosities of the modern world. We live in a time when metal is king. The modern instrument of torture is called a telephone. Men, so proud of their science, and fervent disciples of progress, appear in Lindsay's writing in a light that Aldous Huxley would have understood, such as 'a petty heap of blind, wriggling, three-dimensional, insect-like beings, surrounded by terrific unseen forces' (page 14). The glory of all existence, therefore, is to detach onself from the prosaic reality that surrounds one, in order to communicate with the living forces of the supernatural world. Whatever human tragedy there is lies in this loss of feeling for the supernatural and marvellous, of which only few writers of fantasy have yet shown proof. Men and writers should, according to Lindsay, turn more often to the marvellous. Education does not escape reproach. Lindsay accuses it of running counter to harmonious development, by its intense intellectual and physical demands. The myth of progress is then vigorously denounced. Far from encouraging the reader to look towards the future, Lindsay invites him to turn back to a Golden Age, irrevocably past certainly, but from which he can gain inspiration.

*The Violet Apple* would perhaps be more optimistic if Lindsay had greater faith in human relationships. Between the characters in the book, the bonds are tight, involving cousins, fiancés, children and parents, and yet the author insists upon the severance of these relationships. Once again, we are at the heart of the feminine world, with its plots, rivalries, jealousies and irrational dislikes. 'It was natural for a man to wish to escape for a time from a perpetual atmosphere of censure, antagonism and suspicion', Anthony tells himself, at the moment when he decides to leave Brasted. It is a safe wager that this is an opinion that Lindsay shared.

One cannot fail to notice the recurrence of the theme of broken engagements, assuredly one of the essential ingredients of Lindsay's novels, since it is to be found in *The Haunted Woman*, *Sphinx*, *Devil's Tor* and *The Violet Apple*, not forgetting *A Voyage to Arcturus*, which contains more than one amatory setback. In all these cases, Isbel,

Nicholas, Ingrid, Jim, and, finally, Anthony, a fragile love, built upon good sense, security and routine, is broken by the unexpected meeting with a third party. Does this indicate a tenacious obsession, stemming from a very personal embarrassment, having its roots in the breaking of his own engagement, which he hoped to exorcise through literature?[3] Alternatively, was this interest that Lindsay felt with regard to women prolonged only as far as this institution of marriage, which symbolises the man–woman relationship? At no time had Lindsay expressed his views on marriage with such frankness. For the first time, also, he depicts a couple 'united in the bonds of matrimony', to quote the sacred formula, these being Haidee's parents, Mr and Mrs Croyland.

Behind Lindsay's questioning on the nature of the sexes, therefore, lies the question as to what it is that brings together these seemingly different beings, and makes them live together all their lives? 'Aren't you in love with the poor old chap?' Haidee is asked. 'In love? How medieval! I absolutely have never asked myself. Does one marry for love?' she counters.

It is evident that the question could not be posed more clearly, and Lindsay's answer scarcely leaves any room for ambiguity. In the majority of cases, the inclination is sometimes rooted in admiration, but more often in a degree of flattery. 'For what were marriages? A girl, during the flowering time of her life, met a limited number of men. She more or less admired, or was more or less flattered by, one of them, accepted his hand, fancied herself to be in love, and behaved accordingly. It was sex-instinct first, and the individual second' (*The Violet Apple*, page 209).

One gathers from this that the idea of lovers made for each other dates back to the chivalry of the Middle Ages. Jim Lytham is thus depicted by Lindsay in ironic terms. 'If only he were less of a gentleman! These knights had no place in modern life, they were anachronisms, and a modern girl, with her quickly-changing moods and needs, would never, if she were sensible, place herself in relations with such survivors of former days. A man ought to be able to love without making himself ridiculous about it.' Haidee provides the proof of this. Jim is the fiancé of convenience. A certain Brownhill is her father's preference. Only Anthony shares spiritual affinities with her.

It is worth adding that close spiritual bonds are not frequent among couples depicted by Lindsay. The majority are cast in the mould of Mr and Mrs Croyland, where the husband is authoritarian, a heavy drinker and a womaniser, and the wife is humble and submissive in her rôle as household supervisor.

Can one blame these ill-assorted couples, and allege selfish motives? It is not quite as easy as that. Certainly, between love and like there is more than a mere shade of difference. The esteem and affection felt by a man and woman for one another could be sufficient justification for their union. Let us not forget *Devil's Tor*! It is almost with regret that Ingrid abandons her plans to marry Peter. Anthony is very well aware of the good points of his fiancée, Grace. Might her delicacy, Nordic beauty and refinement not compensate for the lack of any artistic sense? Is there not some satisfaction in marrying a perfect housewife? Equally, if the contemplated marriage of Haidee to Jim is not the ideal union, at least it guarantees her liberty and the prospect of plenty of travel and of never lacking anything.

The ambiguity of marriage is real and justifies every hesitation. It may be necessary to seek its origin in the instability of feminine nature. In this book, one finds the same reflections as before on the mystery of the Eternal Female. This world is made of ups and downs, and of sudden reversals and disconcerting experiences. Nothing seems to fit Haidee Croyland for the rôle of 'Angel of God' which falls to her at the end of the book. Believed to be flirtatious, she proves herself to be passionate. Far from being superficial, she gives evidence of an unsuspected sensibility. Who would have believed that, with her foreign, Southern appearance, she would be able to symbolise the ideal woman? Lindsay has so accustomed the reader to prefer the Nordic type that this choice here cannot be anything but a surprise. Between the pallor of Grace and the exotic richness of Haidee, Anthony is torn two ways. For once, it is the Southern nature that prevails.

Emphasis has already been laid upon the permanence of the theme of upheaval in David Lindsay's books, with its metaphors of explosion and storm, personality flaws, precipices, pits, holes, caves, tombs, pools and the varied countryside of Arcturus. *The Violet Apple* is possibly *the* classic Lindsay novel of rupture. There is the incident at the beginning of the story, for example, of the breaking of the serpent, a glass ornament that Jim Lytham unluckily smashes, and which contains a seed emanating, according to legend, from the tree of Genesis. The broken object unleashes a succession of ruptures, one after the other, upsets the established order of things, and, at the same time, opens a breach by which a metaphysical element can be introduced into the story.[4]

The couples separate, and family ties are severed. Haidee leaves her parents, whilst Anthony becomes estranged from his sisters. Both make their escape from Malfait Street. The writing style adjusts itself to the direction taken by the story. Quite suddenly, dialogue gives way to description. On an interior level, the upheaval is no less intense. There is no actual fracture of the personality, as in the case of Isbel in *The Haunted Woman*, but rather a rejection of one part of the self which is felt to be repugnant. Anthony breaks with a part of himself, and with his past, since he resolves to bring his writing career to an end. Haidee, too, previously so flirtatious, comes to reject triviality. The metaphor of the storm has not completely disappeared. 'These were but the first mutterings of a tremendous storm to come' (page 100), but it tends to be replaced by a new metaphor; the cross. One has to wait until the final pages of the book for the precise meaning of this sign that Anthony has revealed on a picture in his collection. The cross, which can be discerned in the background of the picture, relates to a rupture between man, on the one hand, and his career and his past, on the other. Anthony draws a cross on his past life.

This description of *The Violet Apple* might give the impression of a book that is entirely negative, dominated by quarrels and ruptures. It is nothing of the kind. Novel of rupture it may be, but it is also a novel of union and discovery. For the first time in one of Lindsay's books, the final outcome brings together two people in love with one another. In the case of Maskull and Sullenbode, Isbel and Judge, and Lore and Nicholas, all their idylls ended in disaster. This time, however, in striking contrast, Anthony and Haidee love each other, and prepare to live together. The book offers solutions. The quest for a new way of life leads to the discovery of new values.

Firstly, it is impossible to over-emphasise the deep nostalgia for the past which provides the counter-balance to the disgust felt in the face of contemporary reality. Although he often extols the virtues of invention and initiative, Lindsay remains a conservative at heart, and a man looking towards the past rather than to the future.

The little apple-tree that Virginia succeeds in making grow is the link with the past. The mythical connotations which surround it also serve to widen the scope of the story, which goes beyond

Anthony and Haidee to encompass humanity as a whole. An allusion to Adam and Eve can be seen behind this tale of the eaten apple which constitutes the theme of *The Violet Apple*.

To cite all the allusions to Genesis would be quite impossible here. The pip which gives birth to the violet apple comes from the Tree of Life, in the Garden of Eden. Probably never throughout Lindsay's writing has the fascination with the Golden Age been more clearly exposed. 'I happen to be one of those queer folk who have faith in Eden, or its equivalent. The farther back you go, the lovelier people seem to have been. Somewhere, at some time, there has been a very lofty chain of celestial mountains from which the rivers have been flowing down ever since to water our modern civilisation, and, should they ever run dry, they can never, never be replenished.'

There is a return to the past, therefore, but, more simply, a return to childhood. Lindsay gladly subscribed to the claim that the child is father to the man. The adult has much to learn from his past, such as the innocence of the child, his capacity to be enraptured in a world of adults where the impossible no longer exists, and the benefits of imagination and belief in the marvellous. These ideas reflect the tastes of the time.[5] In this context, the marvellous is not the subject of a game, but of an occupation that is deadly serious.[6]

The return to Paradise Lost, the nostalgia for childhood and the taste for the phenomenal are all precisely the themes of an essay by Marthe Robert on Romantic novelists. For her, novelists are either romantics or realists. The former have the childhood which they have never renounced, the taste for the phenomenal, fairy tales and the impossible. They avoid anything real, and, being mentally childlike, believe in the total power of ideas. As inveterate narcissists, they reject all relationships. They do not confront the father, but disown him. The novel would therefore be the resurgence of what Freud has called 'the family novel of the neurotics', this biographical fable that the child invents to explain the shame of being ill-born, ill-provided and ill-loved, and in which he reconstructs the world to his liking, disowning notably his parents, in order to invent a more glorious relationship.

One can see how closely the subtle analysis of Marthe Robert[7] could be applied to Lindsay. We need not dwell upon all the various elements in this study which support the theories of Marthe Robert, and liken Lindsay to the other authors cited, including Cyrano de Bergerac, Jean Paul, Novalis and others. *The Violet Apple* clearly shows the rejection of relationships. Anthony and Haidee, the 'foundlings' of Marthe Robert, repudiate parents and families in order to achieve a more glorious ascendance, in the manner of Adam and Eve. Through Anthony and Haidee, the experience of Genesis is repeated. This violet apple is, in a sense, a legacy from their ancestors.

Quite often, moreover, this negation of the father leads, in practice, to a veneration of the mother, theoretically destroyed, but reappearing with the characteristics of the spouse. Such is certainly the picture created by Haidee in Anthony's eyes, when the author says 'It was as if she represented for him some unthinkable, lofty, *maternal*, protecting, spiritual influence.'

It is scarcely surprising to find that Nature is another direction in which the search for origins leads. It should not be forgotten that psycho-analysis often makes of Nature a maternal image. *The Violet Apple* confirms once more the movement so often described, from the town towards the country, though the book goes much further. Not only does Anthony abandon his career as a playwright, based firmly in London, but he also finds a vocation as a gentleman farmer. 'I'm going to buy some land, probably in Cornwall, and work on it.' Elsewhere, he reaffirms his spiritual creed in saying 'Woods, hills, streams and meadows, the sun and rain, clouds, breezes, thunder and lightning; they are a man's natural environment, and out of them sprang the true inspirations of Heaven.'

The quest for reality culminates in the affirmation, so sad in a writer, that 'art is the still-born travesty of life.' With Anthony Kerr's experience, Lindsay boldly tackles a question which never ceased to torment him, and which can be found in an almost identical form in Aldous Huxley, whose affinities with Lindsay have not been sufficiently stressed. This question is whether, in view of the problems posed by life, the occupation of a writer can be justified. Is there an intrinsic validity in literature?

The artist, Lore Jensen, has already coloured the debate. Lore was a musician, while Anthony Kerr is a playwright, making him, in Lindsay's scale of values, the most contemptible example of the writer, not only because the theatre, by its very nature, is a dissimulation, but also because its aim is to manufacture truth, to imitate reality, to copy life, and to manipulate characters. Anthony Kerr, as a writer, is redeemed by the use he makes of metaphysical elements, but, at the same time, by doing so, he contradicts the nature of the theatre, which is to copy reality. The tensions of the writer exist between these two poles. In the struggle between the theatre's illusion of truth and the metaphysical illusion of unreality, it is the latter which prevails.

Anthony Kerr is a writer, but one who is ashamed of himself. For him, there is always the unhappy compromise between satisfying a public taste that is scarcely demanding, and thus earning money, and, on the other hand, the desire to express his ideas on the world, and, notably, his belief in the occult. It is from this conflict that there springs the association of realism and fantasy, buffoonery and cynicism, frivolity and determination. The co-existence of these discordant elements is not accomplished without some inner discord. It is from this that there is born this existentialist anxiety already met in Isbel, Hugh Drapier and Lore Jensen; a spiritual discomfort which, in the long term, ends by removing all desire to live, and of which cynicism is, as with Huxley, one of the rare antidotes.

Does art offer a solution to the pain of living? Is it possible to resist the temptation of success, and of money easily earned? How can one avoid despising readers who are too easily satisfied? Do not readers ask to be reassured and flattered? Is it the aim of literature, as the critics wish, to 'assist the progress of goodness', or, as Lindsay wishes, to 'assist the enlargement of the soul'? Is not original literature condemned in advance by the omnipotence of literary critics? Can a writer reconcile the demands of his art with his family obligations? To put it in different terms, is not literature the author's spouse? Is not the true work of art already exposed to us in our contemplation of Nature, rather than in a dead object such as a book? *The Violet Apple* contains all these questions, and Anthony Kerr's answer is scarcely encouraging, in that he finds it necessary to abandon writing, or, at any rate, the writing of plays.

The debate was also that of David Lindsay himself. Hence, the publication to-day of *The Violet Apple* provides the indication that, as early as 1924, five years after he had started writing, Lindsay was already more than sceptical about the value of his calling. To carry the matter a stage further, if, as it seems, he showed little enthusiasm for getting the book published, was it not because it raised problems too intimately linked to the situation of the writer, and that the answers it contained amounted to an avowal of literary suicide? Was it not, perhaps, undesirable to reveal so openly the doubts raised by literature, even while the author was trying to learn about it? To leave the typescript in a drawer was one way of hiding the problem, and not becoming publicly involved in this field so strewn with pitfalls. It would be better to wait for *The Witch* for the doubts to be resolved.

Lindsay's final novel, *The Witch*, must unquestionably be considered as one of his most important books, even if it is not the most successful. When Lindsay died, the book was unfinished, though it lacked only a few concluding chapters. Although J. B. Pick seems to have reduced considerably the size of the typescript, the present edition (Chicago Review Press, 1976) indicates clearly enough what would have been the size of the whole work when finished. Lindsay himself attached exceptional importance to it, and did not hesitate to describe it as 'one of the world's greatest books'. He started to write it in 1932, just after the publication of *Devil's Tor*. The first version was finished in 1934, but refused by Victor Gollancz. During the next five years, Lindsay revised his typescript, day after day, though with little hope of ever finding a publisher. By 1939, the book was practically finished, but the outbreak of World War II inspired Lindsay to a long period of intense activity. The result of this protracted labour is a novel of prodigious complexity, but one which lacks spontaneity.

*The Witch* is not devoid of interest. It recalls *A Voyage to Arcturus* in its philosophy and technique. One finds the same abundance of ideas, and the same attention to every detail of the story, which had contributed to the success of Lindsay's first book. In its way, *The Witch* is a masterpiece of organisation comparable to the most ambitious works, but the novel, as a work of art, is left to suffocate under the weight of the philosophy. If the beginning is more in tune with a traditional novel, the end, which is particularly obscure, is more reminiscent of an esoteric philosophical treatise. It is no less important, in the sense that it constitutes Lindsay's spiritual testament, and brings clarification to the philosophy that has never previously been treated in such a systematic manner. The book also reveals the extent to which Lindsay's preoccupations were removed from contemporary philosophical trends.

Lindsay's doubts regarding the value of literature are certainly not absent from *The Witch*, which offers a very firm conclusion in this respect. For the second time, the book's hero is a writer. Lindsay even goes so far as to attribute to him certain characteristics which cannot fail to be interpreted as being autobiographical, such as, for instance, 'He felt that his condition was abnormal, the inevitable result of these absurd embarkations upon major works of literary imagination. Some devil was in it that he should write his books, read by few, comprehended by fewer, wanted by none!'

Such, then, is Ragnar Pole, the hero of this new novel, whose name is no less bizarre than that of earlier characters. If Lindsay does not emphasise Ragnar Pole's profession, he certainly ensures that other characters express their ideas on literature. Chief among these is Waldo, Ragnar's brother, editor of a magazine currently in difficulties. Far from being treated to any reiteration of the doubts of *The Violet Apple*, the reader is offered a lesson in optimism, and faith in the future of literature. Even reading taste is in a process of evolution, one is told. Serious literature is about to see the light of day. The book form, once threatened by radio, has resisted very well.

The characters described in *The Witch* belong almost exclusively to the worlds of literature and music. We are amongst people of the same background, with affinities and preoccupations that are either identical or very close. We are, one might say, amongst the élite, the aristocracy of the spirit, whose members can lay claim to enlightenment. The tone of the book is accordingly more structured than hitherto. There are no quarrels, and no scandals amongst individuals who respect and admire each other. One of the principal affinities concerns Germany, which cannot fail to appear daring when it is remembered that the book was written in the few years preceding World War II. Three characters who play a vital rôle in Ragnar's adventure are either German or Austrian; namely, Cecilie Toller, Marya Klangst and Urda Noett.

Lindsay certainly wished, in this last book, to pay renewed homage to Germany, and its philosophers, musicians, writers and language. It is also true that *The Witch* marks a return to a genre directly inspired by the German 'fairy tales'. After a series of novels in which 'realistic' elements played a considerable part, *The Witch* is situated more in the realm of the novels written at the beginning of Lindsay's career, *A Voyage to Arcturus* and *The Haunted Woman*, both of which were dominated by metaphysical elements. The influence of the fairy tale is clear. The other world has an extraordinary presence. The reader is taken into a world that is closer to the dream than to the real world. The spiritual adventure is paralleled by an investigation of the nature of reality, conducted in ideological terms. The depiction of characters often gives way to theoretical argument. The writer reveals his preference for spiritual conditions which he then proceeds to reproduce fictionally. This is a kind of literature that had its origin in the German Romantics, notably Novalis and Tieck, and which also inspired George MacDonald.[8]

*The Witch* is the story of a rather unusual man, Ragnar Pole, who is ill at ease in the modern world, and haunted by a young girl with the body of a sorceress, Urda Noett. She first appears to him in a dream. Fascinated by the secret that she conceals behind her enigmatic personality, Ragnar agrees to go to meet her, in company with a young girl, Faustine Gaspary. This amounts, in fact, to a spiritual adventure, similar to Surtur's quest in *A Voyage to Arcturus*. Urda has the same double rôle as Krag in the latter novel, being both guide and object of the quest. Urda is the Surtur of *A Voyage to Arcturus*, the incarnation of the vital principle which assures to the world its essentially spiritualistic nature. The meeting between Urda and Ragnar is, for the latter, the beginning of a process of spiritualisation, consisting of three separate stages; (1) emancipation from the Earth, under the influence of the amorous passion felt for Faustine, (2) discovery of the soul as an entity, in a moment of ecstatic calm, (3) incorporation of the human soul in the universal soul. These three stages are called the 'three musics'.

Apart from the philosophical interest of the book, its value lies in the literary techniques chosen to express almost exclusively the states of the soul. The first chapters serve as an explanation, and naturally appear more realistic. They are, however, particularly symbolic. They serve also to introduce the characters, some of whom will play only a limited rôle in what follows. Conversely, Faustine, who is only a secondary character at the outset, will be seen to assume a vital rôle. There is clearly recognisable here one of Lindsay's theories on fictional creation. 'In fiction, a similitude to real life is effected by a minor character in the opening becoming a major character later on, and finally occupying the centre of interest' (*Philosophical Notes*, Number 390).

The story is presented in traditional Lindsay style, consisting of the journey, firstly out of London to Sussex, and then on foot to the Downs. The journey is the poetic equivalent of the spiritual quest. As regards the geographical framework, its function is to express the states of the soul, and to indicate the progress of the journey. The technique is not new. It is used by G. MacDonald. Very familiar, moreover, is the way in which Graham Greene has capitalised on the equation of the plot and the place in which it unfolds, be this Africa, London or Vietnam.

Lindsay's method is analogous with Hampshire in *Sphinx*, Tormance in *A Voyage to Arcturus*, and Dartmoor in *Devil's Tor*. In *The Witch*, the Sussex Downs, chalky and barren, provide a landscape with a ghostly aspect that is in perfect harmony with the strange adventure being related. The book ends against the background of a part of the Downs, and one follows the progress of Ragnar Pole, as he climbs the slope to detach himself from reality (Chapter 14), crosses a chalky area whose extraordinary nature corresponds to the spiritualistic process that is unfolding (Chapter 15), and surmounts the crest of the Downs to find himself at last on the other side, in the unreal world (Chapter 16). While the earthly background becomes blurred in the mist of the summits, a kind of uncanny house takes shape, with an entrance that symbolises the penetration of a world apart, representing Paradise and a place of the imagination.

The reader will have no difficulty in following the work of the writer in order to shape reality, and to charge it with a significance that is still more subtle. The summit of the Downs becomes a bridge leading to 'the other world'. The shafts of the dawn's light are a divine blessing.[9] The storm is the poetic equivalent of passion, and symbolises the destruction of the world. Each house visited, every character met, signifies much more than might appear to be indicated. Like *A Voyage to Arcturus*, *The Witch* is a book which has hidden meaning.

The example of the 'three musics' is enough to indicate the complexity of the webs woven by Lindsay. Each of these three spiritual states is associated with a multitude of meanings.

In Chapter 12, the first music is associated with Cecilie Toller, at Swayning, and is concerned with the idea of upheaval of the soul, through liberated passion. In Chapter 13, the second music is associated with Marya Klangst, again at Swayning, but the soul is now calm, through the discovery of itself. Finally, in Chapters 18 and 19, the third music is associated with Urda Noett, this time at Morion House, with the soul being in a state of solitude, through integration with the universal soul.

The moving interpretation given by Cecilie Toller to Beethoven's Sonata Opus 31, at the beginning of the book, prepares her to assume later the rôle of liberator of Ragnar's soul. Her profession of translator is already an indication of her function in the book, serving as a guide for the passage from one world to another. These few indications will show the complexity of the book, without it being necessary to develop the symbolism of *The Witch*.

*The Witch* is also a metaphysical novel. The last fifty pages are scarcely anything but a philosophical treatise that is particularly esoteric. The fundamental idea of this philosophy has already been developed, being the reality of the soul, which is capable of existing independently of any material support. Man is, first and foremost, a soul, itself part of a universal soul, divided into as many living beings as exist. The soul, or spirit, possesses its own life, and a means of communication which survives after death. This explains Lindsay's attacks upon a world that could scarcely be more materialistic.

It would take a very long study indeed to examine in detail the philosophy of Lindsay, as revealed in *The Witch*. Certainly, he took a fair number of ideas from earlier books, but he had never previously given so many explanations. It will suffice to consider the main threads. At the beginning of the world, there was a vital source that became divided into a multitude of living beings. Lindsay calls this source a 'soul'. This internal quest has the object of uniting the spirit with the Unself. Between the two, there is an identity of nature, but the separation of these two souls, or spirits, contained in all life is responsible for existentialist solitude. Urda is the intermediary between Divinity and the human spirit. 'In that pale hour before the frame of time, spirit had been shattered. A mystic *avatar*, a Breath, whose earthly phenomenon was Urda, had departed from spirit, so that suddenly it had become a living dust.' Urda, therefore, is a resurgence of the Divine, primitive spirit. Any quest for reality passes through Urda, and notably by experiencing solitude, and then suffering.

The transcendental part of man is composed of the two elements of self and soul. The self is the inferior element, attracted by things that are perishable, and quite valueless, submissive as it is to the demands of the will, and to the satiation of needs. The abolition of the self is a first condition in order to make contact with the divine spirit diffused in the world, Urda. It is to this extent that the world must be considered as being an illusion. The human soul possesses a distinct original nature, both of the self and of the spirit, even though close to the latter. This is, in fact, the covering of 'the spirit', just as the body is the covering of the flesh. 'The soul was but a second interior covering, or flesh, to the impersonal spirit.' From there, Lindsay goes on to assert that the death of the body is not, in itself, sufficient to allow the integration of the spirit. The soul, too, must die.

The end of *The Witch* is certainly didactic, but Lindsay does not present us with the truth. As in the case of *A Voyage to Arcturus*, the reader follows the questioning of the characters. The truth appears gradually, as each metaphysical problem becomes resolved. Solitude is nothing other than the pang of conscience felt in the face of the gulf that separates human beings. On Earth, it is only the bodies that can unite, whereas the souls always remain strangers one to the other, notwithstanding all attempts at fusion, and in spite of the abnegation and devotion which lovers can show for one another. The soul is the prisoner of the body. Not only love, but also work and pleasure, are vain attempts to conceal the immensity of solitude. The disappearance of the body does not signal the end of solitude, as the soul, even when detached from the body, is controlled by the same contradictory tendencies as those found on Earth, and especially the desire for incorporation but rejection of the divine core of the soul.

Solitude, therefore, constitutes the nature of the world, and pain is the expression of it. Pain is not a divine element. This pain, which covers the world like a recurring, obsessive theme, has only one significance, according to Lindsay. It is sometimes a feeling of universal solitude, and of helplessness in the face of the chasm which separates human beings, and sometimes the realisation that human tendencies, especially those designed to satisfy needs and desires, are so easily thwarted. Sometimes, again, this pain springs from the omnipresence of death at every stage, and the fear of the unknown that awaits man at the next juncture, after the death of the body or the death of the soul.

Earthly life can be summarised as a continual struggle between the demands of the self and those of the will, and the resistance offered by the divine element of the soul, the spirit, in face of the satisfaction of immediate needs. Pleasure may be termed the satisfaction of needs, and pain the feeling that is born when desires are not satisfied. If man wants to recapture his divine origin, says Lindsay, he must begin by abolishing the self, that he so recognises the *beneficial* effect of pain. One cannot reach a superior level of consciousness without sacrifice. Moreover, the abolition of the self, although a necessary condition, is not enough to put an end to human solitude, especially in the experience of love, with its ultimate, but quite impossible, aim of the total fusion of the loved ones.

*The Witch* traces the steps taken by Ragnar Pole to regain his divine nature, beginning with emancipation from the Earth, on his becoming aware of the world's illusory nature, and proceeding to the annihilation of the self, under the pressure of passionate love, withdrawal of the soul to itself, and, finally, to fusion with the universal soul, as represented by Urda.

These stages are common to quite a number of mystical doctrines. The real originality of Lindsay seems to lie in his conception of a world first founded upon solitude, and then, in consequence, upon pain, contrary, for example, to the Christian idea of Paradise. No less worthy of notice is the importance attached to the rupture of the spiritual order between the Divinity and its creatures. Lindsay's ideology, in any case, is greatly influenced by the Gnostic doctrine that he was either able to discover directly through original treatises or, more probably, through the writings of authors such as Novalis and Goethe, whose philosophy is riddled with Gnostic spiritualism.

The Gnostic reacts to individual anguish in the world, and aims to achieve salvation for himself. In the process of illumination, the individual can become aware of himself, his nature and his origins. He believes in God, and feels himself to be a stranger in the world. He aims to reunite the world in which he is born. The Gnostic discovers the ways, and the means, of access. In this journey towards origins, the earthly coverings fall, one after another. Man's body becomes first celestial, and then ethereal, before transformation into pure, luminous spirituality.

Any list of the analogies between Lindsay's ideology and the Gnostic cults would be a long one, commencing with the stages of the 'three musics' of death of the body, death of the soul, and fusion with Divinity. It would also be necessary to cite the importance attached to the spirit, the systematic depreciation of the body and the flesh, man as a stranger in the world, the conception of an evil world, indeed an evil God, the cult of the Mother and the Eternal Female, and the condemnation of sexuality. It is certain, for instance, that the 'green sparks' which symbolise the spirit in *A Voyage to Arcturus* are often encountered in Gnosticism. It is from Schopenhauer that Lindsay borrows the theory of a world submissive to the tyranny of the will. As for the omnipresence of suffering, this is derived from Buddhism, as is the need for those strict rules of life, with the object of purification of the soul, in order the better to prepare it for contemplation.

Lindsay wrote several times that death remains the principal mode of access to 'the other world'. Nevertheless, in the conclusion to *The Witch* that Lindsay would have added, he had intended to bring Ragnar Pole back on Earth, after his experiences in the hereafter, as in the novels of MacDonald. *The Witch* thus confirms the existence of other means of communication with the world of the spirits, notably through dreams and the subconscious. Two of the characters, Faustine and Waldo, have the privilege of discovering, confusedly in their dreams, the existence of this other world, even though they never penetrate it. Visions and intuitions have the same function as dreams. Moreover, the same enchanted ground is found in *The Haunted Woman*. The characters are victims of the same psychic confusion. Other characters suddenly appear like ghosts, leaving the reader to doubt their existence. Death lurks in the person of Bluewright, biding his time to come to lead Ragnar to the kingdom of spirits. It is against this background that Lindsay can allow himself to rehabilitate witches, those victims of the materialism of our society, since they would, in fact, be nearer than anyone to the origins of life. 'The witches have helped to keep the world a place for spirits.'

It is impossible to exaggerate the austerity of this ideology. The solitude of human beings reaches cosmic proportions. Death is everywhere, sparing nothing, not even the soul. No matter at what level, the spirit does not escape either pain or solitude. The only ray of hope in this gloomy picture is the importance attached to love, which certainly appears as a chance of salvation. It operates as an intense spiritual union, attainable in its perfection only after the death of the body. This is a false hope, however, as the fusion of souls shows itself to be impossible. The soul clashes with the perpetuity of solitude. 'Love, seeking to overcome loneliness; loneliness necessarily giving birth to love; they must be together from the beginning, and express one nature.' Must one, therefore, conclude total defeat? No, because love on Earth, in the sense that it lives upon disinterestedness, abnegation in favour of the loved one, and sacrifices, is a weapon capable of disintegrating the self, but love *in itself* does not admit of access to 'the other world'.

The rôle vested in music is quite close to that of love. Music allows the individual to break away from the Earth and glimpse the splendour of the superior world. Never before had Lindsay accorded it such a place. The characters are connoisseurs, and sometimes even professional artists. In choosing to call the 'three musics' the stages of the spiritual quest, Lindsay certainly did so because he saw them as affinities. Characters, places and landscapes all end by being lost in music. One need only cite *The Violet Apple* to illustrate the overwhelming effect produced by music. 'The mighty ascending and falling scales electrified his heart, he became pale, forgot to breathe, and before long his brow was again moist with perspiration. He had not remembered what music was like. It was no self-existent thing, but a gigantic magnifying-glass to enlarge a man's emotions a hundredfold. He did not know what he was feeling, but it seemed to him as if he were wrestling with an angel, and as if all the forces of his body and soul were engaged in the life-and-death struggle. In struggling up out of his chair, he fell over, face-forwards, on to the floor' (page 199).

In music, there is an element that is inhuman, or supernatural, which uproots man from the Earth. If love and beauty are re-flections of Divinity, then music is the pure expression of it. It is a language apart, or 'a mysterious power forcing us towards eternity'. It does not seek to pacify, or to reassure man of the well-being of his existence, but rather to make it intolerable for him. 'Music spoils us for the world. It is the worst preparation for it.' It should be stressed that this music referred to has no connection with the composer or the interpreter. It might be better to call it 'the spirit of music', that is the inaudible melody, the pure creation of the spirit of the musician, not yet having taken shape in the senses.

*The Witch* reveals no drastic change in Lindsay's ideology. There is visible, on the contrary, the continuity of an ideology already partially revealed previously. Lindsay, however, by the richness of his explanations, his association of elements hitherto separated, and his care to go to the root of matters, has produced a book of enormous interest to anyone studying his ideology. Perhaps the most striking feature, when one considers his writing, extending over some twenty years, is the homogeneous nature of the whole output. There can be no doubt that *The Witch* will be of value to anyone

trying to interpret the labyrinth of symbols in *A Voyage to Arcturus*.
The essential basis of *The Witch* is already contained in Lindsay's
first novel, with man as the prisoner of the tangible world, the quest
for spirituality, the beneficial effect of pain and sacrifice, music as a
message from the hereafter and as a technique of expression, and the
need to suffer in order to be able to reach a superior level of
consciousness. The distinction between 'spirit' and 'self', as present
in *The Witch*, is analogous to the separation of the 'green sparks' and
the 'whirls' in *A Voyage to Arcturus*. Muspel has become 'The Unself',
whilst Krag has taken the form of a woman in Urda. The pessimistic
outlook inspired by Schopenhauer is varied slightly, even to the
extent of being coloured with Christian mythology in *The Violet
Apple*.

One notable absentee, however, from *The Haunted Woman* onwards, is Crystalman. Although the windfall of one solitary novel,
he will undoubtedly remain Lindsay's most memorable character.
Even though the values that he personified continue to be denounced with no less virulence than before, Crystalman himself
appears no more in the form of such an autonomous character and
unifying symbol. Lindsay's imaginative power, on the contrary,
moved towards his antithesis in the Divinity embodied sometimes in
the Great Mother and sometimes in Urda, or the vital principle.
Along with Crystalman, there also disappeared the conception of an
evil God, the incarnation of a primitive Divinity, reigning over the
visible world. The idea by which the Creator allowed himself to be
contaminated by Evil is still present in *Devil's Tor*. In *The Witch*,
there is no longer any question of it. Evil is inherent in life. The
delusions of man merely serve to increase his unhappiness.

Whatever may be its merits and limitations, one cannot fail to
regard the whole of this work with respect.

# CONCLUSION

The aim of this book has been to shed light on the life and personality of David Lindsay, and, for the first time, to study his work in its entirety, not only because a knowledge of the whole is often necessary for an understanding of each part, but also because several of David Lindsay's books, particularly *The Haunted Woman*, less well-known than *A Voyage to Arcturus*, are in no sense lacking in interest and qualities of their own, and will greatly reward wider study.

Attention has been drawn to the evolution of his thinking, from the total rejection of human values in *A Voyage to Arcturus* to the pitiable perfidy of *The Haunted Woman*, and then to a possible redemption in *Devil's Tor* and *The Violet Apple*. Finally, *The Witch* constitutes the spiritual testament, uniting the elements that have been spread at random throughout the earlier books. *A Voyage to Arcturus* had been written by a man of mature age, so it is not surprising to find that, since this first novel, the writing has scarcely changed at all.

It would be idle to pretend that this writer with whom we are concerned merits a place in the front rank of literature. Even though his work may not be entirely devoid of certain qualities, it nevertheless reveals obvious shortcomings which it is difficult to ignore without risking an allegation of bias. By their very nature, and their obsession with the supernatural and the unusual, Lindsay's novels are situated outside current literary trends. The aim of the novelist, insofar as it can be defined here, is not so much to paint the world as it is, and to represent truth, but rather to convey his own beliefs, and to depict the world as the author wishes that it might be. From this standpoint, the author's point of view and that of the reader constantly threaten to collide. This danger merely intensifies when this writer chooses to set at naught all natural laws, sometimes even going to the extent of preferring a world that is totally unreal. Perhaps a good number of readers will show themselves initially

231

hostile to such a genre. Lindsay's novels, therefore, start with an enormous handicap which the earnest reader must surmount. He must suspend his disbelief. The plots of Lindsay's novels defy all credibility. Everyone knows that magic staircases and back-rays do not exist, just as they know that apples are not violet, and that it takes ten years for a tree to grow, and to bear fruit. Lindsay's novels can interest only those who start by accepting the premises established by the author, and the impossible conventions peculiar to the genre.

The danger, therefore, is to abandon oneself to literature of sheer escapism, in which the anxiety to astonish the reader becomes fundamental. David Lindsay avoids this stumbling-block, not only because his books are imbued with his own personal world-view but also because sheer fantasy is kept within bounds, and confined to his first novel, *A Voyage to Arcturus*. The subsequent books are firmly set in the England of the inter-War years, even if, in essence, the moral judgments on human nature come across more clearly than any picture of contemporary society. Lindsay remains a pitiful chronicler of his period, largely because it is only spiritual life that interests him. Overwhelmed by the evolution of the modern world, he has made no effort to grasp its complexities, preferring to pour scorn upon society, and turning more towards the vagaries of human relationships.

His conclusion is one of total pessimism, to the point of leaving the reader to question the reasons for such baseness. The analysis often lacks a sense of proportion when it does not address itself simply enough to the rôles of the sexes. Behind the excessive disgust, one senses the presence of the lonely hypochondriac reflecting upon the misery of having been born. Between the thinker and the individual, no boundaries exist. One expresses the other. Lindsay's ideology is constantly tainted by his fantasies and his obsessions.

One might also venture to speculate on the extent to which the pessimism simply betrays a certain inability to come to terms with the world. The occult would then be a heaven-sent refuge, as welcome as it was free from unpleasant surprises. Upheaval is the predominant theme running through both Lindsay's books and his life. When he decided, one day in 1919, to abandon his career as an insurance broker, in order to become a writer, it was a personal expression of this phenomenon of break-up which was destined to become so recurrent in his books. Even the basic contrast between the tangible world and the Sublime is merely another form of this dissociation.

It is true that often the musician, the thinker or the dreamer take over from the writer. It does not prevent his books being the reverse of entertaining literature. Each of them reveals an undeniable complexity, sometimes so refined that it becomes misleading. With the possible exception of *The Adventures of Monsieur de Mailly*, none of Lindsay's books are soothing. If excessive length is a valid criticism of him, it is one that can certainly be made very often. It is notably the case with *Devil's Tor* and *A Voyage to Arcturus*. There is no lack of people who consider the shortest of his books, *The Haunted Woman*, as being his best.

Lindsay is also open to criticism for having tried to bring to life ideas, rather than characters, even to the extent of risking descent into allegory, notably in *A Voyage to Arcturus*. If this latter book enjoys modified immunity from such criticism, it is because of the harmony between its ideas and its symbolic invention. Moreover, the message of the book has nothing to do with the genre of escapist literature to which it might seem to belong. Its tenor, indeed, is one of an austerity to make one shudder, since all the values that one holds sacred, such as love, art, beauty, education, and even life itself, are rejected.

It would certainly be an exaggeration to regard David Lindsay as a great writer. His books are all too open to criticism. The style seems antiquated, tortuous and stiff. The characters are far from convincing. As for the ideas, these sometimes assume a rambling aspect that can scarcely fail to make the reader smile. The obscurity that is inherent in the message, and also in the pervading symbolism, makes the reading nothing if not arduous. It would be going too far, however, to conclude that Lindsay should be relegated to oblivion. His books will remain no less interesting for the abundance of thought, the care of symbolic elaboration, and the picture of human relationships, rather than for his notion of a transcendent world. *A Voyage to Arcturus* is still one of the most systematic investigations of Evil that has ever been conceived. In his other books, Lindsay has illuminated the complexity of human relationships, blending, in varying degree, prejudice, the unconscious, the irrational and conventional behaviour.

With all their limitations, Lindsay's books do not lack their followers; indeed, there are those who see in them even the basis of a secret cult. *A Voyage to Arcturus* is to-day recognised as being one of the leading examples of the fantasy novel, and it is worth bearing in mind that, nearly fifty years after their having been written, no fewer than five of David Lindsay's novels have been republished in the United States.

# NOTES

## INTRODUCTION

1 *Translator's note*: in Hove, to be precise.
2 Edition Denoël, 1976.
3 J. B. Pick, E. H. Visiak, C. Wilson, *The Strange Genius of David Lindsay*, John Baker, London, 1970.
4 *Adam International Review*, Volume XXXV, Numbers 346–348 (1971), pp. 39–67.
5 *The Sunday Telegraph*, 20 June 1963.
6 Introduction to *The Violet Apple* and *The Witch*, Chicago Review Press, Chicago, 1976, p. 4.
7 J. D. McClure, 'Language and Logic in *A Voyage to Arcturus*', *Scottish Literary Journal*, Volume I, Number 1 (July, 1974), pp. 29–39. Gary K. Wolfe, 'David Lindsay and George MacDonald', *Studies in Scottish Literature*, Volume XII, Number 2 (October, 1974), pp. 131–145.
8 A. Hoog, *Le temps du lecteur*, P.U.F., Paris, 1975.
9 Sigmund Freud, 'L'inquiétante étrangeté', in *Essais de psychanalyse appliquée*, Gallimard, Paris, 1975, p. 164.
10 G. Bachelard, *La psychanalyse du feu*, Gallimard (Idées), Paris, 1949, p. 9.

## 1. THE LIFE AND PERSONALITY OF THE AUTHOR

1 Unpublished letter from Victor Gollancz to Colin Wilson, dated 7 August 1964. 'Yes, I knew Lindsay, though not well. A very remarkable man, and really more a musician than a writer.' Also a letter from Victor Gollancz to E. H. Visiak, dated 8 October 1962. 'I have always been fascinated by the man.'
2 *Philosophical Notes*, Number 419. Unpublished typescript lodged, 25 July 1972, at the National Library of Scotland, Edinburgh, and registered under Number 5616 (57 pages).
3 All references to *Devil's Tor* relate to the Putnam edition of 1932.
4 E. H. Visiak, *Life's Morning Hour*, John Baker, London, 1968.
5 Ferreira in *Sphinx*, p. 41.
6 All references to *A Voyage to Arcturus* relate to the Gollancz edition of 1968.
7 Frank Swinnerton says of the intellectuals of the period at the beginning of World War I 'Insofar as there was any political leaning on the part of these liberals, it was in the direction of Germany.' Frank Swinnerton, *The Georgian Literary Scene*, Everyman edition, Dent and Sons, London, 1938, p. 259.
8 J. B. Pick, 'The Work of David Lindsay', *Studies in Scottish Literature*, January 1964, p. 173.

9   Letter to E. H. Visiak, dated 21 October 1921, in *Adam*, Volume XXXV, Numbers 346–348, p. 41.

10   Letter to E. H. Visiak, dated 9 May 1922, in *Adam*, Volume XXXV, Numbers 346–348, p. 47.

11   *The Adventures of Monsieur de Mailly*, Melrose, London, 1926, p. 144.

12   Letter to E. H. Visiak, dated November 1929, in *Adam*, Volume XXXV, Numbers 346–348, p. 57.

13   A few years later, Jonathan Cape rejected *Devil's Tor*.

14   Letter to E. H. Visiak, dated 9 May 1922, in *Adam*, Volume XXXV, Numbers 346–348, p. 47.

15   Letter from Victor Gollancz to E. H. Visiak, dated 18 October 1962, in *Adam*, Volume XXXV, Numbers 346–348, p. 67.

16   '*Devil's Tor* represents my best', declared Lindsay to E. H. Visiak, in a letter dated 22 November 1931. He reiterated this judgment, in 1938, when he lent a copy of the book to a friend of the family, Kenneth Gunnell, the translator of this present work.

17   This was a term frequently used by Lindsay to describe *Devil's Tor*.

18   See the section by J. B. Pick in *The Strange Genius of David Lindsay*, pp. 24–26.

19   All references to *The Haunted Woman* relate to the Gollancz edition of 1964.

20   Letter to E. H. Visiak, dated 18 May 1922, in *Adam*, Volume XXXV, Numbers 346–348, p. 48.

21   *Philosophical Notes*, Number 91. See also Number 275.

22   *The Haunted Woman* is set in the Brighton area.

23   His book, *John Milton, Complete Poetry and Selected English Prose*, Nonsuch Library, London, 1938, remains one of the best presentations of the work of Milton.

24   Letter to E. H. Visiak, dated 1 November 1921, in *Adam*, Volume XXXV, Numbers 346–348, p. 42.

25   E. H. Visiak, *Life's Morning Hour*, pp. 198 and 210–211.

26   *Ibid.*, p. 130.

27   Quoted by J. B. Pick in *The Strange Genius of David Lindsay*, p. 20.

28   A novel by Myers, *The Near and the Far*, contains a most violent criticism of Bloomsbury in the portrait of Daniyal and his coterie. See also G. H. Bantock, 'L. H. Myers and Bloomsbury', in *Pelican Guide to English Literature*, Volume 7, Harmondsworth, 1961, pp. 270–279.

29   *The Pelican Guide to English Literature*, Volume 7, p. 551.

30   G. H. Bantock, *L. H. Myers, a Critical Study*, Jonathan Cape, London, 1956, p. 148.

31   R. Harvey, 'Daniyal on Arcturus', in *Delta*, Number 29, February, 1963, p. 26.

32   L. H. Myers, *The Root and the Flower*, Reprint Society, London, 1953, p. 335.

33   Among Lindsay's connections, it is worth mentioning the German writer, Leo Huberman, who stayed with him on several occasions. Although little known, Leo Huberman had gained a not inconsiderable reputation in England, upon the appearance of his book, *Man's Worldly Goods*. This book, inspired by Marxist doctrines, was mainly devoted to questions of a political and economic nature, and was even selected, in April 1937, by the Left Book Club, which had been founded by Victor Gollancz, just a few months previously, in order to counter Fascist propaganda in Western Europe.

34   See L. Bonnerot, *L'oeuvre de Walter de la Mare, une aventure spirituelle*, Didier, Paris, 1969.

35   We have it from Robert Barnes himself that this effigy was of neo-classical style, and far removed, therefore, from the fantasy description given by E. H. Visiak in *The Strange Genius of David Lindsay*, p. 97.

36   F. Scott Fitzgerald, *The Crack-up*, New Directions, New York, 1945, p. 15.

37   E. H. Visiak, *The Strange Genius of David Lindsay*, p. 97.

38   Letter from Victor Gollancz to E. H. Visiak, dated 18 October 1962, in *Adam*, Volume XXXV, Numbers 346–348, p. 67. 'I met him only once, when he struck me as a person of singular charm and gentleness, not at all what one would expect from the pain motif of *A Voyage to Arcturus*.'

39   *The Strange Genius of David Lindsay*, p. 97.

40   Colin Wilson, *The Outsider*, Gollancz, London, 1956, p. 15.

41   Maurice Lévy, 'De la spécificité du texte fantastique', in *Ranam*, Number 6 (1973), pp. 3–13.

42   There seems little doubt that this kind of collapse of the personality, sometimes brief, sometimes prolonged, is due to an inability to accept normal sexuality, indeed to a setback to the attempt at sublimation or acceptance of latent homosexual tendencies that are present in every individual.

43   Lionel Trilling, 'Art and Neurosis', in *The Liberal Imagination*, Penguin Books, Harmondsworth, 1970 edition, p. 179.

44   Unpublished letter from Victor Gollancz to Colin Wilson, dated 7 August 1964.

45   M. Serres, *Jouvence sur Jules Verne*, Editions de Minuit, Paris, 1974, p. 150.

46   See C. N. Manlove, *Modern Fantasy*, Cambridge University Press, Cambridge, 1975, pp. 55–98.

47   '*Phantastes*, and *Lilith* I found endlessly attractive, and full of what I felt to be holiness, before I really knew what it was', *Letters of C. S. Lewis*, ed. W. L. Lewis, George Bles, London, 1966, p. 167.

48   Lin Carter, Introduction to MacDonald's novel, *Lilith*, p. ix. 'David Lindsay, the author of that extraordinary novel, *A Voyage to Arcturus*, found much to use in MacDonald.'

49   Letter to E. H. Visiak, in *Adam*, Volume XXXV, Numbers 346–348, p. 49.

50   E. Burke, *A Philosophical Enquiry into the Origins of our Ideas of the Sublime and the Beautiful*, London, 1756.

51   'He did not succeed, even in *A Voyage to Arcturus*, in producing any work of genius because he despised the medium in which he worked, not merely the novel as a form but the use of words and their exclusion' (*The Times Literary Supplement*, 20 November 1970, p. 1346).

52   *The Times Literary Supplement*, 20 November 1970, p. 1346.

53   *A Voyage to Arcturus*, Gollancz, London, 1946.

54   Letter from Jacqueline Lindsay to Victor Gollancz, dated 1 December 1946. 'A complete fiasco ... most mortifying to hear ... Mr Gerald Bullett was jeering at the scrappy extracts that Miss Sheila Shannon mentioned reluctantly.' The broadcast took place on 29 November 1946.

55   B.B.C. Third Programme, 24 and 30 June 1956.

56   *The Times Literary Supplement*, 'Fantastica', 5 July 1963.

57   *The Sunday Telegraph*, 20 June 1963.

58   Letter from C. S. Lewis to C. A. Brodie, dated 29 October 1944, in *Letters of*

*C. S. Lewis*, p. 205. See also C. S. Lewis, *Of Other Worlds*, George Bles, London, 1966, p. 12.

59   *A Voyage to Arcturus*, Ballantine Books, New York, 1972.

60   J. D. McClure, 'Language and Logic in *A Voyage to Arcturus*', pp. 29–38.

## 2. BACKGROUNDS, SETTINGS AND PLACES

1   Marie Bonaparte, *Edgar Allan Poe, sa vie, son oeuvre, étude analytique*, 2 vols., Denoël et Steele, Paris, 1933, Volume 1, pp. 45, 179. Marie Bonaparte has clearly shown that foul, stagnant water, imbued with all the terrors of the night, is one of the dominant themes of the writing of Edgar Allan Poe.

2   See *A Voyage to Arcturus*, p. 25, and *Devil's Tor*, p. 78.

3   See, for example, *Devil's Tor*, p. 87. 'One entire arm, from shoulder to finger-tips, the neck, both feet and ankles, nothing else, glimmered there in that distance as if lighted from within; exactly *like a lunar lamp* shining through the gloom.'

4   See, for example, the anecdote related by E. H. Visiak in *The Strange Genius of David Lindsay*, p. 100.

5   'Isn't this divine?'
'*Divine* is the word!' (*Sphinx*, p. 252).

6   '"You served in the war, of course?"
"Yes", replied Nicholas shortly' (*Sphinx*, p. 19).
A rough calculation places the date of the plot of *The Haunted Woman* as 1920, and that of *Devil's Tor* as 1927.

7   See the very significant title of the book by Robert Graves and Alan Hodge, *The Long Week-end: a Social History of Great Britain, 1918–1939*, Faber & Faber, London, 1940. (Penguin Books, 1971).

8   The care with which Lindsay describes dress and clothing is in striking contrast to the absence of detail regarding the human environment, such as decorations, articles and furniture.

9   'The gown, according to the prevailing fashion, was cut low across her somewhat full bosom, but lower still in the back' (*The Haunted Woman*, p. 8).

10   Robert Graves and Alan Hodge, *The Long Week-end*, p. 37.

11   See *The Haunted Woman*, p. 7.

12   See *Devil's Tor*, Chapters 6 and 16.

13   *Sphinx*, p. 8. 'Few people were about. They were soon past the houses, but the road for the first half-mile had no feature of interest.'

14   'Not many people were travelling, and she was able to secure an empty first-class compartment' (*The Haunted Woman*, p. 94).

15   'There were few people abroad, and certainly no one she knew' (*The Haunted Woman*, p. 95).

16   'Mrs Moor, for her part, sat as nearly upright as the thickly-padded cushions would permit, staring severely at the throng which gradually thinned as they approached Hove' (*The Haunted Woman*, p. 19).

17   'His cheeks made pale with the unnatural life of London' (*Devil's Tor*, p. 95.)

18   'The suburbs I cannot endure, town flats are prisons, while hotels will be impossible after you've left me' (*The Haunted Woman*, p. 22).

19   'A near approach to the cities of Western Europe always rather disgusted him' (*Devil's Tor*, p. 209).

20  'Devil's Tor is alive and working to an end' (*Devil's Tor*, p. 121).

21  'A big, ancient fireplace occupied the centre of one of the side walls; against the opposite one stood a modern steam-heating apparatus' (*The Haunted Woman*, p. 23).

22  'Each house so far erected stood in its own grounds, and was red-tiled, many gabled, and of fantastic shape' (*Sphinx*, p. 9).

23  'The wide double door was resplendent with dark-green paint and highly-polished brass' (*The Haunted Woman*, p. 22). 'It stood well back from the aesthetic road, with which its glittering new paint, feminine-looking window curtains and pretty garden, gay with roses, were in perfect harmony' (*Sphinx*, pp. 66–67).

24  *Translator's Note*: 'Lynscot', Lindsay's own former home at Porth, Cornwall, is now, alas, a rather garish hotel, and a monument to the kind of utter tastelessness that he so much deplored.

25  O. Marc, *Psychanalyse de la maison*, Le Seuil, Paris, 1972, p. 128.

26  'This is the entrance to my Wilderness!' she informed him, turning in through the opening and pausing for him beyond. 'I keep it for my men friends. Men always feel cramped in a garden.' (*Sphinx*, p. 217).

27  'She was in fact one of those eccentric women, who ought to have been born men. Her tastes were masculine, her knowledge chiefly related to masculine topics' (*The Haunted Woman*, p. 10).

28  Bachelard said that the house offers man 'a dynamic of comfort'. *La terre et les rêveries du repos*, José Corti, Paris, 1948, p. 119.

29  'We afterwards bought and sold residential estates and farm properties together' (*Devil's Tor*, p. 115).

30  'Saltfleet identified it at once as his prison of unutterable boredom for the next couple of days' (*Ibid.*, p. 235).

31  'What are those bigger packets still in the box? It might be a bomb!' (*Sphinx*, p. 50). See also p. 55. 'I don't understand. There is not to be an explosion or a shock?'

32  M. Lévy, *Lovecraft*, Union Générale d'Editions, Paris, 1972, p. 52.

33  *Adam*, Volume XXXV, Numbers 346–348, p. 43.

34  *The Haunted Woman*, p. 23. 'Its age, loftiness, and dim light reminded them of an ancient chapel.'

35  *A Voyage to Arcturus*, p. 20. 'Ladies and gentlemen, you are about to witness a materialisation.'

36  Bachelard, *La terre et les rêveries du repos*. See Chapter 4.

37  See P. Sansot, *Poétique de la ville*, Editions Klincksieck, Paris, 1973, p. 363. 'La dédramatisation de la salle de séjour.' Everything, in modern living, arouses in him the disquiet he felt formerly. Opening on the outside to bays or a terrace, the living-room has become functional. Man is invited there to live for the moment.

## 3. THE HUMAN WORLD

1  Page 287. 'The girl is play-acting according to her breed.'

2  Page 13. 'Go where one will about the house, drapers' catalogues meet the eye!'

3  Thomas Carlyle, *Sartor Resartus*, Everyman edition, Dent & Sons, London, 1973, p. 38.

4  *Ibid.*, p. 54.

5  *Sphinx*, p. 313. 'He was lightly clad in antique-looking garments. Lore disengaged herself, laughing, lightly shook out her graceful draperies.'

6  *A Voyage to Arcturus*, p. 21. *The Haunted Woman*, pp. 94, 101. *Devil's Tor*, p. 171.

7  *Translator's Note*: As an indication that David Lindsay's preoccupation with clothing, and its psychological significance, was not as abstract and academic as might be supposed, I can usefully contribute a first-hand, personal observation. A frequent visitor at Pembroke Crescent in the late 1930's was a tall girl about eighteen called Cynthia, who came from a distinguished naval family. Like the Sturt girls in *Sphinx*, she was a keen tennis-player, and often arrived on her way to, or from, a game, wearing one of her seemingly-endless array of tennis-dresses, all of which were somewhat ahead of their time in extreme brevity. On these occasions, it was most noticeable that the author, now well into his sixties, seemed unable to resist a constant appreciative contemplation of the young visitor's admittedly-shapely thighs, thus unknowingly causing mild amusement to many, including their owner herself. Most significantly, however, the analogy with *Sphinx* was carried a stage further by Lindsay one day, when we were briefly alone together, after one such encounter; he remarked, as much to himself as to me, 'That girl *is* Celia Hantish!'

8  *Devil's Tor*, p. 13. 'Her grey-blue eyes, in their perfect orbits, were the hardest to decipher. Superficially they struck one as tranquil, quiet and simple, but then something *waiting* in them began to appear, and at last one might suspect that they were essentially not in the present at all. They might be the eyes of a prophetess going about her everyday jobs. It gave a marvellous latent power to the whole face.'

9  Even Ingrid's mother was unaware of this aspect of her daughter's personality. See *Devil's Tor*, pp. 97, 140, 285, 349, 350.

10  See, for example, the theme of the split personality in Romantic literature, as analysed by Otto Rank in *Don Juan et le double*, Payot, Paris, 1973.

11  Sigmund Freud, 'La création littéraire et le rêve éveillé', in *Essais de psychanalyse appliquée*, Gallimard, Paris, 1975, pp. 77–78.

12  Sometimes it is more a vicarious catharsis that Lindsay seems to seek; for example, in the numerous portraits of adventurers. One can guess the fascination felt by Lindsay for the conquest of the Himalayas by Saltfleet, the exploration of space by Maskull, and the wanderings across Asia of Hugh Drapier. It can have been no mere coincidence that Michael Strogoff was one of his favourite heroes in his youth. There was no more beautiful end than the death which came to him in the far North, during a bear hunt. These adventurers of modern times are the noble descendants of the Vikings whom Lindsay so much admires. Even an office-worker may dream of his distant ancestors!

13  These are in striking contrast to artistic occupations, such as those of writers, musicians and painters.

14  *Devil's Tor*, p. 10. 'My mode of life has deprived me of the necessary experience of women. They put fear into me.'

15  *Adam*, Volume XXXV, Numbers 346–348, p. 56.

16  The sole example is provided by the pair Saltfleet and Arsinal in *Devil's Tor*, but, in their case, a disagreement soon ensues. They quarrel and separate.

17 Sigmund Freud, *Introduction à la psychanalyse*, Payot, Paris, reprinted 1972, pp. 141–144.

18 Isbel, too, compares herself with a drug-addict, unable to resist the attraction of the haunted room. In *A Voyage to Arcturus*, pp. 120–121, perfume is again a weapon for the young girl who tries to seduce Hator.

19 *A Voyage to Arcturus*, pp. 245–247. 'He perceived a dim, vast shadow without any distinguishable shape, but *somehow throwing out a scent of disgusting sweetness*. Nightspore knew that it was Crystalman.'

20 *The Haunted Woman*, p. 18. 'a thick sentimental syrup'. The metaphor of sugar appears again on pages 17, 102, 130 and 151.

21 *Sphinx*, p. 178. 'I have been sweet quite long enough. To be in their house affects me like drinking *eau sucrée*, and my digestion isn't overstrong.'

22 *Sphinx*, p. 156. See also *The Haunted Woman*, p. 62. 'A woman's natural impulse is to look for faults in her sisters.'

23 In her article, 'Monsieur Vénus et l'ange de Sodome' (*Revue française de Psychanalyse*, Number 7, October, 1973, pp. 63–69), Françoise Cachin interprets the resurgence of the theme of the androgyne at the turn of the century as a subconscious fear in face of the new woman, as personified by the woman agitator and the suffragette.

24 *Devil's Tor*, p. 224. 'There was a sort of effeminacy in the obsession, too, for the man.'

25 *Ibid.*, p. 146. 'It's like being unmanned by the slow effect.'

26 *Ibid.*, pp. 452–453. For a more detailed consideration herein, see Chapter 5, pp. 194–196.

27 Wilhelm Reich sees in such opposing impulses, the overrating and the extreme depreciation of women, the sign of neurosis, having its origin in some major disillusionment, such as either an amatory disappointment or dissatisfaction as regards the mother.

28 *A Voyage to Arcturus*, p. 131. At the end of the book, Nightspore feels a similar shame when he finds, all around him, human beings corrupted by pleasure (p. 245).

29 G. MacDonald's *Lilith*, and Lewis Carroll's *Through the Looking Glass*, for example.

30 O. Rank, *Don Juan et le double*.

31 Letter quoted by J. B. Pick, in *The Strange Genius of David Lindsay*, p. 6.

32 Maurice Lévy, *Lovecraft*, pp. 33, 38.

33 Letter to E. H. Visiak, in *Adam*, Volume XXXV, Numbers 346–348, pp. 56–57.

34 Felix Boehm, 'Le complexe de féminité chez l'homme', *Revue française de psychanalyse*, Number 7 (Spring, 1973), p. 283.

35 Sigmund Freud, 'Quelques conséquences psychiques de la différence anatomique entre les sexes', in *La vie sexuelle*, P.U.F., Paris, 1969, pp. 131–132.

36 J. Markale, *La femme celte*, 2nd edition, Payot, Paris 1973.

37 *Devil's Tor*, pp. 80–82. 'The emasculated crest had been blotted out by the weather.'

## 4. THE WORLD OF CRYSTALMAN

1 Eric S. Rabkin, *The Fantastic in Literature*, 2nd edition, Princeton University Press, Princeton, 1977, p. 45.

2   Mark R. Hillegas, ed., *Shadows of Imagination*, Southern Illinois University Press, Carbondale, 1969, p. xiv.

3   Eric S. Rabkin, *The Fantastic in Literature*, p. 45.

4   Kingsley Amis, *New Maps of Hell*, Gollancz, London, 1961, p. 16.

5   M. R. Hillegas, *Shadows of Imagination*, p. xiv.

6   We are indebted to C. S. Lewis for an anthology of MacDonald's writings (Collins, London, 1946). Lewis readily acknowledged his debt to H. G. Wells, whom he quotes several times in *Out of the Silent Planet*.

7   *Out of the Silent Planet*, London, 1938, republished by Pan Books, 1952, p. 180.

8   W. L. Lewis, ed., *Letters of C. S. Lewis*, p. 205.

9   C. S. Lewis, *Of Other Worlds*, George Bles, London, 1966, p. 12.

10  Lindsay's originality needs to be qualified, because, long before him, writers had used distant worlds with an identical aim. As early as the seventeenth century, Francis Godwin had made the Moon's inhabitants creatures of superior morality (see Kingsley Amis, *New Maps of Hell*, p. 29). Without having recourse to a planet, Jonathan Swift adopts this method in his picture of the Houyhnhnms (*Gulliver's Travels*, Part 4). C. S. Lewis expressed what were manifestly the same sentiments in a letter to Ruth Pitter, dated 4 January 1941, in which he wrote 'From Lindsay, I first learnt what other planets in fiction are really good for; for spiritual adventures. Only they can satisfy our craving which sends our imagination off the earth, or, putting it another way, in him I first saw the terrific results of fiction hitherto kept apart, the Novalis, G. MacDonald, James Stephens sort and the H. G. Wells, Jules Verne sort. My debt to him is very great.'

11  See C. S. Lewis, *Out of the Silent Planet*, p. 35, and H. G. Wells, *The First Men in the Moon*, Collins edition, London, 1973, pp. 58–63.

12  The propulsion of airships has always posed problems for novelists. In his book, *From the Earth to the Moon*, Jules Verne conceives an enormous cannon, capable of firing a rocket. C. S. Lewis is very reticent about the technique, no doubt because it is scarcely satisfactory. He refers to 'the less observed properties of solar radiation' (*Out of the Silent Planet*, p. 27). Finally, H. G. Wells invents a sphere that can resist the force of gravity, and which can be steered in space with the aid of a system of 'blind rollers' (*First Men in the Moon*, p. 46). The technique used by Lindsay is quite close to that of Cyrano de Bergerac. The latter propelled his machine by means of flasks full of dew, which the heat of the sun lifted in the air. It is common knowledge that the sun absorbs dew. (*Le voyage dans la lune*, p. 115).

13  The back-rays which serve to propel a torpedo were equally in the author's symbolic imagination, since he said (*A Voyage to Arcturus*, p. 246) that they represented the movement of beings towards Crystalman. The return in reverse is a symbol of degradation. It is clear, therefore, that the choice of the star, Arcturus, cannot be attributed to a desire to astonish the reader, as claimed by J. van Herp (*Panorama de la science-fiction*, Marabout Collection, Verviers, 1975, p. 44), 'Where, then, should one go in the solar system? It was outside the system that one could still go to find planets suitable for adventures.'

14  On this point, see Hélène Tuzet, *Le cosmos et l'imagination*, José Corti, Paris, 1965.

15  J. van Herp *Panorama de la science-fiction*, p. 39.

16  'No insect-like, vermiculate or crustacean Abominable, no twitching feelers,

rasping wings, slimy coils, curling tentacles, no monstrous union of superhuman intelligence and insatiable cruelty seemed to him anything but likely on an alien world' (*Out of the Silent Planet*, p. 39).

17   *A Voyage to Arcturus*, p. 46. See also p. 75. As regards these problems of communication, see Kingsley Amis, *New Maps of Hell*, pp. 20–21.

18   Some credit must be given to this allusion. 'Maskull; that name must have a meaning, but again thought is a strange thing. I connect that name with something, but with what?' (*A Voyage to Arcturus*, p. 58.)

19   *Ibid.*, p. 170. As regards the metamorphoses of organs, see also pp. 74, 85, 104, 119, 132–133, 157.

20   P. Brunel, *Le mythe de la métamorphose*, A. Colin, Paris, 1974, p. 160.

21   *A Voyage to Arcturus*, p. 61. 'Sporting is the blind will to become like Shaping.' 'Sporting' is a term used by Lindsay to denote the mutations of the beings on Arcturus, and Shaping is one of the numerous names of Crystalman. In horticulture, the word 'sporting' denotes an abnormal variation of a plant which mutates.

22   'He's great and brawny, and can hold his own with other men' (*Ibid.*, p. 151).

23   'His body was like a prison. He longed to throw it off and become incorporated with the sublime universe which was beginning to unveil itself' (*Ibid.*, p. 225).

24   It seems probable that Dreamsinter is none other than Krag in disguise. Were this not so, how could Dreamsinter possibly know of the existence of Nightspore? (*Ibid.*, p. 134.)

25   'Yes, we must fight Krag, the author of evil and misery, whom you call Devil' (*Ibid.*, p. 54).

26   *Ibid.*, pp. 27, 40, 229. In contrast, Maskull feels pleasure in contact with the creatures of Crystalman (*Ibid.*, pp. 23, 45).

27   *Ibid.*, pp. 55, 144, 165, 169, 195.

28   Proof of this seems to be provided by the indistinct noise which rises from the Gap of Sorgie, and which is afterwards heard on the star, Arcturus (*Ibid.*, pp. 61–62).

29   'I was tired of vulgarity' (*Ibid.*, p. 58).

30   'Oh, mine is a decrepit world, where nature takes a hundred years to move a foot of solid land. Men and animals go about in flocks. Originality is a lost habit' (*Ibid.*, p. 82).

31   '"Krag treats me like a child", he remarked presently, "and perhaps I am a child"' (*Ibid.*, p. 33).

32   See what Sullenbode says later in the book. 'That grand-souled girl I admire the most of all. She listened to her inner voice, and to nothing else besides. Which of us is strong enough for that?' (*Ibid.*, p. 219).

33   In Lindsay's philosophy, the forest often symbolises error. In this connection, see *Devil's Tor*, p. 408, 'a forest of illusions'. See also *A Voyage to Arcturus*, p. 122, 'a forest of false ideas is waiting for your axe'.

34   *Ibid.*, pp. 61–62, 113, 132–135, 192, 224–225, 241, 243.

35   'The sound appeared to him to belong to a different world from that in which he was travelling. The latter was mystical, dreamlike, and unbelievable, the drumming was like a very dim undertone of reality. It resembled the ticking of a clock in a room full of noises, only occasionally possible to be picked up by the ear' (*Ibid.*, p. 62).

36   *Ibid.*, pp. 61, 113. It is interesting to compare this drumming with the sound of the orchestra heard in *The Haunted Woman* (pp. 26–29). Both are manifestations of the parallel world.

37   *A Voyage to Arcturus*, p. 185. 'I'm not a student. My journey is no holiday tour.'

38   H. R. Ellis Davidson, *Gods and Myths of Northern Europe*, Penguin Books, 1974 edition, Harmondsworth, pp. 27, 235. See also *Philosophical Notes*, Number 471.

39   See E. H. Visiak, '*Arcturus* and Christian Dogma' in *The Strange Genius of David Lindsay*, pp. 109–111.

40   *A Voyage to Arcturus*, p. 242. 'They continued to approach the wall of darkness, straight towards the door. In a few minutes, they were before the gateway. The entrance was doorless.'

41   Vohn Bunyan, *The Pilgrim's Progress*, Butler & Tanner, London, 1910, p. 35.

42   E. H. Visiak, *The Strange Genius of David Lindsay*, p. 111. 'There are no churches in Tormance, no symbology or ceremonial, which seems a pity. Otherwise, it might have been shown how that kind of beauty, on Lindsay's argument, obscures sublimity by sentimentalising it, as in pictures on sacred subjects, even by Great Masters.'

43   'If you live as we live, you will assuredly grow like us.'
     'Do you mean food and drink?'
     'We eat no food, and drink only water' (*A Voyage to Arcturus*, p. 170).

44   'In this book, the situation is complicated by the fact that it is impossible, until the very last episode, to know what the author is telling us.' J. D. McClure, 'Language and Logic in *A Voyage to Arcturus*', p. 37.

45   Leehallfae's explanations of the creation of the universe (*A Voyage to Arcturus*, p. 176–177) are largely false.

46   The use of recollection in Polecrab's account is remarkable in this respect. 'As far as I can remember, that is what Broodviol said, but perhaps, as I was then a young and ignorant man, I may have left out words which would explain his meaning better' (*Ibid.*, p. 146). Moreover, this character, in his entirety, is a good example of the conspiratorial ignorance to which reference has been made.

47   In connection with James Joyce's *Ulysses*, Joseph Frank writes 'All the factual background, so conveniently summarised for the reader in an ordinary novel, must be reconstructed from fragments sometimes hundreds of pages apart, scattered through the book. As a result, the reader is forced to read *Ulysses* in exactly the same manner as he reads poetry, continually fitting fragments together, and keeping allusions in mind until, by reflexive reference, he can link them to their complements. A knowledge of the whole is essential to an understanding of any part.' Joseph Frank, 'Spatial Form in Modern Literature', *Sewanee Review*, LIII, 1945, pp. 221–240.

48   *A Voyage to Arcturus*, p. 67. We are clearly in the classic mystical tradition here. The inversion of the two worlds, for instance, is one of the essential elements of Gnosticism. Compare the Lindsay quotation with the following description of mystical experience. 'In the deepest religious experience, whether it be Christian, Buddhist, Hindu, or Mohammedan, when all ideas, thoughts, sensations, and volitions which make up the self are exhausted, there is found to remain only a Void, the One of Plotinus, the Godhead of Eckart and Ruysbroeck, the Brahman of Hinduism. The Void is not only Emptiness. In mystical experience,

it is found to be a Plenum-Void. The Emptiness and the Fullness are one.' F. C. Happold, *Mysticism*, Penguin, Harmondsworth, 1970, p. 80.

49  See H. Leisegang, *La Gnose*, Payot, Paris, 1951 (republished, 1971), pp. 7–46; S. Hutin, *Les Gnostiques*, P.U.F., Paris, 1958.

50  *Monsieur, or The Prince of Darkness*, Faber and Faber, London, 1974.

51  *Philosophical Notes*, Number 338. See also Number 252. 'Every ugly person is eccentric in mind; one need never look for good balance except in handsome people.'

52  *Ibid.*, Number 3. 'Pleasure is the only self-subsisting quality, i.e. the only sufficient reason for the world's existence.' See also *A Voyage to Arcturus*, p. 232. 'The world could not go on being without pleasure.'

53  *Philosophical Notes*, Number 151. 'Society and solitude are both forms of pleasure but the former dissipates while the latter concentrates our energies.'

54  'If there were a Devil, of all his inventions, *ennui* might be the one on which he would chiefly pride himself.' (*Ibid.*, Number 111).

55  *A Voyage to Arcturus*, p. 236. This picture is equally applicable to the musician in *The Haunted Woman* (p. 131).


## 5. THE SUBLIME WORLD

1  *Philosophical Notes*, Number 192. 'To attain the sublime oneself, and bring it within the grasp of others, this is the grandest of all ambitions.'

2  Letter to E. H. Visiak, dated 25 November 1921, in *Adam*, Volume XXXV, Numbers, 346–348, p. 45. 'Long since, for my own use, I have postulated the existence of a "sublime" world, this word being employed for want of a better.'

3  Edmund Burke, *A Philosophical Enquiry into the Origins of our Ideas of the Sublime and the Beautiful*.

4  Schopenhauer, *The World as Will and Idea*, London, 1788. Clément Rosset, *L'esthétique de Schopenhauer*, P.U.F., Paris, 1969, pp. 49–52.

5  *Philosophical Notes*, Number 337. See also Number 204. 'The sublime world must not be conceived as more vague, formless and undefined than the physical, three-dimensional world, but, on the contrary, as far more real, vivid and substantial. To keep this in mind is a key to the understanding of world-life.'

6  *Ibid.*, Number 545.

7  In *A Voyage to Arcturus*, Maskull notices, at the bottom of a lake, a region of fire which is none other than Muspel (*A Voyage to Arcturus*, p. 239).

8  Colin Wilson, *The Outsider*; and *Religion and the Rebel*, Gollancz, London, 1957.

9  *Devil's Tor*, p. 160. See also p. 407. 'Sublimity should not represent a natural state of the soul, but be, as it were, its homesickness.'

10  An example of this is to be found in Ferreira's father in *Sphinx*. See also *Devil's Tor*, p. 396. 'Such a civilisation of decay will resume its old evil work with the earliest *visit of the doctor*, the earliest paid caresses of the *hired nurse*.' (Our italics.)

11  *Philosophical Notes*, Number 113. 'The beautiful may be enjoyed in society, but the sublime demands solitude, the reason being that it is an emancipation from individuality, and other persons serve to remind one of this individuality.'

12  *A Voyage to Arcturus*, p. 101. 'This adventure of yours will scarcely come to an end until you have made some sort of sacrifice.'

13  To understand this point, it is necessary to remember the myth of the primitive androgyne, to which Lindsay often refers. The division of the sexes always fascinated and interested him. In *A Voyage to Arcturus*, he conceives a rather astonishing bisexual character in Leehallfae.

14  *Ibid.*, p. 103. 'I feel that the only thing worth living for is to be so magnanimous that fate itself will be astonished at us. Understand me. It isn't cynicism, or bitterness, or despair, but heroism.'

15  'A coquette, for instance, would know how to flatter his vanity, and use her eyes to the best effect, but it's extremely unlikely that she would consent to throw overboard all other society for his. That would be one test. Then there's the question of sacrifice. Is she not only ready but eager to sacrifice her happiness for his, not in one or on one occasion, but in all their relations and at all times?' (*The Haunted Woman*, p. 63).

16  '"No. No, I'm not happy. Love is not happiness."
    "What is it, Maskull?"
    "Restlessness, unshed tears, thoughts too grand for our soul to think"' (*A Voyage to Arcturus*, p. 223).

17  See also pp. 268, 296, 297, 305.

18  J. Russier, *La Souffrance*, P.U.F., Paris, 1963, pp. 17–26.

19  *Philosophical Notes*, Number 278. 'The Viking spirit to treat death, pain, work, trouble, etc., as jokes; this is certainly the easiest way to get through the world.'

20  *Ibid.*, Number 88. Pain is so universal that it does not spare the Creator. In the struggle in which Crystalman and Surtur engage, the latter is far from playing a beautiful rôle. In the later books, although Lindsay abandons his earlier conception of Muspel, he nevertheless retains the idea of a suffering God. If pain be the nature of man, he admits in *Devil's Tor*, it can only originate with the Ancient, creator of the world and humanity. Hence, suffering is both the means of recovering one's origins and the evidence of man's origins. 'That Ancient was both torturer and tortured', writes Lindsay. (*Devil's Tor*, p. 476. See also p. 334.)

21  Nietzsche, *La volonté de puissance*, Volume II, Gallimard, Paris, 1947, Introduction, p. 15.

22  'Surtur's world does not lie on this side of the *one*, which was the beginning of life, but on the other side; and to get to it we must re-pass through the *one*, but this can only be by renouncing our self-life, and re-uniting ourselves to the whole of Crystalman's world' (*A Voyage to Arcturus*, p. 146).

23  Colin Wilson, *The Strange Genius of David Lindsay*, p. 33.

24  E. H. Visiak, letter dated 1 November 1956, to *The Listener*.

25  See also pp. 154–158.

26  J. Przyluski, *La grande déesse*, Payot, Paris, 1950, p. 36.

27  'With regard to the Occult, I have no recollection of hearing any of his opinions, neither did he report any personal occult experience. Obviously, he must have given much attention to the subject. Nevertheless, he regarded "spiritualism" with distaste; resulting from his character of mind devoted towards spirituality of another kind. However, David Lindsay's mother and her sister occasionally exchanged ideas of spiritualism, rather on the level of superstition, and at times had sessions with a "planchette".' (Letter from Robert Barnes, dated 18 August 1975.)

28  'Saltfleet had always conceded that the universe was a very queer place, full of unlighted holes and corners.' (*Devil's Tor*, p. 210). See also p. 52, where Hugh

Drapier adds 'It's fast leading me to believe that the universe as a whole is very odd.'

29   Letter to E. H. Visiak, dated 9 May 1922, in *Adam*, Volume XXXV, Numbers 346–348, p. 47.

30   This interpretation is reinforced by the reference to the ancient nature of the character (p. 131). 'He looks like an ancient Saxon come to life.' See also the description of his clothes.

31   T. Todorov, *Introduction à la littérature fantastique*, Le Seuil, Paris, 1970, p. 61.

32   R. Caillois, *Images, Images*, José Corti, Paris, 1966, p. 26.

33   L. Vax, *L'art et la littérature fantastique*, P.U.F., Paris, 1970, p. 29.

34   *Devil's Tor*, p. 180. 'He is Celtic and psychic as well.'

35   *Devil's Tor*, p. 12. 'Maybe our inadequate modern occult faculties no more than represent some atrophied sixth sense, then rich and splendid. I mean, just as there have been mammoths, mastodons, megatheriums, so there may have been seers.'

36   'Like everyone else, no doubt, your enjoyment is strictly demarcated? You don't pretend to rise to a sympathetic appreciation of all forms of musical art? No outsider does' (*Sphinx*, p. 71).

37   *Philosophical Notes*, Number 26. 'Its true name is the Supernatural Symphony. Its character is peculiar, weird and mysterious; a long dream. One can hear it for ever, and yet not understand it.' One can see with what exactitude this definition could be applied to *The Haunted Woman*.

38   Compare the beginning of *Devil's Tor*, with the storm, to this description by Emile Ludwig of the First Movement of the Ninth Symphony. The resemblance is quite astonishing. 'The Ninth Symphony rises out of chaos. Whilst the other eight are provided with a long introduction, or commence directly with the principal theme, we are overwhelmed this time by the formless noise of the elements, as if in the middle of a humane landscape, dotted with frightful volcanoes, seemingly extinct, but which can erupt suddenly. Here, Fate knocks at no door; it roars in a deformed world, and *finally finds an enormous rock on which to strike*.' Emile Ludwig, *Beethoven*, Flammarion, Paris, 1945, p. 272. The italics are ours.

39   See also other comparisons, *A Voyage to Arcturus*, pp. 46, 72, 75, 88, 230.

40   *Ibid.*, pp. 36, 113, 133, 135, 239, 241–244.

41   *Ibid.*, pp. 153–154. The passage, on Lindsay's own admission, was inspired by Beethoven's music. 'On reading the chapter, "The Wombflash Forest", I was always shaken with emotion. He told me that he was inspired to so write that chapter by the Fifth Symphony of Beethoven, especially the *drumming* passage linking the scherzo to the finale.' Letter from Robert Barnes to J. B. Pick, quoted in *The Strange Genius of David Lindsay*, p. 23.

42   'Presently, they met a fantastic little creature, the size of a new-born lamb, *waltzing along on three legs*' (*A Voyage to Arcturus*, p. 55). See also p. 51. In the human scale of values, dancing is the form of this degeneracy.

## 6. *THE VIOLET APPLE* AND *THE WITCH*

1    *The Violet Apple* and *The Witch*, edited by J. B. Pick, Chicago Review Press, Chicago, 1976. *The Violet Apple*, Sidgwick and Jackson, London, 1978. All references to this book relate to the Sidgwick and Jackson edition.

2  See Chapter 3 herein, under the heading of 'Human relationships. The theatre.'
3  See the biographical section herein, p. 17.
4  One should remember that the very nature of fantasy is itself a rupture. Roger
   Caillois, for example has said 'Fantasy reveals a scandal, a fissure, an unusual
   eruption, that is almost intolerable in the real world.' Roger Caillois, *Images,
   Images*, p. 15.
5  See, for example, Bettelheim's book, *The Uses of Enchantment*, Penguin Books,
   Harmondsworth, 1978.
6  In his book, *The Game of the Impossible*, University of Illinois Press, Urbana, 1976,
   W. R. Irwin likens fantasy literature to a game, which leads him to regard it as a
   diversion in a writer's career, consequently disowning part of its value.
7  Marthe Robert, *Roman des origines et origines du roman*, Grasset, Paris, 1977.
8  Gary K. Wolfe, 'David Lindsay and George MacDonald', in *Studies in Scottish
   Literature*, Volume XII, Number 2, October, 1974, pp. 131–145.
9  *The Witch*, p. 366. 'In their destructive height, those rays were the pure pain of
   heaven, but, in their cold beauty of the dawn, they were music.'

# BIBLIOGRAPHY

## 1. WORKS BY DAVID LINDSAY

When a more recent edition has been used, this is indicated in parentheses.

*A Voyage to Arcturus*, Methuen, London, 1920 (Gollancz, London, 1968).
*The Haunted Woman*, Methuen, London, 1922 (Gollancz, London, 1964).
*Sphinx*, John Long, London, 1923.
*The Adventures of Monsieur de Mailly*, Melrose, London, 1926; as *A Blade for Sale* in the U.S.A., R.M. McBride & Company, New York, 1927.
*Devil's Tor*, Putnam, London, 1932.
*The Violet Apple*, Sidgwick and Jackson, London, 1978.
*The Violet Apple* and *The Witch*, edited by J. B. Pick, Chicago Review Press, Chicago, 1976.
*Philosophical Notes*, typescript now at the National Library of Scotland, Edinburgh, Number 5616, 57 pages.

Latest American editions
*A Voyage to Arcturus*, Ballantine Books, New York, 1977.
*A Voyage to Arcturus*, reprint of 1920 edition, Gregg Press, Boston, 1977.
*The Haunted Woman*, Newcastle Publishing Co., Hollywood, 1975.
*Devil's Tor*, Reginald, R. & Menville, Douglas, eds., Arno Press, New York, 1978.
*The Violet Apple and The Witch*, Chicago Review Press, Chicago, 1976 (paperback edition, 1977).

## 2. LETTERS

Letters of David Lindsay to E. H. Visiak have been published in *Adam International Review*, Volume XXXV, Numbers 346–348 (1971).

*Lines Review*, Number 40 (March 1972), edited by Robin Fulton, contains extracts from *The Witch*, *The Violet Apple* and *Philosophical Notes*.

## 3. CRITICISM

Christopher, Joe R., 'Touring *The Dark Tower*', *CSL: the Bulletin of the New York C. S. Lewis Society*, New York, Volume 9, Number 6, April 1978, pp. 9–13.
Harvey, Robert, 'Daniyal on Arcturus', *Delta*, Number 29 (February 1963), pp. 22–27.
Jeanes, Geoff, 'Other Worlds in Fiction: Reflections on a Body of Literature', *CSL: the Bulletin of the New York C. S. Lewis Society*, New York, Volume 6, Number 8, June 1975, pp. 1–4.
Linden, William, 'Tormance and G. S. Lewis', *CSL: the Bulletin of the New York C. S.

*Lewis Society*, New York, Volume 5, Number 7, 1974, pp. 4–5.

Lindsay, Maurice, *History of Scottish Literature*, Robert Hale, London, 1977, pp. 417–421.

McClure, John Derrick, 'Language and Logic in *A Voyage to Arcturus*', *Scottish Literary Journal*, Volume 1, Number I, July 1974, pp. 29–39.

'"Purely as Entertainment"? *Adventures of Monsieur de Mailly* as a Representative Work of David Lindsay', *Studies in Scottish Literature*, April 1974, pp. 226–236.

Pick, J. B., 'The Work of David Lindsay', *Studies in Scottish Literature*, January 1964, pp. 171–182.

'A Sketch of Lindsay's Life as Man and Writer', *The Strange Genius of David Lindsay*, John Baker, London, 1970, pp. 3–32.

Rabkin, Eric S., 'Conflation of Genres and Myths in David Lindsay's *A Voyage to Arcturus*', *The Journal of Narrative Technique*, Number 7, 1977, pp. 149–155.

Raff, Melvin, 'The Structure of *A Voyage to Arcturus*', *Studies in Scottish Literature*, Volume XV, pp. 262–267.

Schofield, Jack, 'Cosmic Imagery in *A Voyage to Arcturus*', *Extrapolation*, Number 13, 1972, pp. 146–151. Review of *The Strange Genius of David Lindsay*, *Studies in Scottish Literature*, Volume X, Number 1, July 1972, pp. 59–61.

Scholes, Robert, & Rabkin, Eric S. *Science Fiction: History, Science, Vision*, Oxford University Press, New York, 1977, pp. 207–212.

Visiak, E. H., *The Strange Genius of David Lindsay*, John Baker, London, 1970, pp. 95–135.

Wilson, Colin, 'Lindsay as Novelist and Mystic', *The Strange Genius of David Lindsay*, John Baker, London, 1970, pp. 35–91.

Wolfe, Gary K., 'David Lindsay and George MacDonald', *Studies in Scottish Literature*, Volume XII, Number 2, October 1974, pp. 131–145.

'Symbolic Fantasy', *Genre*, Number 8, 1977, pp. 194–209.

## 4. GENERAL BIBLIOGRAPHY

Amis, Kingsley, *New Maps of Hell, a survey of science fiction*, Gollancz, London, 1961.

Bachelard, Gaston, *La terre et les rêveries du repos*, José Corti, Paris, 1948.

*La psychanalyse du feu*, Gallimard, Paris, 1949.

Bantock, G. H., *L. H. Myers, a Critical Study*, J. Cape, London, 1956.

'L. H. Myers and Bloomsbury', *Pelican Guide to English Literature*, Volume 7, Harmondsworth, 1961, pp. 270–279.

Bergonzi, Bernard, *The Early H. G. Wells, a Study of the Scientific Romances*, Manchester University Press, Manchester, 1961.

Burke, Edmund, *A Philosophical Enquiry into the Origins of our Ideas of the Sublime and the Beautiful*, London, 1756.

Caillois, Roger, *Images, Images, essais sur le rôle de l'imagination*, José Corti, Paris, 1966.

Carlyle, Thomas, *Sartor Resartus*, London, 1836 (Dent and Sons, London, 1973).

Cyrano de Bergerac, *Histoire comique des états et empires de la lune et du soleil* (*L'autre monde*), Paris, 1650 (*Le voyage dans la lune*, Galic, Paris, 1962).

Eliott, R. C., *The Shape of Utopia*, University of Chicago Press, Chicago, 1970.

Ellis Davidson, H. R., *Gods and Myths of Northern Europe*, London, 1964 (Penguin Books, Harmondsworth, 1974).

Frank, Joseph, 'Spatial Form in Modern Literature', *Sewanee Review*, LIII (1945), pp. 221–240.

Freud, Sigmund, 'La création littéraire et le rêve éveillé', *Essais de psychanalyse appliquée*, Gallimard, Paris, 1975, pp. 69–81.

Freud, Sigmund, *La vie sexuelle*, Presses Universitaires de France, Paris, 1969.
Gillie, Christopher, *Movements in English Literature 1900–1940*, Cambridge University Press, Cambridge, 1975.
Green, R. L., *Into Other Worlds, Space Flights in Fiction from Lucian to Lewis*, A. Schuman, London, 1957.
Haggard, H. Rider, *She*, London, 1887 (Hodder Paperbacks Ltd., London, 1971).
Happold, F. C., *Mysticism*, Penguin Books, Harmondsworth, 1970.
Herp, J. van, *Panorama de la science-fiction*, Marabout Collection, Verviers, 1975.
Hillegas, Mark R. (ed.), *Shadows of Imagination*, Southern Illinois University Press, Carbondale, 1969.
Hutin, Serge, *Les Gnostiques*, Presses Universitaires de France, Paris, 1958.
Irwin, W. R., *The Game of the Impossible, a Rhetoric of Fantasy*, University of Illinois Press, Urbana, 1976.
James, Henry, *The Turn of the Screw*, London, 1898 (Dent & Sons, London, 1963).
Kelley, L. P. (ed.), *The Supernatural in Fiction*, McGraw-Hill, New York, 1973.
Leisegang, H., *La Gnose*, Payot, Paris, 1951.
Lévy, Maurice, *Lovecraft*, Union Générale d'Editions, Paris, 1972.
   *Le roman 'gothique' anglais, 1764–1824*, Faculté des Lettres, Toulouse, 1968.
Lewis, C. S., *A Voyage to Venus*, London, 1943 (Pan Books, London, 1952).
   *Out of the Silent Planet*, London, 1938 (Pan Books, London, 1952).
   *That Hideous Strength*, London, 1945 (Pan Books, London, 1955).
   *Of Other Worlds, Essays and Stories*, ed. W. Hooper, George Bles, London, 1966.
Lewis, W. L. (ed.) *Letters of C. S. Lewis*, George Bles, London, 1966.
MacDonald, George, *Lilith*, London, 1895 (Ballantine Books, New York, 1969).
   *Phantastes*, London, 1858 (Ballantine Books, New York, 1969).
Machen, Arthur, *Tales of Horror and the Supernatural*, John Baker, London, 1964.
Manlove, C. N., *Modern Fantasy*, Cambridge University Press, Cambridge, 1975.
Marc, Olivier, *Psychanalyse de la maison*, Le Seuil, Paris, 1972.
Markale, Jean, *La femme celte*, 2nd edition, Payot, Paris, 1973.
Myers, L. H., *The Root and the Flower*, Reprint Society, London, 1953.
*Nouvelle Revue de Psychanalyse*, 'Bisexualité et différence des sexes', Number 7 (printemps 1973), Gallimard, Paris.
Przyluski, Jean, *La grande déesse*, Payot, Paris, 1950.
Rabkin, Eric S., *The Fantastic in Literature*, 2nd edition, Princeton University Press, Princeton, 1977.
Rank, Otto, *Don Juan et le double*, Payot, Paris, 1973.
Robert, Marthe, *Roman des origines et origines du roman*, Grasset, Paris, 1977.
Rosset, Clément, *Schopenhauer*, P.U.F., Paris, 1968.
   *Schopenhauer, philosophe de l'absurde*, P.U.F., Paris, 1967.
   *L'esthétique de Schopenhauer*, P.U.F., Paris, 1969.
Schul, P. M., *L'imagination et le merveilleux*, Flammarion, Paris, 1969.
Schopenhauer, Arthur, *The World as Will and Idea*, London, 1818.
Todorov, Tzvetan, *Introduction à la littérature fantastique*, Le Seuil, Paris, 1970 (*The Fantastic: A Structural Approach to a Literary Genre*, Richard Howard, transl., Case Western Reserve University Press, Cleveland, 1973).
Tuzet, Hélène, *Le cosmos et l'imagination*, José Corti, Paris, 1965.
Urang, Gunnar, *Shadows of Heaven: Religion and Fantasy in the Fiction of C. S. Lewis, Charles Williams and J. R. R. Tolkien*, S.C.M. Press, London, 1971.
Visiak, E. H., *Life's Morning Hour*, John Baker, London, 1968.
   *Medusa*, Gollancz, London, 1963.
Wells, H. G., *The First Men in the Moon*, London, 1901 (Collins, London, 1973).
Wilson, Colin, *The Outsider*, Gollancz, London, 1956.
   *Religion and the Rebel*, Gollancz, London, 1957.

# INDEX